NEW YORK UNIVERSITY STUDIES IN COMPARATIVE LITERATURE

General Editor: **Robert J. Clements**

Cartoon by S.A. Tsivinskii in *Segodnia*, 26 August 1924, p. 21.

Blue Evenings in Berlin
Nabokov's Short Stories of the 1920s

Marina Turkevich Naumann
Douglass College
Rutgers University

New York · New York University Press · 1978

The publication of this work has been aided by a grant from the Andrew W. Mellon Foundation.

Library of Congress Cataloging in Publication Data

Naumann, Marina Turkevich, 1938
Blue evenings in Berlin.

(New York University studies in comparative literature ; v. 9)
Bibliography: p.
Includes index.
1. Nabokov, Vladimir Vladimirovich, 1899-1977—
Criticism and interpretation. I. Title. II. Series:
New York University. Studies in comparative literature; v. 9
PG3476.N3Z795   1978   891.7'3'42   77-82751
ISBN 0-8147-5753-7

Manufactured in the United States of America

To the memory of my grandparents

Militza M. Buketoff

The Right Reverend Constantin Buketoff

His Eminence Leonty,
Archbishop of New York, Metropolitan of North America

who lovingly shared and bequeathed to me
their Russian tongue

Preface

Vladimir Nabokov's brilliant literary career spanned over half a century, three major languages, and numerous genres. Yet, in spite of this international reputation, a full twenty years of Nabokov's work remain essentially unexplored today. Ironically, Nabokov's work in his native Russian dating from 1924 has been forgotten. This earliest Russian creative output is so exceptionally rich that at the time of its first publication in émigré newspapers it evoked excited responses from critics of that day. In those formative years Nabokov clearly tested his skills and probed his talents while seeking his artistic niveau. "The special pattern or unique coloration" [1] of Nabokov's prose then appeared in its simplest configurations; his debt to world literature and to Russian literature in particular was genuine and straightforward.

Nabokov's Russian period, however, came to an abrupt end in May 1940. World War II not only silenced his critics and physically destroyed many of the Russian newspapers and journals bearing Nabokov's original works and their companion critiques but forced the gifted author to leave Europe for America. At this point Russian literature lost a talented writer and English literature gained one. In speaking of this transition Nabokov wrote:

None of my American friends have read my Russian books and thus every appraisal on the strength of my English ones is bound to be out of focus. My private tragedy, which cannot, and indeed should not, be anybody's concern, is that I had to abandon my natural idiom, my untrammeled, rich, and infinitely docile Russian tongue for a second-rate brand of English, devoid of any of those apparatuses—the baffling mirror, the black velvet backdrop, the implied associations and traditions—which the native illusionist, frac-tails flying, can magically use to transcend the heritage in his own way.[2]

Although twenty years have passed since Nabokov wrote these words, his literary craft still remains unfocused. Contemporary scholars are not always aware that Nabokov's English work is only half of his total; and Nabokov's critics have been appraising his fiction in a more or less complete vacuum, neglecting his fundamental Russian work. The reasons for this may be practical: the texts of Nabokov's Russian fiction are not easily obtainable, this Slavic language is not readily understandable, and no study exists that indicates or bridges this serious cultural gap.

The purpose of my book is to remedy this deficiency. It draws attention to Nabokov's earliest Russian prose, viewing it with the hindsight that his fifty-year career affords. The introductory chapter gives a résumé of Nabokov's entire literary career, focusing on his expatriate beginnings and emphasizing the Berlin milieu in which his art developed and first received acclaim. The three following chapters represent the heart of my study. Here Nabokov's short stories of the 1920s are analyzed in detail. The sheer number and diversity of these refreshing and unaffected pieces indicate that this decade was Nabokov's "short fiction" phase. Some of these stories recently became available in translation by the author; others are virtually unobtainable even in Russian. The aim of these chapters is to discuss the full body of these many stories inasmuch as they are the visible foundation of Nabokov's creative genius. As individual efforts they reveal the author's nascent artistry better than one long novel possibly could. My emphasis on these stories of the 1920s is particularly motivated by Nabokov's broad artistic approach, characteristic of that decade. Beginning in 1930 his perspective shifted exclusively to symbolism. The final chapter of the study discusses the degree to which these stories have reemerged in the fabric of Nabokov's late novel, *Transparent Things,* and shows that his artistry in the end came full circle.

Nabokov clearly cherished his earliest stories. Shortly before his death he revised, translated, and published some of this fiction.[3] American critics are now beginning to appreciate its value, albeit in translation. In a recent issue of *The Atlantic Monthly* Edward Weeks noted: "I have sometimes wondered if among his several accomplishments Mr. Nabokov was not at his best in the short story, and the appearance of this collection of his earliest work confirms me in my belief." [4] The present study is thus both timely and critical; it complements Nabokov's publication of the English versions of some of these stories.

My monograph reunites these newly translated stories with those early pieces which are available only in Russian. Furthermore, since the translations of the 1970s are literary anachronisms, it examines them in their proper historical perspective; these are the initial ventures of a young émigré in prewar Berlin, not the mature works of a famous author living in Switzerland who was for many years a leading candidate for the Nobel Prize in literature.

Many of these earliest Nabokov stories have never been reviewed in depth either in Russian or in English criticism. Consequently, in this study some of these stories are evaluated for the first time, and all are finally considered together as the foundation for Nabokov's contribution to modern letters.

My transliteration of Russian words, texts, literary titles, and personal names is based on System II as given by J. Thomas Shaw in *The Transliteration of Modern Russian for English Language Publications* (Milwaukee, Wisc.: Univ. of Wisconsin Press, 1967). The major exceptions are the familiar names, Dostoevsky, Gogol, Gorky, and Tolstoy, which are rendered according to System I, but are also acceptable under the rules of System II. Nabokov had his own unique transliteration scheme, and took particular liberties when translating/transliterating the names of his characters. These authorial peculiarities will be noted in text.

It is a pleasure to acknowledge first my debt to Nina Berberova of Princeton University. Mrs. Berberova not only acquainted me with Nabokov's early work and suggested this study but also patiently guided my initial thoughts and several early drafts. I also wish to thank my teacher, colleague, and friend, Professor Murl G. Barker of Rutgers University, for his many contributions and scrupulous review of my first versions. Professor Gleb Struve of the University of California very kindly read and corrected my later manuscripts and supplied me with invaluable information and source material which would have been otherwise unavailable to me. I am indebted to him. Miss Jean MacLachlan's editorial assistance transformed my stylistic infelicities into grammatical prose. My last thanks go to the one who gave the most, my dear husband Robert. His firm belief that the Russian language can also flourish in a German milieu sustained and encouraged me as I worked. For all of this very special help I am truly grateful.

Princeton, New Jersey   M.T.N.

Contents

Foreword

The late Vladimir Nabokov launched his dazzling and unique literary career as far back as the early 1920s, and his best work of this early phase was done in the short story. He wrote in Russian under the pseudonym of V. Sirin while living on meager financial resources as a member of the Russian emigré community in Berlin; and the stories were published by emigré journals of that time— *Russkoe Ekho, Rul', Segodnia* and the like—which could not afford to pay well a young writer just beginning.

It would, however, be a mistake to think of the Berlin stories as mere apprentice work or to assume that Nabokov's life in Berlin was a miserable and frustrated one. From his great novel of 1938, *Dar (The Gift)*, which is in considerable part about its author's artistic and personal growth in Berlin during the 1920s, we learn that for Nabokov the period constituted an intensely exciting epoch of creativity. During those years Nabokov shaped his style, defined his artistic individuality, worked out his complex relationship to Russian literature and culture of the past, from his cult of Pushkin to his scapegoating of Chernyshevsky, and, moreover, fell deeply in love with the woman whom he married and who yet survives him.

The shock of the emigration ordeal, beginning in revolutionary terror and ending in painful severance from the Russian homeland, followed by the further trauma of his father's assassination in 1922, had to be assimilated or otherwise dealt with by the writer's sensitive psychic economy. But such are the ways of artistic genius, and such the spiritual resources which underlie genius that Nabokov responded to these grievous losses, not with despair or even bitterness, but with a copious outpouring of imaginative work of which the early stories are the first fruits. With most of the familiar world of his youth gone or going, he set about making a new world. The first order of created beings in that new world was formed by those narratives which Marina Turkevich Naumann intensively studies in *Blue Evenings in Berlin*

Marina Naumann brings an unusual combination of gifts and accomplishments, and a special advantage, to her work on the Nabokov texts. She is genuinely bilingual in Russian and English and of course bases her analyses and interpretations on the Russian originals of the nineteen stories she treats. Her own translations of substantial passages (which are always given in both languages) are close yet graceful and idiomatic, and her discussion of stylistic features—Nabokov's rhythmic phrasing and syntax, his sometimes lavish employment of such "poetic" devices as assonance, alliteration and buried rhyme, and his extraordinary treasure house of color words and recurrent images—are full and sensitive. She is in a position to check the originals against English versions prepared by Dmitri Nabokov in consultation with his father during the early 1970s, and to take note of certain changes between Russian and English versions. In the original of "Rozhdestvo" ("Christmas"), first published in 1925, the reader must surmise that the father has just come from a funeral service by inference from the telling detail of candle wax hardened on the back of his hand. In the recently published English version (*Details of a Sunset and Other Stories*, New York: McGraw-Hill, 1976), the information of his attendance at the funeral is supplied, with consequent change of emphasis and reduction of emotional impact.

Dr. Naumann is an authority on Russian literature as a whole. This serves her well in her charting of some of the moves of the complicated and frequently ironical game Nabokov plays in his

stories with the Russian literary past. She appreciates the nuances
of his handling of certain traditional themes—the duelling theme
from Pushkin and Lermontov in "Podlets" ("An Affair of Honor"),
or the Chekhovian theme of the heartbroken, isolated father in
"Rozhdestvo." The speech and behavior of the rather sinister
narrator of "Bakhman" is sharply illuminated by her lucid
summary of a peculiar story technique call "skaz," which she traces
to the 19th century folk novelist, Leskov. And a traditional four-
fold division of Russian story forms into *povest! novella, rasskaz* and
skazka is equally well used to show how Nabokov balances generic
requirements against innovative features in the design of particular
narratives.

From the brilliant Russian Formalist school of literary analysis
Dr. Naumann borrows the now familiar distinction between *fabula*
and *siuzhet,* or the distinction between the order of events and the
order of their presentation in a story, and also takes the concept of
ostranenie, or "making strange," which was originally developed for
the study of Tolstoi. To *ostranenie,* both at the level of verbal style
and in larger aspects of compositional strategy, is perhaps owed
that special hallucinatory or phantasmagoric quality in Nabokov's
fiction, that process by which things, actions, persons and even
atmospheres are simultaneously lucid and distinct yet disturbingly
dreamlike and bizarre. Whatever it meant in Tolstoi, in early
Nabokov this strangeness or alienation effect seems inevitably to
reflect the experiences of uprooting, loss of status and security, and
partial deracination that were the frequent fate of Russian exiles in
Nabokov's generation. In "Zvonok" ("The Doorbell") and
"Sluchainost'" ("A Matter of Chance"), the poignant strangeness of
reunions long dreamed of but now to end in bitter disappointment
in the first story, and to be missed altogether in the second,
expresses a real historical anguish as well as the imaginative power
of the young man who wrote these deeply affecting works. Perhaps
that is why Dr. Naumann categorizes both these stories as
Realistic-Symbolic in her convincing and helpful division of her
material into Realistic, Realistic-Symbolic, and Symbolic
groupings.

I mentioned a special advantage enjoyed by this young American critic and that is the fact of her Russian ancestry. This puts

her in essential rapport, if not complicity, with her subject and guarantees that in her expert investigation of Nabokov's subtle art the human and cherishable traits of a lost Russian generation which that art reveals will never be taken for granted or forgotten. She shows us how Nabokov in his last completed novel, *Transparent Things,* returned to his artistic beginnings by incorporating into it the essential plot line of "Vozvrashchenie Chorba" ("The Return of Chorb"), a story dating from 1925 that is about loss of the beloved and a compulsive return. *Blue Evenings in Berlin* is a return to beginnings also but not at all compulsive or at a loss. In fact it is a great success and is one of the very few works of Nabokov criticism known to me which every Nabokov admirer should read and own.

Julian Moynahan

Blue Evenings in Berlin

I

An Introduction to Nabokov's Early Life and Work

Vladimir Vladimirovich Nabokov was nineteen when his family emigrated from Russia. Most of the families who were evacuated from the Crimea left in the fall of 1920; unlike them, the Nabokovs emigrated in March 1919. They traveled from Sevastopol to Constantinople, continued by way of Greece, France, and England, and finally settled in Berlin. Nabokov and his younger brother Sergei were left at English universities. Vladimir entered Cambridge University, where he studied English and concentrated on Russian literature. He wrote of that time: "My fear of losing or corrupting, through alien influence, the only thing I had salvaged from Russia—her language—became positively morbid. . . . I used to sit up far into the night, surrounded by an almost Quixotic accumulation of unwieldy volumes, and make polished and rather sterile Russian poems not so much out of the live cells of some compelling emotion as around a vivid term or verbal image that I wanted to use for its own sake." [1] Nabokov sent these poems to Berlin to be published in *Rul'*.

Rul' was a Russian émigré newspaper that had just been founded by Nabokov's father and was edited by him and Iosif V. Gessen, his former colleague in the Duma Kadet party and on the newspaper *Rech'* in St. Petersburg. Of the forty-odd Russian journals and newspapers in Berlin at that time, *Rul'* was the most important daily newspaper and was an average of four to six pages long, running to ten pages on Sunday.[2] The editor, V. D. Nabokov and the other contributors had strong connections with the Duma Kadets, and because of this the paper had a liberal cast. However, there were many literary and artistic pieces in *Rul'*, and young Nabokov's early poetry readily found a place in its pages.

At this time, to avoid confusion with his father, the young Nabokov assumed a pen name, Sirin, the name of a mythological multicolored bird of ancient Russian literature with a feminine face and breast, and the connotation of a good omen. Nabokov explained his choice: "In 1920, when casting about for a pseudonym and settling for that fabulous fowl, I still had not shaken off the false glamour of Byzantine imagery that attracted young Russian poets of the Blokian era." [3] It was never a secret who V. Sirin was, as most of the copyrights to his work were in the name of V. Nabokoff [sic]. Despite the fact that the elder Nabokov was assassinated in March 1922, scarcely two years after young Nabokov assumed the name, he continued to use it until 1940.

After his graduation from Trinity College, Cambridge, in the spring of 1923, Nabokov returned to Berlin. He had been sending his poetry to Gessen from England, and now he started bringing it there in person. His deceased father's colleague, it appears, accepted these early poems graciously. Nabokov wrote: "Hessen [sic], allowed me with great leniency to fill his poetry section with my unripe rhymes. Blue evenings in Berlin, the corner chestnut in flower, lightheadedness, poverty, love, the tangerine tinge of premature shoplights, and an animal aching yearn for the still fresh reek of Russia—all this was put into meter, copied out in long hand and carted off to the editor's office, where myopic I. V. would bring the new poem close to his face and after this brief, more or less tactual, act of cognition put it down on his desk."[4]

The period from Nabokov's return to Berlin until 1930 was the first of four stages in his literary career. Although it might be labeled his immature Russian period, it was a prolific stage. In addition to plays and abundant poetry, Nabokov published his first three novels. *Mashen'ka,* written in 1925, enjoyed a *succès d'estime* when it appeared in 1926.[5] *Korol' dama valet*, written between June 1927 and June 1928, followed; [6] and in 1929 a major literary step was taken by Nabokov with the serialization of *Zashchita Luzhina* in *Sovremennye Zapiski* in Paris.[7] However, the most significant developments in Nabokov's first literary decade occurred in the short-story genre. During the five-year period between 1924 and 1929 he published twenty-two short stories. Considering that Nabokov has written some fifty short stories all told, this high output of the 1920s indicates that proportionately this was his short-story period. It is these stories of the 1920s that form the subject of the present study.

It was a short story that launched Nabokov's prose career. In January 1924 "Udar kryla" ("The Stroke of a Wing") appeared in the Russian émigré weekly *Russkoe Ekho* in Berlin. This piece was followed by twenty-one other stories in rapid succession.[8] These were published variously in Russian-language newspapers and journals. In 1930 Nabokov republished fifteen of these stories in his first collection, entitled *Vozvrashchenie Chorba (The Return of Chorb)*.[9] It seems likely that this volume contained the author's favorites. Unfortunately, six other early stories have never been published in separate editions. Consequently, "Draka" ("The Fight"), "Britva" ("The Razor"), and "Rozhdestvenskii rasskaz" ("The Christmas Story") are buried in the faded and crumbling issues of *Rul'*.[10] The aforementioned "Udar kryla," "Mest'" ("Vengeance"), and "Bogi" ("The Gods"), which were published in the émigré publications *Segodnia* and *Russkoe Ekho* and whose existence was recently mentioned by Field, [11] are now unobtainable. A fourth forgotten story "Sluchainost'" [12] ("A Matter of Chance"), was translated by Nabokov in *Tyrants Destroyed and Other Stories* in 1975. [13] Whether there are other early missing stories that have perished or were forgotten even by Nabokov himself remains an intriguing problem for Nabokov aficionados. Although I can only suppose that these elusive stories were not among Nabokov's best, I hope that someday more of them will surface.

In addition to "Sluchainost'," many other early stories have recently been translated into English. Five stories appeared in the two Nabokov collections published in 1973 and 1975: [14] "Kartofel'nyi El'f," [15] "Podlets," [16] "Bakhman," [17] "Skazka," [18] and

"Uzhas." [19] Nabokov's English versions of "Vozvrashchenie Chorba," "Passazhir," [20] "Katastrofa," "Pis'mo v Rossiiu," "Putevoditel' po Berlinu," "Zvonok," "Groza," and "Rozhdestvo" have all been included in *Details of a Sunset and Other Stories.* [21] This, Nabokov's final short-story collection, was published after this study was completed [22] and underscores the extent to which Nabokov's English-language readers are now being exposed to his earliest work.

In order to appreciate these stories fully, it is crucial for the English-language reader to understand the Russian émigré audience for which they were originally created. These exiled compatriots of his not only enjoyed Nabokov's work but, more importantly, surrounded and influenced him. With the 1920 Crimean evacuation many Russians fled to Berlin or Paris. Nabokov recalled: "As I look back at those years of exile, I see myself, and thousands of other Russians, leading an odd but by no means unpleasant existence, in material indigence and intellectual luxury, among perfectly unimportant strangers, spectral Germans and Frenchmen in whose more or less illusory cities we, émigrés, happened to dwell." [23] Most of the liberal-minded and creative forces left Lenin's Russia. Some left of their own accord; others, like Berdiaev, were "sent out." Thus during this Berlin period Nabokov was part of a particularly thriving intellectual émigré community. [24] He described this as an itinerant but exhilarating life, with an abnormal frequency of literary readings in homes or hired halls. During this early period he came in close contact with numerous literary figures, among them, Khodasevich, Bunin, Aldanov, Remizov, Kuprin, Tsvetaeva, Aikhenval'd, and Fondaminskii. [25] This bubbling and exciting society of the early 1920s is artistically recorded in his novel *Dar,* first published in the 1930s. [26] In the foreword to the English translation, Nabokov wrote: "The tremendous outflow of intellectuals that formed such a prominent part of the general exodus from Soviet Russia in the first years of the Bolshevist Revolution seems today like the wanderings of some mythical tribe whose bird-signs and moon-signs I now retrieve from the desert dust." Nabokov added: "That world is now gone."

This Berlin émigré community was at the peak of its growth and

development in 1922-23. Thus when Nabokov completed his
university studies, he returned to a stimulating Russian Berlin. But
this vibrant Russian circle was to be short-lived. In 1923 the
German reichsmark began to devalue quickly, prompting a
number of émigrés to leave Berlin. That fall some moved to
Prague; others went to Paris; and some, like Pasternak, Belyi, and
Erenburg, returned to Russia. It was, however, the 1924 revalua-
tion of the reichsmark that forced the major outflow of Russians
from Berlin. Nevertheless, Nabokov chose to remain in this smaller
Russian community. In May 1925 he married a fellow Russian,
Vera Slonim, and as a young émigré writer he "supplemented
chance subsidies" by teaching tennis and tutoring in French and
English. He mentioned that he received five dollars, "quite a
sum," [27] for his Russian translation of *Alice in Wonderland.* [28] He
helped to compile a Russian grammar for foreigners, made up
chess problems and crossword puzzles for *Rul'*, and held public
readings of his works. His real love, however, was serious writing,
and he continued to publish his poems and reviews and began to
submit short prose pieces to *Rul'*. But *Rul'*, like the circle to which it
catered, began to fade away. The daily issues became erratic. In
September 1931 hoodlums ransacked its offices, [29] and *Rul'* ceased
publication on 12 September 1931.

Although Nabokov remained in Berlin as a resident alien until
1937, he started to visit Paris, the new émigré capital, regularly in
1933. As early as 1927 one of his stories, "Uzhas," appeared there
in *Sovremennye Zapiski*. I have already noted the serialization of
Zashchita Luzhina, begun in 1929, in that same periodical.

The earliest stories nearly all reflect this German milieu.
Ironically, at that time Nabokov claimed that he "spoke no
German, had no German friends, had not read a single German
novel either in the original or in translation." [30] If one is to believe
implicitly Nabokov's own statement, he had not even been able to
read the 1928 German edition of *Korol' dama valet*. This complete
isolation from the surrounding milieu proved, however, to be an
asset for Nabokov. In this regard, he said that "in art, as in nature,
a glaring disadvantage may turn out to be a subtle protective
device." [31]

Thus the restricted backdrop of this early work is Germany,

often Berlin. The time framework of these stories is in most cases the post-World War I and post-Russian Revolutionary era, when European society was changing and enduring cataclysmic upheavals at all levels. In the case of the Russian émigrés, this unrest was compounded by the trauma of the loss of a homeland, with consequent displacement, emigration, and, in some cases, a new displacement. This early Nabokovian literary background is unifying but limited when compared with the scenarios of Nabokov's later works. In "Sogliadatai," [32] for instance, the backdrop becomes multileveled and the narrator's role shifts. In *Dar*, "Ultima Thule," [33] "Solus Rex," [34] and *Pale Fire*, [35] on the other hand, the epoch wavers between the present and a historical, almost mythical, past.

The unchanging background of these early stories is generally complemented by solitary heroes. More often than not, they are sensitive young Russian men whose problems are tacitly those of their creator. Many are nascent artists in one medium or another. There are no true heroines; in fact, they are notable for their absence. This is particularly curious in view of the degree to which women dominate Nabokov's later works *Lolita* [36] and *Ada*. [37] In the early stories women exist only in the memories that they have created for the heroes.

In many of these stories the young émigrés are content to seek a Proustian remembrance of things past. This theme is, of course, the germ of the themes of buried treasures and of Russia as a paradise lost that dominates Nabokov's novel *Podvig* [38] and nearly all of his subsequent work. As yet this myth is at its lowest denominator. The young heroes, like Nabokov, are not yet longing for their homeland, nor do the stories reflect any antagonism between the hero and his milieu. Most of Nabokov's earliest heroes are merely wistful and sorrowful; their break with the past, like Nabokov's, is not yet clear and absolute.

By the 1930s the grim psychological realization that Russia was lost had struck the émigrés, authors and heroes alike. Their pessimism was aggravated by the growing Fascist movement. Nabokov's works of the 1930s contrast with those of the preceding decade in that his heroes are hostile toward their cold, insensitive German surroundings. Fedor, the hero of *Dar,* is at odds with the

Germans around him. Ironically this novel is set in the milieu of the more sympathetic 1920 Berlin circle. However, in *Dar* Nabokov endowed his hero with the attitude of a Russian émigré of the 1930s. Thus, as Nabokov himself noted in the foreword, he anachronistically transposed a 1930 hero into a 1920 setting. In the fine story "Oblako, ozero, bashnia," [39] dated "Marienbad, 1937," the hostile German community is pictured as psychologically destroying a mild Russian bachelor named Vasilii Ivanovich.

In this connection it is appropriate to remember the language in which Nabokov wrote these stories. He was using his native tongue when his ties to it were most recent, fresh, and, as evidenced by his Russian studies, emotional. This closeness is reflected in the old Russian orthography in which early émigré literature was printed and Nabokov always wrote. Never again was Nabokov to be so close to his native tongue.

It is not surprising that Nabokov's first prose piece was a short story. From a practical point of view, such short pieces could readily be included in *Rul'*. More basically, Russian literature's strong tradition of short-story writing was well developed by the time that Nabokov turned to it. Gogol; Turgenev; and, more immediately for Nabokov, Chekhov and Bunin were masterful storytellers. In Russian literary history there have been varieties of story forms: the *povest'* (novelette); the *novella* (a short story which often focuses on an unusual event); the *rasskaz* (a slightly shorter short story which often concentrates on an everyday event); and the *skazka* (fairy tale). The stories of the 1920s are not *povesti* as Nabokov labeled "Sogliadatai." [40] Only one of the earliest pieces is a fairy tale, and it is appropriately entitled "Skazka." All of the other stories are called *rasskazy*, which points to an auctorial emphasis on everyday events.

As a point of reference, I understand the classic short story to be as defined by one of Nabokov's favorite authors, [41] Edgar Allan Poe: "A skilful literary artist has constructed a tale. If wise, he has not fashioned his thoughts to accommodate his incidents; but having conceived, with deliberate care, a certain unique or single *effect* to be wrought out, he then invents such incidents—he then combines such events as may best aid him in establishing this preconceived effect. If his very initial sentence tend not to the outbringing of this effect, then he has failed in his first step. In the whole composition there should be no word written of which the tendency, direct or indirect, is not to the one pre-established design." [42]

Flaubert, another of Nabokov's favorite writers, [43] stressed the importance of a masterpiece's subjectivity: "One is not at all free to write this or that. One does not choose one's subject. That is what the public and the critics do not understand. The secret of masterpieces lies there, in the concordance between the subject and the temperament of the author." [44]

All of these early Nabokovian stories are remarkable variations of this genre. For Nabokov the story was a particularly appropriate medium. As a highly subjective form, his artistic credo could find expression within it. Like Shakespeare, Cervantes, Pushkin, Flaubert, Baudelaire, and Blok, Nabokov wrote for pleasure and artistic satisfaction. [45] He forcefully stated his belief in *l'art pour l'art* in his afterword to *Lolita*. [46] Although Nabokov did not care for the slogan *l'art pour l'art,* he wrote that "there is no question that what makes a work of fiction safe from larvae and rust is not its social importance but its art, only its art." [47] His views on the role of inspiration have been recently presented in his article "Inspiration." [48] His novel *Dar* is a magnificent expression of a writer's introspection and gift of inspiration. I quote a passage from that novel as an example:

> Fyodor thought with heavy revulsion of the verses he had written that day, of word-fissures, of the leakage of poetry, and at the same time, with proud, joyous energy, with passionate impatience, he was already looking for the creation of something new, something still unknown, genuine, corresponding fully to the gift which he felt like a burden inside himself. (p. 106)

Art was central to Nabokov's work from the start. His early critics were quick to note precisely this aspect of his writings. In 1936 Weidlé wrote in the first issue of *Krug:* "The theme of Sirin's art is art itself—this is the first thing that one must say about him." [49] In 1937 Khodasevich added that the life of the artist and the creative process itself were Sirin's theme. [50]

The artistic and subjective quality of the story, coupled with its brevity, readily allowed Nabokov to probe his talents and experiment with his artistic tools. Thus these first stories provided sound training for his mature and better-known works. These precious stories, through their sheer number and diversity, reveal many facets of Nabokov's early artistry that might never have been uncovered by one or two long novels. These are in a sense uncomplicated exercises or sketches by Nabokov. The critic Nikolai Andreev understood them as such when he wrote in 1930: "And if occasionally similar images are repeated which are familiar from the novels [*Mashen'ka, Korol' dama valet, Zashchita Luzhina*], then it is the echo of his own writer's world and maybe in these stories there are preparatory études for the author's later thoughts" (IV). [51]

The disparate images of cigarette cases, treasure chests, butterflies, gurgling water, chess games, ascending shadows, mirror reflections, letters, and knobbed walking sticks are only a few of the recurring materials that characterized Nabokov's earliest prose. These images have become familiar and take on symbolic meaning in his later work, but in the early stories they appeared as Nabokov first envisioned them. They were the raw material for his later, more elaborate motifs. They were beautiful, refreshing, simple elements of Nabokov's prose that in the 1920s served as distinctive features of his style, linking the short stories together into one prose unit. These artistic devices have survived intact in Nabokov's mature works, acquiring deeper significance and complexity in the interim.

At the core of Nabokov's earliest work was his broad artistic modus operandi. Many authors tend to depict life and its manifestations either realistically or symbolically. Some, like Tolstoy, employ one approach when they are young and mature to the opposite approach when they grow older. Others never shift their artistic method. Like Bunin, they are consistently realists; or like Belyi, they remain symbolists. Such classifications are almost nullified when a rare artist is able to see life both realistically and symbolically at one and the same time. Here I note, of course,

Gogol who, with his descriptions of minutiae in *Dead Souls,* [52] was considered a realist, even though much of the novel, especially its galloping troika, are symbolic views of Russia. Not surprisingly, Nabokov was interested in Gogol and in 1944 published a study on this Russian giant. [53] This affinity may be grounded on the fact that both writers were able to view life in real and symbolic terms simultaneously.

In Nabokov's earliest literature realistic and symbolic aspects coexisted. Mochul'skii in his review of *Mashen'ka* in *Zveno,* observed that these two levels existed at once in this first Nabokov novel. [54] Struve, in considering this work, noted: "But there is always in his work a blending of realism and artifice. Not content with recreating the natural flow of life, he artificially organizes his real life material. His artificiality is deliberate, a part of his artistic credo, which he has on more than one occasion formulated in the prefaces to his works in English." [55] Thus Struve contended that Nabokov in his early work mixed realism with artificiality. Andreev saw the action of Nabokov's earliest work as existing on two levels: in reality and in recollection (II), while Petr Pil'skii, in his review of the *Vozvrashchenie Chorba* collection, chose to call it a melding of realism with illusion. [56] In short, Nabokov's earliest critics recognized the two-planed quality of his art. All agreed that one method was realistic, and for the complementary method each chose his own term. I regard this second, unrealistic, element in Nabokov's art as symbolic. Here I am viewing symbolism in its broadest sense: an approach balancing realism. It incorporates artifice, illusion, Proustian recollection, as well as fantasy, and symbolism in its traditional metaphoric meaning, to name but a few of its elements. These diverse techniques, realistic and symbolic, coexisted in distinct fashion in Nabokov's earliest stories, which are the subject of this study. [57]

By way of a brief introduction, let us note that Nabokov's direct, realistic manner was very much a part of his early craft. His near-photographic modus operandi was inherited from his Russian predecessors Gogol,[58] Turgenev, Tolstoy, Chekhov,[59] and Bunin.[60] The last he knew personally as well as artistically.[61] In the Western tradition Nabokov followed the manner of Balzac, Flaubert, and de Maupassant. Objectivity, impartiality, and impersonality prevailed. Life was pictured from the exterior and separate and excessive detail predominated. In reflecting later on *Korol' dama valet,* a novel that represented this realistic method of the 1920s, Nabokov made some relevant observations that held for his realistic approach during the decade as a whole.[62] Retrospectively he claimed to have been unfamiliar with Balzac's "preposterous stuff" during that early period and protested that he was not parodying Balzac. I would argue, however, that this traditional approach was implicitly there and that the vehemence of Nabokov's denial speaks for itself. On the other hand, Nabokov openly acknowledged his debt to Flaubert. He observed that his own technique was "assignable to the French 'human document type', " and he specifically added that "my amiable little imitations of *Madame Bovary,* which good readers will not fail to distinguish, represent a deliberate tribute to Flaubert." He then cited specific examples.

This Flaubertian manner is particularly evident in the wealth of detail in the early stories. For example, like Flaubert, Nabokov drew attention, not only to the attire of his characters, but to the state of their fingernails. He was fascinated by the furnishings and trappings of the mini-worlds of his characters; even the paintings and poster letterings hanging on the walls attracted both Flaubert and Nabokov. Thus, like his mentors, Nabokov did not always stop with functional or even poetic detailing in his art; he went beyond. Details were added for details' sake. In view of the succinctness demanded by the short-story genre, this overabundance was all the more pronounced. The overall effect of Nabokov's realistic creations was a plethora of minutiae. The description of a minor character in the early story "Putevoditel' po Berlinu" is a case in point:

Pochtal'on podstavil meshok pod kobal'tovyi pochtovyi iashchik, natsepliaet ego snizu i taino, nezrimo, s pospeshnym shelestom, iashchik oporazhnivaetsia, i pochtal'on zakhlopyvaet kvadratnuiu past' otiazhelevshego meshka. (p. 98)

A postman, who has placed the mouth of a sack under a cobalt-colored mailbox, fastens it on from below, and secretly, invisibly, with a hurried rustling, the box empties and the postman claps shut the square jaws of the bag, now grown full and heavy. (p. 95)

Nabokov's symbolic manner echoed that of Gogol, Tolstoy, and Dostoevsky, as well as Belyi and his *Petersburg*. [63] Like these Russian masters, Nabokov could present a profound picture of life. Erich Auerbach would label this approach "internal realism" as opposed to the "external realism" of Balzac and Flaubert discussed in the paragraph above. [64] Nabokov's art lay below the text as well as within the text. In some of the early stories Nabokov's approach intimated the existence of something oblique and beyond the visualized object or printed word. For Nabokov's reader this modus operandi connoted artifice, illusion, beauty, grandeur, poetry, irony, fantasy, laughter, and fear. This particular approach found its expression in parodies, masks, and allegories. Nabokov used the stream of consciousness technique which he admittedly inherited from Tolstoy [65] and placed stylistic missing links in his stories. Often his more modern method revealed a disjointed, visionary, and even absurd world. The following sentence is a clear example of Nabokov's symbolic manner as it is fragmented in both form and content:

Ia uvidel ego [mir] takim, kakov on est' na samom dele: ia gliadel na doma, i oni utratili dlia menia svoi privychnyi smysl; vse to, o chem my mozhem dumat', gliadia na dom . . . arkhitektura . . . takoi-to stil' . . . vnutri komnaty takie-to . . . nekrasivyi dom . . . udobnyi dom . . . vse eto skol'znulo proch', kak son, i ostalsia tol'ko bessmyslennyi oblik,—kak poluchaetsia bessmyslennyi zvuk, esli dolgo povtoriat', vnikaia v nego odno i to zhe obyknovenneishee slovo. ("Uzhas," p. 202)

I saw the actual essence of all things. I looked at houses and they had lost their usual meaning—that is, all that we think when looking at a house: a certain architectural style, the sort of rooms inside, ugly house, comfortable house—all this had evaporated, leaving nothing but an absurd shell the same way an absurd sound is left after one has repeated sufficiently long the commonest word without heeding its meaning: house, howss, whowss. ("Terror," p. 119)

Nabokov's wide-ranging method was within the frame of his aesthetics of *l'art pour l'art.* The presence of both realistic and symbolic stories attested to this very point, for it indicated that Nabokov was not bound to any rigid technique. He stated: "No creed or school has any influence on me whatsoever. Nothing bores me more than political novels and the literature of social intent." [66] Further, he has remarked that he saw no distinction between literary schools and for this reason abhorred classifications such as realist and symbolist. [67] Although Nabokov's pronouncements must frequently be taken *cum grano salis,* his earliest work certainly did reflect an unrestricted, broad approach to art.

Nabokov's emphasis on the supremacy of art per se was also demonstrated by the fact that beauty always supplied the prevailing tone. Nabokov's realism never extended to the naturalism of Gogol or Zola, or to the neo-realism of his contemporary Zamiatin. There was nothing unseemly, morbid, or pathological in Nabokov's realism, even in his most precise detailing. Likewise, the symbolic depiction was never completely ugly, horrible, or grotesque. Tragedies, nightmares, and fears were frequently expressed in images of grace, fragility, and delicacy. Even death, a recurrent theme in the early stories, was treated without pessimism. This was due in part to Nabokov's youth; in addition, he was striking an artistic pose in choosing such a standard literary motif, and thus the theme lacked a negative bite. [68]

Although the realistic and the symbolic modi operandi coexisted in the early stories, they were not completely integrated. The realistic and symbolic levels could be distinguished and readily differentiated. In some stories the two methods were mutually exclusive; in others, both artistic procedures appeared in varying proportions. This diversity of approach undoubtedly indicates that Nabokov was seeking a way to meld realistic and symbolic perspectives. More pertinent here is that Nabokov may have been toying with his devices in an attempt to find a natural balance for his own subjective view of art. This balance was soon achieved.

The 1930 publication of "Sogliadatai" marked the end of

Nabokov's earliest period. With this work his fascination with
realia ended, and his interest in excessive detail waned. In short, in
"Sogliadatai" Nabokov's career reached a turning point. He
completely freed himself from the traditions of Tolstoy and Bunin
and began his mature Russian period, which was more in the spirit
of the modern symbolic literature of Belyi. Only a few subsequent
exceptional stories published in the 1930's, such as "Pil'gram,"
indicated his earlier interest in minutiae, and there is an indication
that even this story may have been written in the 1920s.[69]

Nina Berberova has noted that "Sogliadatai" overflows its
covers. In her excellent article she points to symbolic devices and
elements that coalesce in "Sogliadatai" for the first time, remaining in harmony in Nabokov's subsequent creations.[70] Indeed, the
period from 1930 to 1940 was rich in output. Nabokov published
twenty-six short stories and five novels: *Podvig, Kamera obskura,* [71]
Otchaianie,[72] *Priglashenie na kazn',*[73] *Dar,* and the first chapters of his
projected novel, "Solus Rex." Of all of the work of that decade,
Dar was the jewel. Appropriately, in it Nabokov revealed his own
true gifts. It was a multiplaned novel, rich in its motifs. It centered
around a hero who was a poet and writer, a theme with which
Nabokov had been experimenting in his earliest stories and in
Podvig. In *Dar* his talent for satire, poetry, and free-flowing
narrative predominated. His vision of a disjointed, even disintegrating world and his own creative process came to the fore. A
talent for literary parody that was first intimated in some of the
early stories became fully developed in *Dar.* In this novel Nabokov
even parodied the literature of the Russian realists whom he had
seriously emulated in his earliest work. This parody of literature
continued to develop throughout Nabokov's career, culminating
fully in his American novels *Lolita* and *Ada.*

Parodic elements blossomed in Nabokov's final, unfinished
Russian novel, "Solus Rex." In this fragmentary work he mocked
Russian and foreign authors, and various literary styles. Pertinent
here is his parody of Bunin's realistic manner, a technique that
Nabokov seems to have genuinely valued in the overdone descriptions found in some of his realistic stories. The following parodic
passage from "Solus Rex" is valuable as a context for my category
of realistic stories below:

V den' progulki pogoda stoiala kholodnaia i bespokoinaia, letelo perlamutrovoe nebo, sklonialsia lozniak po ovragam, kopyta vyshlepyvali bryzgi iz zhirnyhk luzh v shokoladnykh koleiakh, karkali vorony, a potom, za mostom, vsadniki svernuli v storonu i poekhali rys'iu po temnomu veresku, nad kotorym tam i siam vysilas' tonkaia, ushe zhelteiushchaia bereza.

On the day of the outing the weather was cold and restless, a nacreous sky skimmed overhead, the sallow bushes curtseyed in the ravines, the horsehooves plapped as they scattered the slush of thick puddles in chocolate ruts, crows croaked; and then, beyond the bridge, the riders left the road and set off at a trot across the dark heather, above which a slim, already yellowing birch rose here and there.[74]

Mention should be made here of Nabokov's third working tongue—French. In 1937, in addition to his Russian work, he published some French translations and a critique of Pushkin's poetry. Although this French output was very limited, it did point to Nabokov's facility in this Romance language and indicated a certain adjustment to his Parisian émigré home, an adjustment never manifest in Berlin.

However, the Nazi invasion of Paris in 1940 brought an abrupt end to Nabokov's very fruitful period in his European home. In May of that year Nabokov and his family departed for the United States, and Russia's leading émigré writer became America's new and promising one. This transition from the "infinitely docile Russian tongue" to a "second-rate brand of English"[75] was signaled by the author's switch from Sirin to Nabokov as his pen name.

The two American periods were not as productive as the Russian ones. His immature and more academic English period lasted from 1940 until 1955. During that time Nabokov taught at Wellesley College and Cornell University. He wrote his autobiography, some eight short stories, and his first American novels. *The Real Life of Sebastian Knight*,[76] his first novel written directly in English, and *Bend Sinister*[77] hinted at the complexity of Nabokov's artistic world

view, which was to be revealed in the later *Lolita* and *Ada*. As late
as 1951, while he was writing his autobiography, *Conclusive
Evidence*,[78] Nabokov's English was being checked.[79]

The publication of *Lolita* in 1955 marked Nabokov's transition
from college professor to mature author of world repute. This
fourth, final Montreux period included the publication also of
Pnin,[80] *Pale Fire, Ada, Transparent Things*,[81] and *Look at the Harlequins*.[82] Nabokov's literary art flowered in these novels. *Pnin*, the
novel about an absentminded émigré professor, was an exception.
As Nabokov's critics have already noted, it was a realistic
throwback which easily paired itself with *Mashen'ka* and with the
realistic stories of the 1920s which depicted émigré life.[83]

At the height of his career, Nabokov seemed to have become
fully aware of the synthesis in his art of realism and symbolism. He
noted: "I tend more and more to regard the objective existence of
all events as a form of impure imagination—hence my inverted
commas around 'reality.' Whatever the mind grasps, it does so with
the assistance of creative fancy, that drop of water on a glass slide,
which gives distinctness and relief to the observed organism." [84] In
Transparent Things Nabokov's creative fancy merged with his
objective observations in a manner very reminiscent of his earliest
prose—this after a fifty-year hiatus.[85]

What is the pattern of his earliest prose? The stories of the 1920's
fall into three categories. Six stories belong to the realistic modus
operandi: "Vozvrashchenie Chorba," "Port," "Blagost'," "Pis'mo v
Rossiiu," "Putevoditel' po Berlinu," and "Passazhir." In eight
other stories the realistic and symbolic approaches are combined:
"Groza," "Zvonok," "Sluchainost'," "Britva," "Rozhdestvenskii
rasskaz," "Skazka," "Podlets," and "Kartofel'nyi El'f." Five early
stories are purely symbolic: "Bakhman," "Draka," "Uzhas,"
"Katastrofa," and "Rozhdestvo." These divisions are not to be
viewed as exclusive or absolute. Realism and symbolism are
subjective concepts, not only for the writer, but for the reader as
well. Within these categories, the stories are not graded, particularly as Nabokov's chronology had no pattern or significance.
Realistic stories appeared after symbolic ones and vice versa.

Within the framework of the realistic, realistic-symbolic, and symbolic approaches, each of these stories stands as a distinct technical treasure. Each story is a singular creation. The diversity of artistic modi operandi and literary techniques that they evince supports my contention that in the 1920s Nabokov tried his skills both at the broad level of authorial focus and at the narrow level of minute aesthetic craftsmanship.

II

The Cathedral Tower

THE REALISTIC STORIES

Most artists shrink from explaining literary concepts such as realism. Flaubert wrote to de Maupassant: "Do not speak to me of realism, naturalism or of the experimental: I am full of it. What empty ineptitudes!" [1] Nabokov detested literary labels [2] and put quotation marks around "reality." Nevertheless, he once remarked: "Reality is a very subjective affair. I can only define it as a kind of gradual accumulation of information; and as a specialization. . . . You can get nearer and nearer, so to speak, to reality; but you never get near enough because reality is an infinite succession of steps, levels of perception, false bottoms, and hence unquenchable, unobtainable. You can know more and more about one thing but you can never know everything about one thing: it's hopeless." [3]

Critics try to define literary terms, but each has his own specific view. Auerbach has a broad concept of realism that virtually includes symbolism. His "external realism" falls into my category of realism and his "internal realism" into what I understand as symbolism. Perhaps the clearest recent literary definition has been made, if metaphorically, by Zamiatin. In considering Russian literature, Zamiatin asked a French journalist: "What is after all

19

realism? If you examine your hand through a microscope you will see a grotesque picture: trees, ravines, rocks—instead of hairs, pores, grains and dust. . . . To my mind that is a more genuine realism [neo-realism] than the primitive one. To follow up the comparison: while neo-Realism uses a microscope to look at the world, Symbolism used a telescope, and pre-Revolutionary Realism, an ordinary looking glass. This naturally conditions the whole imagery, the entire formal structure." [4]

In his earliest realistic stories Nabokov looked at life with the pre-Revolutionary looking glass. He noted that he did not make broad generalizations.[5] His early method produced an objective and accurate representation of nature and real life. In the tradition of Chekhov, Nabokov described what he saw and was exact in his observations and detailed in his descriptions. Within this context, on November 2, 1930 Bunin remarked that Nabokov had presented a "new kind of literary art" and "discovered a whole universe for which one can only be grateful to him." [6] His realism, however, in no way met Wellek's strict criterion that realism be "didactic, moralistic, reformist." [7] Nabokov was an aesthetic realist. For instance, his figurative and literal [8] emphasis on detail goes beyond the functional. It is decorative and copious. Obliquely he justified some of his excessive use of trivia. For him, ordinary details did not merely have a value of their own, nor serve only a descriptive or poetic purpose. They play a subtle, aesthetic role in his plots. It is precisely these seemingly irrelevant aspects of everyday life that are crucial for many of Nabokov's central characters. Trivia are essential as tangible and sacred souvenirs for the émigré heroes, the artists in particular. However, Nabokov varied this Proustian theme. In *A la recherche du temps perdu,* a work that Nabokov considered one of the greatest prose achievements,[9] the hero unexpectedly effects remembrance through an accidental or insignificant occurrence. In Nabokov the hero consciously as well as unconsciously searches out these minutiae. It is this theme that underlies nearly every Nabokovian realistic story of the 1920s.

1. "Vozvrashchenie Chorba"

The remembrance of things past is the central theme of Nabokov's exquisite story, "Vozvrashchenie Chorba" ("The Return of Chorb"). A young Russian is depicted emotionally confronting memories of his dead wife. Chorb has been widowed on his honeymoon. In an effort to keep his wife's image alive, he chooses to immortalize her by sleeplessly retracing the steps of their wedding trip.[10] As the title indicates, the principal event of the story is Chorb's return to the town where he had met, courted, and married his wife. Chorb settles in the hotel where they spent their wedding night. By coincidence he is given the room they had shared. This return to the very source of his memories thus presents an even more bittersweet test. In order to survive this last night and live down his sorrow, Chorb finds a prostitute who will simply keep him company. He falls asleep without touching her. A few hours later when he momentarily mistakes the prostitute for his wife, he recaptures the memory of his wife and thus survives his trauma.

In his effort not to contaminate his grief, Chorb has purposely withheld the tragic news from his parents-in-law, the Kellers. He has only left a cryptic message at their house announcing his return and the fact that their daughter is ill.[11] The Kellers, upon learning of Chorb's return, go to the hotel, where they find him with the prostitute and the Kellers enter as she leaves the room. The door is shut and only silence emanates from the room.

To appreciate the intricate composition of "Vozvrashchenie Chorba" we must look not only at its *fabula,* or story, but at its *siuzhet,* its narrative structure.[12] In "Vozvrashchenie Chorba" these elements are very distinct, and this formal difference and the consequent temporal dislocation lend the story aesthetic complexity.

The *siuzhet* of "Vozvrashchenie Chorba" is classically balanced and can be patterned ABA. A brief exposition describes the Kellers returning home to learn that their son-in-law has come back. Questions are raised concerning Chorb's arrival, and the Kellers set off for the hotel. This exposition is objectively, almost journalistically narrated from the very first sentence:

Suprugi Keller vyshli iz teatra pozdno. (p. 5)

The Kellers left the opera house at a late hour. (p. 59)

A narrative shift marks the end of this section.

The central section of this story, Chorb's drama, follows his stream of experience. I understand this narrative method as "the continual presence of a character through whom the writer can transmit the experience and, assuming the writer's imaginative ability to shed all of himself but his ability to record and get into that character and feel the experience through the character's sense, a kind of expanded mental discourse.[13] The reader is admitted to Chorb's personality almost completely in this section. He hears and sees only what Chorb hears and sees. For example, Chorb's motives for not telling his parents-in-law the entire story seem completely justified and understandable. They are in no way masked. The drama is particularly highpitched because there is no narrator or intruding author to filter Chorb's story, and the action is a unique occurrence: Chorb returns but once. His tragedy seems real and immediate, and as a result the story gains emotional momentum. It flashes back to his happy marriage, his wife's sudden death, his grief, and his subsequent decision to immortalize her image. The rising action is marked by his determination to share his grief with no one, but to keep her death secret. The story of his three-week-long return unfolds as Chorb arrives in the town, and it slowly accelerates up to the climax, when he successfully conjures up his wife's image. The brief falling action is his realization that he has survived the test.

In conclusion, the narrative shifts back to the objective method. The reappearance of the Kellers links the beginning with the conclusion in a subtle frame. This structural link is to become a frequent device in Nabokov's later works, allowing him to resolve riddles raised in the opening of his dramas at their conclusion, as in *Zashchita Luzhina*, for example. Once again Keller is carrying his top hat and Frau Keller is wearing the same veil that she wore in the exposition. They are ready with their questions. Ironically, in surviving the night, Chorb may fail in this second, unexpected confrontation with his past. The silence behind the closed door conveys the shock of the Kellers and Chorb. It seems likely the Kellers will never believe Chorb's explanation, and no one can imagine what will transpire. This scene with a group of characters wondering about the silence behind the door is repeated by

Nabokov in the concluding scene of *Zashchita Luzhina.* Structurally this second conflict remains unresolved.

The ending *en l'air* may appear too harsh. O'Faolain has noted that the merit of a short story is not in its clever ending.[14] The essence of this particular story lies in all aspects of Chorb's return, not in this one predicament. The ending even implies a continuation of Chorb's woe rather than an arbitrary and abrupt cessation. In commenting later on zero endings, Nabokov wrote: "And yet the ear cannot right now part with the music and allow the tale to fade; the chords of fate itself continue to vibrate; and no obstruction for the sage exists where I have put The End: the shadows of my world extend beyond the skyline of the page, blue as tomorrow's morning haze—nor does this terminate the phrase." Such a poetic open ending concludes *Dar* (p. 378), as well as *Ada.* Thus, the stunning dramatic effect of Chorb's return lies precisely in the continuing vibration of these chords of fate.

Intimately connected with this future-implied ending is the structural use of time in the *siuzhet* of "Vozvrashchenie Chorba." Although Chorb's story is brief—fourteen pages—it spans a period of six months. Numerous flashbacks are combined with frequent indications of seasons, months, and hours that convey a realistic sense of extended time in a very few pages. Moreover, this impression of the passage of time provides the momentum that a short story requires.

Nabokov used the element of suspense three times in "Vozvrashchenie Chorba" to heighten the drama. In the exposition, the reader, like the Kellers, is unaware of the couple's tragedy. The information is withheld until Chorb's story unfolds. The second instance of suspense is complex in that the reader, but not the hero, foresees a new predicament. Chorb is so engrossed in memories of his wife that he forgets that his message may bring the Kellers to his room. The reader, although fully aware of this possible meeting, is disoriented because of the flashbacks and consequent disordered time. Further, Chorb's drama is so absorbing that the Keller theme is readily forgotten. Chorb's dilemma in explaining to his parents-in-law becomes more complicated when he takes the prostitute. Ironically, the prostitute leaves early after a chaste night, but not before the Kellers appear. Thus Chorb's problem is compounded. The story ends on a new note of suspense as the reader, the porter, and the prostitute wonder about the silence behind the door.

"A good short story should have two or three well conceived and sharply drawn characters." [15] There are six figures in "Vozvrashchenie Chorba." Three service characters play a minor role and are described by a few concise adjectives: the frightened maid, the pale and pert hotel porter, and the prostitute with her short, fair hair. The remaining figures are immediately named: Chorb, Keller, and his Russian wife Varvara Klimovna. Here I must stress that the essence of a classic short story is "its comment on human nature, on the permanent relationships between people, their variety, their expectedness and their unexpectedness." [16] Because of the brevity of the classic short story's form, the characters do not generally develop or change, but are revealed in critical situations. Unless the story is a fantasy, they must be very real and must stand for particular values. In "Vozvrashchenie Chorba" the hero's personality is so realistically portrayed that it may be said to reflect the creator's personality. Chorb, like Nabokov, is a young Russian littérateur who lives in Germany in the 1920s and is surrounded by strangers such as Keller. Chorb was a readily understandable everyday figure with whom the Russian reader abroad could easily relate.

Chorb is introduced through the eyes and opinions of his father-in-law in the exposition. Keller considers Chorb to be an émigré who is suspect, criminal, mad, and, above all, an inappropriate match for his daughter. But Chorb is none of these. His distinctive virtue is his love for Keller's daughter. Chorb's personal sorrow over her death is gradually revealed by his thoughts and actions. His motives are clear. His desire to endure his grief alone so as not to contaminate her memory reflects the depth of his love for her. As he gathers all of the moments of their life together, his quest acquires religious overtones.

The depth of Chorb's agony is intensified by his extraordinarily responsive senses. During his courtship, happiness had a scent for him:

Kak khorosh byl zemlianoi, vlazhnyi, slegka fialkovyi zapakh
vialykh list'ev pokryvavshikh panel' . . . i emu kazalos', chto
vot tak, kak pakhnut vialye list'ia, pakhnet samo schast'e. (pp.
10-11)

How good was the earthy, damp, somewhat violety smell of
the dead leaves strewing the sidewalk! . . . and it seemed to
him that happiness itself had that smell, the smell of dead
leaves. (pp. 64-65)

He was prompted to speak of Russia when he saw birches.
(These birches develop into a fuller symbol of the lost homeland by
"childishly smelling of Russia" for Nabokov's hero in *Dar* [p. 344].)
Now as Chorb returns to the source of his memories, physical and
emotional exhaustion amplify his impressions. Small, meaningful
details become progressively more vivid and bittersweet: the
southern beach, the Swiss hotel, the cliffs, the little house and
stream in the Black Forest. Finally, in the hotel room the familiar
painting on the wall, the glare of the light bulb, the perfumed
clothes in the trunk, and the noisy mouse strike all of Chorb's
senses. The distraught hero is driven outside.
   Chorb's emotional state is apparent not only in his sensitivity
but in his mannerisms. Silent and distracted expressions reflect his
inner turmoil. His repeated indifference, his mad expression, and
his climactic scream frighten the prostitute into leaving him. His
emotional state is matched by the agitation of the Kellers when
they hear of Chorb's arrival and their daughter's "illness." Frau
Keller's face shivers and reddens with worry. The couple are
excited when they appear at the hotel room. Fear and anxiety are
experienced by even the tertiary figures as they eavesdrop without
success.
   The unflattering portrayal of the Kellers serves as a stark
contrast to the picture of Chorb. Nabokov emphasizes the external
rather than the spiritual facets of their personalities, noting their
physical appearance, gestures, speech, attire, and the furnishings of
their home. He uses an overabundance of details, and this
technique serves to stress their apparent artificiality, insensitivity,
and *poshlost'*.[17] A disparity between the staid German and the

emotional Russian temperament may also be inferred. Thus the Kellers' poor opinion of Chorb is immediately discredited.

The formal, festive attire of the couple, marked by Keller's starched shirt, pearl stud, and top hat and his wife's beaded gown and veil, convey opulence. They live in a mansion and go to the opera and the most fashionable night club. During their daughter's wedding reception they eagerly show off the room prepared for the newlyweds. Nabokov uses diminutives to underscore facetiously that everything is ever so correct:

[Varvara Klimovna] ukazyvala na ispolinskuiu perinu, na apel'sinovye tsvety, na dve pary noven'kikh nochnykh tufel',— bol'shie klechatye i malen'kie krasnye s pomponchikami,— postavlennykh riadyshkom na kovrike, po kotoromu goticheskim shriftom shla nadpis': My vmeste do groba. (p. 9)

[Varvara Klimovna] with tender emotion, whispering under her breath . . . pointed out the colossal eiderdown, the orange blossoms, the two pairs of brand-new bedroom slippers—large checkered ones, and tiny red ones with pompons—that she had aligned on the bedside rug, across which a Gothic inscription ran: *"We are together unto the tomb."* (p. 63)

In contrast, the bridal couple assert their independence and escape to a shabby hotel whose salient details imply anything but respectability and propriety: rooms can be rented by the hour; the front door is never locked; the halls smell of sauerkraut and resound with the creaking of beds. Thus, for the Kellers, the hotel will represent the memory of a crime; for Chorb, it is the source of all his lost happiness. This contrast of memories accentuates the difference between the Chorbs and the Kellers. The older generation is completely blind to the love felt by the younger.

Chorb's wife never appears physically in the action of the story. Her primary role is her effect on Chorb as a memory of love and life. Because she is Chorb's blithe spirit, he never calls her by name. On the other hand, she is realistically remembered. He recalls:

On videl ee malen'koe litso, splosh v temnykh vesnushkakh, i glaza, shirokie, blednovato-zelenye, tsveta stekliannykh os-kolkov, vyglazhennykh volnami. (p. 8)

He saw her small face with its dense dark freckles, and her wide eyes, whose pale greenish hue was that of the shards of glass licked smooth by the sea waves. (p. 61)

He recollects her childlike sleep and her light-footedness. The latter points to a graceful spontaneity lacking in her parents:

. . . bystro stupali ee vysokie sapozhki,—i vse dvigalis', dvigalis' ruki . . . legkie smeiushchiesia ruki, kotorye ne znali pokoia. (pp.7-8)

. . . her little boots stepped rapidly, and her hands never stopped moving, moving . . . light, laughing hands that knew no repose. (p. 61)

Ona prygala i smeialas'. (p. 11)

She was jumping and laughing.

Ona pobezhala k sebe pereodetsia. (p. 9)

She ran to her room to change.

She touches stones, rocks, and cliffs and catches leaves and branches on the run. She has run off with Chorb from the banal surroundings of the Keller home. This action in itself indicates a remarkable quality in her personality. It is her dancing and attraction to the elemental and the natural that brings her to her premature death by electrocution:

. . . ona, smeias', tronula zhivoi provod burei provalennogo stolba. (p. 7)

... she had touched, laughing, the live wire of a storm-felled pole. (p. 60)

This was, as Chorb notes, fated. She herself had pointed out to him:

... to, chto bylo, pozhalui, rokovym proobrazom,—luchevoi razmakh pautiny v telegrafnykh provolokakh, unizannykh biserom tumana. (p. 7)

... and something which one might be inclined to regard as a kind of fatidic prefiguration: the radial span of a spider's web between two telegraph wires that were beaded with droplets of mist. (p. 61)

In the Keller home the scatter rug with the words "Together unto the tomb" was not just an indication of the Keller's *poshlost'*; it was also a grim sign of what lay ahead for the couple.

Technically, in a classic short story nothing, even death, should happen by chance.[18] The electrocution of Chorb's wife is incredible. Nabokov justifies this death structurally by having Chorb reflect on its strangeness; Chorb goes so far as to rationalize that his wife was fated to die this the purest and cleanest form of death. In *Lolita* Nabokov returns to the same image of death. Humbert explains that his "very photogenic mother died in a freak accident (picnic, lightning)" (p. 12). Later Humbert notes: "When my mother, in a livid wet dress, under the tumbling mist (so I vividly imagined her), had run panting ecstatically up that ridge above Molinet to be felled there by a thunderbolt, I was but an infant" (p. 289).

Symbolically, death by lightning has mythological overtones and assumes epic proportions. However, in "Vozvrashchenie Chorba" the manner of this death is not as important as the hyperbolic effect that it has on Chorb. The bolt separates Chorb from the rest of the world:

—ves' mir dlia Chorba srazu otshumel, otoshel,—i dazhe mertvoe telo ee, kotoroe on nes na rukakh do blizhaishei derevni, uzhe kazalos' emu chem to chuzhim i nenuzhnym. (p. 7)

Chorb's entire world ceased to sound like a world: it retreated at once, and even the dead body that he carried in his arms to the nearest village struck him as something alien and needless. (p. 60)

The setting of "Vozvrashchenie Chorba" is convincingly presented. What appears particularized to today's reader—a German town—was generalized for many Russians living in Germany when the story was published in 1925. Only a few sharply chosen details were necessary to create an authentic scene: facades of theaters, hotels, and stately homes; silhouettes of the cathedral tower and statues; tree lined streets and park allées. Structurally, the setting is all the more vivid because it is united with the action. The Kellers and more particularly Chorb not only move through this locale but are affected by it. Indeed the hero's motives for returning are to gather all that which his bride had noted:

I tak zhe, kak na iuzhnom pliazhe, on staralsia naiti tot edinstvennyi, kruglyi, chernyi, s pravil'nym belym poiaskom, kamushek, kotoryi ona pokazyvala emu nakanune poslednei progulki,—tochno tak zhe on otyskival po puti vse to, chto otmetila ona vozglasom: osobennyi ocherk skaly, domishko, krytyi serebristo-serymi cheshuikami, chernuiu el' i mostik nad belym potokom. (p. 7)

And just as he had tried, on the southern beach, to find again that unique rounded black pebble with the regular little white belt, which she had happened to show him on the eve of their last ramble, so now he did his best to look up all the roadside items that retained her exclamation mark: the special profile of a cliff, a hut roofed with a layer of silvery-gray scales, a black fir tree and a footbridge over a white torrent. (p. 60)

In this excerpt, Chorb seeks mundane objects to substantiate his happy memories and thereby to recapture his past. Nabokov

repeated this realistically detailed passage with few changes in
Podvig. The hero, Martin, confronts his past when he searches
"with Lida, on the shingly beach, for seaside curios (a round
pebble with a colored belt, a little horseshoe, grainy and red-brown
with rust; pale-green sea-polished fragments of bottle glass that
reminded him of his early childhood and Biarritz)" (p. 17). Even
the introductory image of the unique pebble is repeated.

Intricately linked with the story's setting is its atmosphere.
"Vozvrashchenie Chorba" is emotionally charged because of the
hero's distraught spiritual condition. Clearly, Chorb's memories of
his happy departure contrast sharply with his agonizing return.
Stylistically this mood is accentuated by Nabokov's use of
chiaroscuro. The light-infused beaches of Nice [19] and snow-covered
Switzerland mountains contrast with the pointedly quiet, dark,
dead German town. Many images of shadows and highlights
produce an atmospheric effect of gloom and fright. Foggy figures,
white shadows, black silhouettes, reflections, and transparency
surround Chorb. Sometimes this play of light and dark describes a
dark diagonal falling on an illuminated background. The inverse
effect also is implemented for tone: light falls into darkness. Often
it is a window or door that casts its light:

Za shtoroi rama byla otvorena, i v barkhatnoi bezdne ulitsy
viden byl ugol opery, chernoe plecho kamennogo Orfeia,
vydeliavsheesia na sineve nochi, i riad ogon'kov po tuman-
nomu fasadu, naiskos' ukhodivshemu v sumrak. (p. 14)

Behind the curtain the casement was open and one could
make out, in the velvety depths, a corner of the opera house,
the black shoulder of a stone Orpheus outlined against the
blue of the night and a row of light along the dim facade
which slanted into darkness. (p. 68)

As with Dostoevsky and Flaubert, a light can intensify or
spotlight a significant scene. The sole description of Chorb's
physical agony is depicted in this manner:

On byl bez shapki . . . i svet ot fonaria padal emu na lob, i lob
byl mokryi ot pota, i volosy ko lbu pristali. . . . U nego glaza

ochen' strashno blesteli, i on kak budto davno ne brilsia. (p. 12)

He had no hat . . . and the light of the streetlamp fell on his forehead, and his forehead was all sweaty, and the hair was glued to it by the sweat. . . . His eyes were blazing, their look terrified me, and he seemed not to have shaved for quite a time. (p. 66)

Significantly, his wife's death is marked by a raylike cobweb in the telegraph wire and the clean, white, bright bolt of light. When her image is immortalized, light and dark again cast their rays and shadows. Chorb looks into the well-lit room from behind the dark diagonals of his outstretched fingers and understands that he has survived the test. In Nabokov's subsequent work, light falls not only in beams, shafts, and diagonals but also in rectangles and chinks of light *(Lolita,* p. 296).

In "Vozvrashchenie Chorba" some trivia acquire symbolic proportions. Ordinary objects in the hotel room become symbols of Chorb's life with his wife. The yellow trunk is the most salient item. The cabby clutches the trunk, which, significantly, Chorb has not left behind in Nice. When he arrives at the hotel, he opens it up and the memories it evokes send him outside. Later the prostitute notes the slightly open trunk, feels around inside it, and touches the lovely clothes that smell of fine perfume. She is saddened and now understands Chorb's motives.

Nabokov retained and in some cases developed this image of the chest full of treasured trivia in his novels. In *Mashen'ka* there is a comparable image when the hero, Ganin, packs his worldly belongings in two suitcases. These belongings include, among other things, dirty clothes, Russian books, and, most critically, four love letters from Mashen'ka, Ganin's only tangible link with his loved one. The author then elaborates: " . . . and all those trivial yet somehow precious things which become so familiar to our sight and touch, and whose only virtue is that they enable a person condemned to be always on the move to feel at home, however slightly, whenever he unpacks his fond, fragile, human rubbish for the hundredth time" *(Mary,* p. 126). The importance of these treasure chests both reflects and prophesies the transiency of

Nabokov's own life. In *Dar* (p. 93) the treasure-chest image is more intangible; Fedor's illegal treasure *(klad)* is his gift for poetry and, secondarily, his memories of his lost homeland. In *Zashchita Luzhina* (p. 66), as in *Lolita* (p. 217), the box is real and holds chessmen. Luzhin's chess box is buried, as is the Prince's precious box of toys in *Pale Fire* (p. 124). In his analysis of Gogol, Nabokov observed that "Chichikov's aura is continued and symbolized by his snuffbox and his traveling case" (p. 89); he expanded on this point, thereby revealing his own link with the Russian master.

Objects meaningful to Chorb are also found in his hotel room. The pink painting of the bathers and the washbasin with the light hair in it not only point to the dinginess of the hotel but serve as structural links between Chorb, his wife, and the prostitute. Chorb's wife had laughed at the cheap painting and the exquisite hair they found in the basin. Now when Chorb returns, he remembers his bride's reaction and notes not only the pink painting but the fair hair of the prostitute who is with him. In this manner, all three characters are figuratively joined.

The green couch is also a linking image. The play of light and shadows on the couch attracts Chorb's attention. He recalls that on their wedding night he had let his bride gently fall asleep alone and that he had slept on the nearby couch. Now on his return Chorb awakens to find that the prostitute, not his wife, has crept into bed next to him, Horrified, he flees to the green couch. Thus the couch may represent Chorb's nights of unconsummated love. Nabokov emphasized these objects by coloring them: the yellow trunk, the pink painting, the green couch.

The language of "Vozvrashchenie Chorba" is a fine example of the poetic prose that is the keystone of Nabokov's work. Nabokov himself noted the union of poetry and prose: "Poetry includes all creative writing; I have never been able to see any generic difference between poetry and artistic prose. As a matter of fact, I would be inclined to define a good poem of any length as a concentrate of good prose, with or without the addition of recurrent rhythm and rhyme. The magic of prosody may improve upon what we call prose by bringing out the full flavor of meaning, but in plain prose there are also certain rhythmic patterns, the music of precise phrasing, the beat of thought rendered by recurrent peculiarities of idiom and intonation." [20]

The poetry of Nabokov's prose is a distinctive feature of his early artistic period. Poetic tropes color his prose. These figures of speech are created by using the method of *ostranenie,* "making strange." This is Nabokov's heritage from Tolstoy.[21] Nabokov clearly recognized "making strange" as a device when he spoke of "beats of thoughts being rendered by recurrent *peculiarities of idiom and intonation."* (The italics are mine.) Although Khodasevich wrote that young Nabokov used "making strange" to characterize the artist-heroes of his early novels,[22] the device was surely at the base of his work in his very language.

In the narrative passages of Nabokov's prose adjectives and nouns and/or nouns and verbs are unusually combined into diverse tropes to form striking new effects; for example:

... avtomobil' legkomyslenno osveshchennyi iznutri, prim chal ikh po mert vym ulitsam k zheleznoi kalitke stepennogo osobniachka. (p. 5)

... their car, flippantly lit on the inside, sped through lifeless streets to deposit them at the iron wicket of their small but dignified private house. (p. 59)

These new realistic images rejuvenate hackneyed images and ideas, enriching the language itself.

As "Vozvrashchenie Chorba" is primarily narrative, various poetic figures of speech are threaded through the entire story. Metaphors (in the narrow sense), personifications, and synesthesia are most prevalent. Similes, hyperboles, and alliterations follow in descending order of frequency. All of these tropes are short in length. Many, but not all, are in "made-strange" combinations. By conveying the aesthetic contrasts of light and dark, of mat and gloss, of transparency and reflection, these tropes serve an artistic purpose.

A related facet of Nabokov's language is his use of color. Although the emphasis of the story appears to be on black and white, color plays a major part in the language of "Vozvrashchenie Chorba." Many colors are used attributively in the aforementioned tropes or as modifiers of significant objects such as the yellow trunk. The verbal use of color is limited to: *nepodvizhno i miagko zhelteli derev'ia* (motionlessly and softly the trees showed yellow). The sole nominal example of color is: *ot mutnoi sinevy maiskoi nochi* (from the dulled blue of the May night). In examining the colors of this story, I am struck by the lack of emphasis on any one hue. Generally, in these early stories Nabokov introduced many shades, thus employing Russian's particularly extensive color vocabulary. This keen and purely artistic use of color was, at times, so broad that it extended to the creation of double colors. In "Vozvrashchenie Chorba" there are: *serbristo-seryi* (silvery gray), *blednovato-zelenyi* (palish green), *tusklovato-belyi* (dullish white).

Nabokov wrote in *Speak, Memory* (and also in *Dar*, p. 86), that from childhood he had been fascinated by color: "On top of all this I present a fine case of colored hearing. Perhaps 'hearing' is not quite accurate, since the color sensation seems to be produced by the very act of my orally forming a given letter while I imagine its outline. The long *a* of the English alphabet (and it is this alphabet I have in mind farther on unless otherwise stated) has for me the tint of weathered wood, but a French *a* evokes a polished ebony" (p. 34). This association of color with letter outlines leads me to Nabokov's Belyi-like interest in letter shapes in "Vozvrashchenie Chorba." The two examples are: *krasnye bukvy afishi: Parsifal,* (the red letters of the poster: Parsifal); *goticheskim shriftom shla nadpis': My vmeste do groba* (in Gothic script ran the slogan: We are together unto the tomb).

In this story Nabokov's prepositions and adverbs often imply diagonals and longitudinals: *poperek* (across), *vdol'* (along), *naiskos'* (obliquely, slantwise). This is unusual and perhaps reflects his love of chess, in which the moves are diagonal, vertical, and horizontal. The more prosaic elements of Nabokov's language—colloquialisms, diminutives, Slavonicisms—are effective by their infrequency. When implemented they underline a distinctive feature. I noted above that diminutives point specifically to the *poshlost'* of the Kellers. Slavonicisms are used with reference to Chorb's wife and add a sacred aura to his quest. Here the double meaning inherent in the Slavonic vocabulary adds still another dimension. For instance, *vossozdat'* (to reconstruct, reconstitute, re-create, renew) points not only to Chorb's reconstruction of his wife's image but to its renewal as well. Other Slavonicisms accenting the sanctity of

Chorb's experience are: *vozglas* (cry, proclamation), *iskus* (ordeal, test), *bessmertnyi* (immortal).

"Vozvrashchenie Chorba" is an exceptionally fine piece. The high value Nabokov himself placed on it is indicated by the fact that it is the title story of his first collection, *Vozvrashchenie Chorba*. Although emotional expressions and outbursts color this story, the essence of the work is Chorb's quest for the salient details of his married life, culminating in the reincarnation of his wife. The bits that Chorb seeks become still more meaningful when contrasted with the details that describe the Kellers. Nabokov's overstated description of the Kellers and their home emphasizes their overdone, false, bourgeois way of life. The final confrontation between them and Chorb provides the ironic twist of this story: Chorb's confrontation with his past has not yet ended.

The recapture of memories and/or confrontation with the past were evocative themes for Nabokov's audience. Like many of his characters, Nabokov's readers were expatriated Russians for whom memories were meaningful and sometimes painful. This mood was reflected in much of the Russian émigré literature, which was flooded with an outpouring of reminiscences—a phenomenon that continued for forty years. Readers and writers subsisted on their memoirs of Russia, and there was a dearth of belles lettres in the Russian literature created abroad.

2. "Port"

Chorb's cataclysmic confrontation with his past is unique. In most of Nabokov's early stories, the searching heroes in finding their past attain an inner peace. An atmosphere of tranquillity and contentment pervades them—an attitude in the spirit of Nabokov's direct and balanced outlook. "Port" is just such a measured story. The theme, again man's encounter with his past, concerns a Russian coming upon fellow émigrés.

At first reading the plot seems to be a realistic slice of a Russian's life, and as Field (p. 144) has suggested, the story is a single, strikingly poetic image with no complexity of exposition. However, there is a structural design in "Port." Nikitin arrives in a southern French port hot and exhausted. His seemingly aimless meanderings there have a definite pattern. He goes down the sloping streets of the seaport four times. These walks are interspersed with his search for refuge: in a barbershop, in a restaurant, in a hotel, and finally in a tavern.

The opening barbershop scene immediately depicts Nikitin receiving physical relief from the seething daytime heat. The haircut and shampoo that cool his head are graphically and sensitively described in one metaphoric sentence:

> Vkusnyi kholodok proshel po makushke, pal'tsy krepko vtirali gustuiu penu,—a potom grianul ledianoi dush, eknulo serdtse, mokhnatoe polotentse zarabotalo po litsu, po mokrym volosam. (pp. 17-18)

> A delicious chill passed over the crown, fingers firmly rubbed in the thick foam—and then an icy shower burst forth, the heart missed a beat, a Turkish towel started to work on the face, on the wet hair.

By contrast the street into which he steps is hot and deserted. The sea is bright and blinding to Nikitin and he feels dizzy looking at the blue water. He seeks comfort in the depths of a Russian restaurant. Although it is dirty and hot, it offers both physical and emotional relief. After leaving Russia and then Constantinople, Nikitin now finds himself jobless in this strange, sultry port.[23] Here, in this restaurant, he finds relief from the heat as well as Russian food and a group of expatriates like himself.

These six secondary characters vary in age and are described in the sympathetic manner in which Nikitin views them. All have apparently adjusted, not only to exile, but also to the heat of the port. The old man in the gold-rimmed spectacles enjoys his soup off in a corner. The mistress of the restaurant welcomes Nikitin with a maternal glance, and one of the dogs answers his whistle and affectionately nuzzles his lap. She looks up at Nikitin with kind eyes. The two sailors are suntanned, windburned, and seem oblivious to the heat; unlike Nikitin in his sweaty shirt, they are cool in their net shirts. They convey a sense of well-being and strike up a conversation with the new visitor. They describe enthusiastically their work as coal stokers on a French ship [24] and tell of their travels to faraway ports in Ceylon and China. The heat and grime of both their job and their ports of call do not in anyway diminish their enthusiasm. They take pride in their scientific manner of stoking and appear unperturbed by the hothouselike climate in Shanghai: to them it is warm rain and red sand. They encourage Nikitin to join them and assure him of work. Nikitin notices the moderation, restraint, and evenness of their speech. This measured manner reflects their wholesomeness.

Lialia, the young daughter of the mistress, enters the restaurant in a broad white hat. The hero turns to look at this young girl. Although she does not have a pretty face, it is kind and smiling. He notes that the motion of her low hips gives her away as being Russian. Her name phonically accentuates this lilt. She greets the two dogs, then the sailors. Her admirer appears in the open window. He too is Russian and, judging by his clothes, he has done well. Through the window he imparts a refreshing image in his white jacket and panama. His face is soft and well shaven, and his shoulders are round. As Nikitin sits over his wine and borsch, he observes this hospitable Russian microcosm and overhears snatches of Lialia's conversations with those around her. For Nikitin she transforms the restaurant into Russia with her birches:

Bylo v nei chto-to trogatel'noe, uezdnoe, khotelos' dumat' o fialochnom myle, o dachnom polustanke v berezovom lesu. Konechno, za dver'iu nikakoi Frantsii net. Kiseinye dvizheniia. Solnechnaia chepukha. (p. 20)

There was something touching, provincial in her; one wanted to think about violet soap, about the small country railway station in the birch forest. Of course, beyond the door there is no France. Posturing of a young miss. Sunny nonsense.

Tak i pakhnulo,—pochti narochito, slovno kto-to zabavlialsia tem, chto vydumyvaet etu baryshniu, etot razgovor, etot russkii restoranchik v chuzhezemnom portu,—pakhnulo nezhnost'iu russkikh zakholustnykh budnei. (pp. 21-22)

And so it smelled—almost deliberately, as if someone were amusing himself by fabricating this young lady, this conversation, this little Russian restaurant in a foreign port—it smelled of the tenderness of the Russian backwoods, humdrum existence.

The image of the small station is added here. In *Dar,* Fedor too has a convergence of thoughts, which includes "the memory of a sunny evening at a Russian small railway station" (p. 175).

As Lialia strokes the dog's ear, even the dog seems to be thinking in Russian. This happy and content Russian world prompts Nikitin to daydream about wandering over the seas in search of other such inviting fabled ports, where he can happily eavesdrop on the souls of others. He leaves the restaurant after the sailors and goes out into the glare of the street.

Now Nikitin appears to be better adjusted to his new surroundings. In a shabby hotel reminiscent of Chorb's, the sunlight evokes a new, almost pleasurable response in him as he falls asleep. He dreams he is in the southern Russian port of Yalta and is wandering through the bushes on a slope. This subconscious image links his past walks with his present ramblings. He awakens with a laugh. Perhaps he has noticed this similarity. In a sense, the Russia of his past and his present have coalesced in this central section of "Port." The dream has also served as a transition from the hot day to the cooler night. The port that Nikitin now sees from his window is dusky and cool. He imagines that among the streetwalkers in the road below there must be Russian ones as well. He goes outside again, this time to wander and, significantly, to enjoy his solitary festive spirit.

The formerly oppressive street is now populated. Children are playing. The shop merchant is smoking and relaxing. The officers are walking their young ladies on the boulevard above. Cafés and bars attract Nikitin with their sentimental fiddle, harp, and accordion music and the smell of their fish and wine. Nikitin is lured into a tavern for a cool mug of beer. But the street woman at the adjoining table attracts his attention, first with her shoes, and then with her emerald-green ensemble. As a result, Nikitin is not altogether sure that he wants to spend his last five-franc note on the cool beer after all. Nikitin's repeated attraction to the woman's shoes reflects Nabokov's Pushkinesque interest in "dear little feet."

The nocturnal familiarity and hospitality of the port setting extend to this doll-like woman, the only non-Russian character in the story. Even that detail is not immediately clear. Nikitin imagines that she is someone he knows. He convinces himself of this as he looks at her eyes, long legs, and the swing of her hips. His memories jump as he glances at her kindly face and the moist gleam of her tiny teeth. Nikitin follows her out into the shadows of the port and finally confronts her under a raspberry light.[25] In a steady voice Nikitin reminds the woman that he knows her. Her answer in broken English and then in Provençal testifies that Nikitin has been carried away by wishful thinking. He laughingly gives up and thrusts his last franc note into her hand. She scurries off. A flutter of paper behind him makes Nikitin think that she has followed him. But this is not the case. Nikitin's mistake does not destroy his lighthearted mood. Once again he goes down the street to the sea.

This final scene on the wharf echoes some of the images of the first scene. His head is cooled as the wind rustles through his hair. Again his skipping heartbeat is described. In contrast to the first walk to the sea, this final one is refreshing and satisfying. Nikitin has been infected by the contentment displayed by his compatriots in his brief meeting with them. His mood is now at one with his new environment—the seaport:

Tam, nad lunnym plavnym kolykhan'em voln, na kamennoi grani starinnoi pristani, on sel, svesil nogi i tak sidel dolgo, otkinuv litso i opiraias' na ladoni nazad otognutykh ruk. Prokatilas' paduchaia zvezda s neozhdannost'iu serdechnogo pereboia. Sil'nyi i chistyi poryv vetra proshel po ego volosam, poblednevshim v nochnom siianii. (p. 26)

There, above the moonlit flowing heave of the waves, on the stony edge of the pier, he sat down, lowered his legs and sat thus for a long while, throwing back his face and leaning back

on the palms of his bent hands. A falling star rolled by with
the unexpectedness of a heart stoppage. A strong and clean
gust of wind passed over his hair, which was faded in the
nocturnal radiance.

The image of the falling star has been forecast. Twice a bright
star has been associated with Nikitin's dreams of having a Russian
woman. In the final scene he notes the heavens and watches the
shooting star. This final image and its overtone of "wishing on a
falling star" imply that Nikitin will have to content himself with
dreaming and wishing for a woman. It also adds a universal
dimension to this story. Nikitin's contented experience is extended
beyond the confines of this port.

The plot line is accentuated by the contrast, not only of day and
night, but of heat and cold, past and present, reality and dream.
The traditional rising and falling actions and conclusion of the
classic story form are dropped. The exposition--Nikitin's first day
in the French port—is expanded. This structure is in the spirit of
Chekhov's twentieth-century novella.

The narrative form is the stream-of-experience method. The
entire action is seen from Nikitin's point of view. On the second to
last page, the narrative and dialogue slip unobtrusively into
Nikitin's stream of consciousness for the first time. Significantly
this occurs during his daydreams about the woman in green.

Nikitin, the central figure in "Port," is immediately described. In
keeping with the stream-of-experience narrative, Nabokov described him as he saw himself, first in the barber's mirror:

Pered soboi, v tusklovatom stekle, Nikitin videl svoe zagoreloe
litso, lepnye priadi iarkikh volos, sverkanie nozhnits,
strekotavshikh nad ukhom,—i glaza ego byli vnimatel'ny i
strogi, kak eto vsegda byvaet, kogda smotrish'sia v zerkalo. (p.
17)

Before him, in the dull glass, Nikitin saw his own tanned face,
the molded strands of glossy hair, the glisten of the scissors,
chirring above his ear—and his eyes were intent and severe, as
it always is, when you look at yourself in the mirror.

Later Nikitin sees his shadow as a sapphire brilliance, growing large in the depths, between the building walls. Although not photographic, these depictions create a highly realistic effect.

"Port" is the title of the story, and the atmosphere of that port, as it strikes Nikitin, is set in the first three sentences of this ten-page story:

> V nizkoi parikmakherskoi pakhlo prelymi rozami. Zharko i tiazhelo zhuzhzhali mukhi. Solntse luzhami toplenogo meda gorelo na polu, shchipalo bleskom flakony, skvozilo skvoz' dolguiu zanavesku v dver'iakh: zanaveska—glinianye busy da trubochki iz bambuka, vperemezhku nanizannye na chastye shnury—rassypchato pozviakivala i perelivalas', kogda kto-nibud', vkhodia, plechom ee otkidyval. (p. 17)

> In the low barbershop it smelled of moldy roses. The flies buzzed hotly and heavily. The sun burned on the floor in pools of melted honey, it pinched the bottles with its brilliance, it showed through the long curtain in the doors: the curtain—clay beads and little tubes of bamboo, alternately threaded on dense cords—clanked and shimmered as if spilled, when someone entering would throw it over his shoulder.

No questions are raised in this passage. No characters are introduced. Instead it is a striking example of the poetic language that Nabokov will use throughout the story. "Made-strange" adjective-noun and noun-verb combinations form a substantial part of the narrative of "Port." Conversely, in the dialogue in the middle of the story there are no such images. The images tend to be a full sentence, not merely a clause long. The wealth and compression of the expressions not only compensate for the story's lack of dynamism but emphasize the impressionist tone of Nikitin's experience. Metaphors and personifications abound. Similes and synesthesia may also be found. There are at least ten alliterative phrases. Consider the repeating sound clusters of these phrases: *skvozilo skvoz'; busy da trubochki iz bambuka; biuro truda brodil; uzkimi ulochkami; stoial solomennyi stol; razyskivat' russkii restoranchik; za sosednim stolikom sideli; dva lokhmatykh shchenka lopocha lapkami.*

Color plays a strong role in "Port," chiefly in the attributive function. Some thirty-odd polychromatic elements are found in the story; on the average there are four colors per page of the text. Violet is the major color and is mentioned in three different hues: *fioletovyi*, *lilovyi* (twice), and *sirenevyi*. There is an associative image: *fialochnoe mylo* (violet soap). Purple in all its shades is Nabokov's favorite literary color. In his study of Gogol he wrote: "It was Gogol (and after him Lermontov and Tolstoy) who first saw yellow and violet at all" (p. 86). This color dominates *Mashen'ka*, *Lolita*, *Ada*, and *Transparent Things* and is used often in images in *Dar* and *Speak, Memory*. In *Dar*, Fedor notes that Tolstoy preferred purple, and later this young hero smells the "Turgenevian odor of heliotrope" in his lady's bedroom (p. 162). Thus Nabokov unotrusively indicated that he shared his penchant for purple with other Russian masters.

Stylistically, the restaurant scene contains only two colloquialisms, perhaps reflecting upon the intelligence of the émigrés, which Nikitin himself has been quick to note. However, when the sailors speak of their stoking they use short sentences and thus not only describe their task but convey its sense of rhythm:

Napolnite bad'iu, stavite ee na telezhku. Podkatyvaete k starshemu kochegaru. Tot udarom lopaty—raz!—otpakhivaet pech'—dva!—toi zhe lopatoi brosaet, znaete, shiroko, veerom, chtoby rovno leg. Rabota tonkaia. Izvol' sledit' za strelkoi, a esli ponizitsia davlenie . . . (p. 20)

You fill the tub, place it on a wagon. Roll it up to the senior stoker. That one with a blow of the shovel—one!—tosses the oven open—two!—with the same shovel he throws, you know, widely, fanlike, so that it lies evenly. It's delicate work. If you please, follow the arrow and if the pressure falls. . .

Incidentally, I note here another, more poetic phrase of one of these sailors: "Teplyi dozhdik, krasnyi pesochek" (p. 22) ("Warm rain, red sand"). Reddish grains are a recurrent Nabokovian motif, and this is its initial appearance. In "Rozhdestvo" this minuscule detail will reappear as cinnamon scattered on the snow. I have already cited a passage from *Podvig* in which a little horseshoe is grainy and brown with rust (See above, p. 30.) In *Dar* this detail reappears: ". . . on the soft red sand one could make out the sigla of a summer day" (p. 97). The image even resurfaces in *Ada:* " 'Do you want a sprinkle of cinnamon on your *lait caillé*? ' asked Marina. 'You know, Belle' (turning to Mlle. Larivière), 'she used to call it "sanded snow" when she was a baby' " (p. 155).

Although in "Port" there is no direct mention of letter shapes, Nabokov did not miss an opportunity to play with the alphabet. When Lialia speaks French, presumably with a strong Russian accent, the phrase is expressed in Cyrillic characters: "Zhe vu zasiur" (p. 21). Later Nabokov linguistically underscored the fact that the prostitute whom Nikitin meets is French. When she speaks her native tongue, Provençal French, it is written in the Latin alphabet: "T'es polonais, alors?" (p. 26). When she speaks a foreign language, it is written in an alphabet that is alien to her. Thus her remark in broken English is rendered in Cyrillic: "—Inglish? Iu spik inglish?" (p. 25).

The chiaroscuro effect dominates the style of "Port," but not as strongly as in "Vozvrashchenie Chorba." It does not reflect Nikitin's mood or actions. Rather, it conveys the mood of the port. The related images of curtains, doors, and windows are used throughout "Port," particularly in the daylit half of the story. Curtains separate the cooler interiors from the hot external world of the port. The windows and doors are also dividers. They frame significant views for the hero, such as the man in a panama hat, the port from the hotel room, sunlight in the doorways of the barbershop and restaurant, or the dark depths [26] of the cafés and taverns. Another image that is threaded through this story is movement downward, often along diagonals. The streets slope. Streams run down these streets, and children send paper boats down the currents. The sun casts angular shadows, and finally the shooting star falls through the sky. This image lends a feeling of action to the fairly static plot of "Port" and gives the story momentum. Nabokov used this technique to a lesser degree in "Vozvrashchenie Chorba."

I disagree with Field concerning the nature of the concluding scene of "Port." Field has written about Nikitin: "Here it is the character himself who, in a manner wholly in keeping with his aimless way of life, confuses dream and reality, past and present." Field then continues: *"Port* ends with Nikitin, who has no clear past, present, or future, sitting on a wharf and looking up at the sky through which at that moment a shooting star is falling" (p. 144). I maintain that the crux of "Port" is not Nikitin's aimless way of life. It is precisely the opposite. In the French port this Russian émigré finds familiar details of his past in the microcosmic restaurant, epitomized in Lialia. The contentment that he derives from this encounter extends to the world beyond the restaurant door. He is now able to find peace and well-being with nature itself down on the pier, in the lightly blowing wind under the shooting star.

3. "Blagost' "

In "Blagost' " ("Benevolence") another Russian émigré finds similar contentment in the seemingly unimportant but tangible aspects of his exile. The central theme of "Blagost' " is, as indicated by the title, the sense of well-being acquired by the hero-narrator. Thus the predominating feature of this eight-page story is its atmosphere.

As in "Port," there is no intricate plot. Rather, the story is a slice of a sculptor's life as described by him in a mental message to his loved one. The simple plot line and the classical narrative structure of the story are at one: the *siuzhet* and the *fabula* coalesce. The exposition sets the scene, as the hero moves out of the darkness of his studio into the light of breaking dawn. Like many of Nabokov's heroes, he looks through his window:

V shirokii prolet okna vidny byli cherepichnye kryshi Berlina—ochertaniia ikh menialis', blagodaria nevernym vnutrennim perelivam stekla, i sredi krysh bronzovym ar-buzom vzdymalsia dal'nyi kupol. (p. 158)

In the broad expanse of the window the tile roofs of Berlin were visible—their outlines changed, thanks to the irregular interior tints of the pane, and among the roofs a distant cupola swelled like a bronze watermelon.

He has spent all night thinking of "her." His mind flashes back to their quarrel two weeks before and his subsequent phone call to arrange a rendezvous at the Brandenburg Gate. The rising action consists of the walk that the lovelorn artist takes to this meeting and his unpleasant reaction to the dry air and the sun's rays. He knows that his loved one, who has already once been unfaithful, will stand him up.

The climax of the story takes place appropriately under the massive gate. As the hero waits in vain, he observes the German passersby. In particular, he identifies himself with an old woman vendor who, like him, is stationary and waiting. She waits for customers for her colorful postcards, guidebooks, and maps. In the brisk autumn wind, the old woman is given a cup of hot coffee by a watchman in the nearby guardhouse. Her bliss while drinking this coffee deeply and delicately suffuses the hero's soul. She responds to the watchman's kindness by offering him two of her postcards, whereupon the hero himself suddenly views the entire world through his newly felt happiness and bliss. The realization that his love will not come is more than compensated for by this smiling old vendor. Through a chain of events and effects from everyday life, she has infused a glorious sense of benevolence into the artist-hero.

The falling action of the story consists of the hero's homeward journey. He catches the contented glances of the passersby as he makes his way. The rising action with its sunny background and the departing heartbroken artist are now opposed to this dark rainy evening with the returning happy hero. The contrasts between the surroundings and the hero are transposed, and the way is prepared for a positive ending. The conclusion of "Blagost'" is marked by the resurgence of the hero's creative powers that this contented moment has given him:

... v pal'tsakh ia oshchutil miagkuiu shchekotku mysli, nachinaiushchei tvorit'. (p. 164)

... in my fingers I sensed the gentle tickling of a thought, beginning to create.

This ending is accelerated and pushed to its height by the hero's hopping from the rainy darkness of the Berlin streets into an illuminated, dry, fast-moving tram. His anticipation of the rhythmic "tok tok" of the round chestnuts falling and rolling on the tram roof bring the story to an end. Thus, as the hero appeared out of the night's darkness in the exposition, now in the conclusion he recedes back into it.

The lyrical atmosphere of the story is furnished by a sculptor who is not only sensitive and impressionable but needs a sense of well-being in order to create. The opening paragraph is an unobtrusive accumulation of significant details: the studio, clay models, dusty fog, debris, splinters of plaster of paris, plasticine dust, and a figure resembling his loved one. It is covered by a wet rag, in the process of being sculptured. The source of his inspiration is his love for this woman. This inspirational image unfolds as a poetic memory:

> . . . udar chernoty, dushistoe i sil'noe dvizhenie. (pp. 157-58)

> . . . a stroke of blackness, a perfumed and intense movement.

As the hero's thoughts focus on his loved one, it becomes clear that she is deceitful and does not value his love, but his equivocal appraisal in no way tempers his affection. While waiting, he repeats six times that she will not come. She has deceived him before, and he does not dare to peek around the corner of the Brandenburg Gate to learn the unpleasant truth—that she is not coming. His emotions are particularly well delineated in his cigarette smoking. He agitatedly puffs. The cigarette smolders crookedly and bitterly. He finally casts it down and then catches it with the end of his walking stick. It is flaming sparks. Even when he sees that she will not come and when he is filled with a new contentment, his love still has a place in his thoughts. The source of happiness hides somewhere secretly in her. Contrary to her agreement, she never appears at the Brandenburg Gate, and as such she never figures in the story. She is the first of Nabokov's phantom heroines. Mashen'ka and Chorb's wife follow soon after.

The artist's contentment abides not only in his loved one but in the image of the old woman who accepts her lot with smiles and radiating kindness. She is realistically and colorfully described:

Ona zabyla svoi lotok, otkrytki, kholodnyi veter, ameri-cantsa,—i tolko potiagivala, posasyvala, vsia ushla v kofe svoi, tochno tak zhe, kak i ia zabyl svoe ozhidanie i videl tol'ko pliushevyi tulupchik, potusknevshie ot blazhenstva, glaza, korotkie ruki v sherstianykh mitenkakh, szhimavshie kruzhku. Ona pila dolgo, pila medlennymi glotkami, blagogoveino slizyvala bakhromku penki, grela ladoni o tepluiu zhest'. I v dushu moiu vlivalas' temnaia, sladkaia teplota. Dusha moia tozhe pila, tozhe grelas',—i u korichnevoi starushki byl vkus kofe s molokom. (p. 162)

She forgot her kiosk, the postcards, the cold wind, the American—and only sipped, sucked, completely disappeared in her coffee; in exactly this same way I forgot my waiting and I saw only the plush cape, the eyes, dimmed from bliss, the short hands in the woolen mittens, clutching the mug. She drank for a long while, drank with slow swallows, reverently licked the fringe of the foam, warmed her palms against the warm pewter. And into my soul poured a dark, sweet warmth. My soul also drank, also warmed itself—and the brown, little old woman had the taste of coffee with milk.

This old woman, the street noises, and nature, in short, the petty snatches of life, blend. Together they create a peaceful montage which evokes an artistically meaningful response in the hero:

Togda ia pochuvstvoval nezhnost' mira, glubokuiu blagost' vsego, chto okruzhalo menia, sladostnuiu sviaz' mezhdu mnoi i vsem sushchim,—i ia ponial, chto radost', kotoruiu ia iskal v tebe, ne tol'ko v tebe taitsia, a dyshit vokrug menia povsiudu, v proletaiushchikh ulichnykh zvukakh, v podole smeshno podtianutoi iubki, v zheleznom i nezhnom gudenii vetra, v osennikh tuchakh, nabukhaiushchikh dozhdem. Ia ponial, chto mir vovse ne bor'ba, ne chereda khishchnykh sluchainostei, a mertsaiushchaia radost', blagostnoe volnenie, podarok, neotsenennyi nami. (pp. 162-63)

Then I sensed the tenderness of the world, the deep benevolence of everything that surrounded me, the sweet bond between me and everything real—and I understood that the joy which I sought in you, not only hides in you, but it breathes everywhere, all around me, in the street sounds which fly past, in the hem of the amusingly pulled-up skirt, in the iron and tender howl of the wind, in the autumnal clouds, bulging with rain. I understood, the world is absolutely not a struggle, not a series of horrid matters of chance, but a fleeting joy, a benevolent agitation, a present, unappreciated by us.

Ironically, this smiling old woman with her short yellow plush jacket, gathered at the waistband; her brown skirt with the pulled-up hem; her smiling, brimmed hat and worn ducklike shoes, is the heroine of this story—not the more romantic, love-inspiring, faceless, and poetic figure in the veil, black silks, and perfume. The old woman is the personification of benevolence. However, the hero finds that benevolence lies not in the old woman and the soldier alone but in the smiles, in the marvelous gestures of the passersby, and in the divine sorrow of the horse's lilac-tinged eyes. The last image recalls the dog's eyes in "Port." All the passersby are scurrying and rushing, as are the buses. Like Chorb, the hero tries to catch and gather these evanescent moments of happiness.

Nature is woven into the story as well. The autumn wind is visible by its effect. Morning flickers; clouds fly and break through the morning sky; reddish leaves run; the hero is forced to put up his collar; and the soldier is prompted to give the old woman a warming cup of coffee. The wind ruffles the postcards, turns the pages of the guidebook, abuses the city maps. It slants the rain. Its effect is seen in in the hurrying, hunched-over pedestrians. Finally the forces of the autumn wind and large clouds combine, and rain starts falling with accelerating frequency, wetting the hands of the hero. These natural elements join with the street noises, which are, as often, pinpointed in Nabokov's ever-present tram. First the hero sees the amber-colored panes of the tram and then he sees them as dark-colored windows. Here Nabokov in a realistic, yet unusual fashion, indicated that the hero has hopped from the outside to the inside of the tram. Inside he hears the "tok tok" of the chestnuts. This is a synthesis of the street sounds, the kind wind, and the accelerating rain. The hero is thus rushed home to his cool studio, no longer in need of his love.

The language of "Blagost' " is poetic, suiting the lyrical timbre of its theme. I have discussed the large central theme of *blagost'* as personified by the old woman. The autumn wind and its effect are also poetic. In considering the more detailed aspects of Nabokov's language, I note that in this very early prose piece he already employed a number of "made-strange" adjective-and-noun combinations. Most of them are metaphors and personifications; one is synesthesia: *v kholodnoi teni* (in the cold shadow); and there are other lesser-used tropes. The more expanded noun-and-verbal combinations are extensive in their use and in their variety of poetic devices. These poetic elements have not only an aesthetic value but a functional one in this particularly subjective story. For instance, the intangibility of the hero's image of his loved one can only be expressed metaphorically:

. . . molchanie i slezy, i teplyi shelk tvoikh kolen. (p. 158)

. . . silence and tears, and the warm silk of your lap.

This fragment conveys credibly and succinctly what the hero feels. Progressive synecdoches are employed to describe what the hero sees. He views the old woman in the brown skirt first as the "brown old woman" as she has, both for herself and for his drinking soul, "the taste of coffee with milk." After her bliss has been transmitted to the hero she becomes "my coffee old woman." Finally she is uniquely, almost affectionately, characterized as "the pulled-up skirt hem." Likewise, the hero is introduced first to the green watchman; then he sees a green shoulder turn into the depth of the guardhouse, and later only the green cuff on the sleeve reaches out. Here the poetic figure is used more to focus on what the hero actually sees rather than on what he feels. This same device is employed in "Port," when Nikitin only sees the white rounded shoulders of Lialia's admirer through the restaurant window. Alliterations serve a structural purpose. These devices are concentrated in the final paragraph and push the story to a satisfying end—fading out on a rhythmic, onomatopoetic repetition of "tok . . . tok. . . ."

Colors are used primarily for characterization: the black of the loved one, the yellow and brown of the old coffee lady, the green of the soldier, and the red hat of the passing woman. Nabokov's favorite lilac occurs twice. Chiaroscuro and the related contrast between flickering brightness and dull fogginess are interwoven into the story as an aesthetic device. Reflecting and transparent windows are also a motif.

A few archaic Slavonicisms serve to underline the exalted quality of "Blagost'," itself a Slavonic word meaning "benevolence" or "goodness." Some examples are *blagogoveino* (reverently), *blagostnoe* (benevolent), *blazhenstvo* (bliss), *bozhestvennoe* (divine). The first three words also carry the root of the title, *blago-* (bene-). Diminutives are used to paint a sympathetic portrait of the old woman. Otherwise, the style of this interior monologue is neutral.

In summary, "Blagost'," like "Port," is lyrical in tone. A lone man, in this story a sculptor, is able to overcome sadness by finding contentment in his immediate surroundings: Berlin, its weather, edifices, trams, and, above all, its people. A kindly old lady becomes the embodiment of benevolence for the hero. The sculptor catches and gathers the smiles radiating on the faces of pedestrians and the movements of their shadows. The cumulative effect of these urban details is not merely the contentment that it engenders but the inspiration that it prompts. The sculptor is once again able to sense in his fingers the urge to create. Therefore in "Blagost' " trivia are important not only as tangible and sacred souvenirs for Nabokov's émigré hero but as aesthetic observations and inspiration for his artistic hero; a slight twist in Nabokov's realistic approach.

4. "Pis'mo v Rossiiu"

The satisfaction derived from valuing the small details of a man's life is the germ of still another early story. In "Pis'mo v Rossiiu" ("A Letter to Russia," translated by Nabokov as "A Letter that Never Reached Russia") the loving message characterizing "Blagost'" is concretized. "Pis'mo v Rossiiu" opens appropriately as a traditional love letter: "Drug moi dalekii i prelestnyi" (p. 43) ("My charming, dear, distant one" [p. 84]), addressed to the young woman whom the narrator sweetly kissed behind a wax figure in the Suvorov Museum. This missive also has a strong autobiographical element. In Chapter 12 of *Speak, Memory,* Nabokov recalled his first love, Tamara.[27] He described their point of rendezvous: "So from these great museums we graduated to smaller ones, such as the Suvorov, for instance, where I recall a most silent room full of old armor and tapestries, and torn silk banners, with several bewigged, heavily booted dummies in green uniforms standing guard over us" (p. 236). Nabokov, like his letter writer, had left Russia eight years earlier. He describes this departure in *Speak, Memory* as more a departure from Tamara than a departure from his homeland: "—and the sense of leaving Russia was totally eclipsed by the agonizing thought that Reds or no Reds, letters from Tamara would still be coming, miraculously and needlessly, to southern Crimea, and would search there for a fugitive addressee, and weakly flap about like bewildered butterflies set loose in an alien zone, at the wrong altitude, among an unfamiliar flora" (p. 251). "Pis'mo v Rossiiu" may be considered Nabokov's answer to these unreceived letters. Originally this story was envisaged as a part of the second chapter of Nabokov's projected novel *Schast'e (Happiness).* The plan was dropped, and the excerpt was included in the collection *Vozvrashchenie Chorba.*

In writing about Nabokov's early stories, Mikhail Tsetlin noted that the tradition of the typical Russian story required that nothing should occur.[28] Tsetlin found, however, that Nabokov's stories contained either a strong external plot or an intense internal experience. Using Tsetlin's criteria, I find that "Pis'mo v Rossiiu" and "Blagost'" are traditional Russian stories but atypical Nabokov stories. As in "Blagost'," so in "Pis'mo v Rossiiu" the atmosphere is the primary element. Man's happiness as evoked by his surroundings is the crux of the story. The final paragraph summarizes this theme.

Slushai, ia sovershenno schastliv. Schast'e moe—vyzov.
Bluzhdaia po ulitsam, po ploshchadiam, po naberezhnym
vdol' kanala,—rasseianno chuvstvuia guby syrosti skvoz'
dyriavye podoshvy,—ia s gordost'iu nesu svoe neob"iasnimoe
schast'e. (p. 48)

Listen: I am ideally happy. My happiness is a kind of
challenge. As I wander along the streets and the squares and
the paths by the canal, absently sensing the lips of dampness
through my worn soles, I carry proudly my ineffable happiness. (p. 87)

There is no strong plot or intense internal experience in "Pis'mo
v Rossiiu." It is a calm and tranquil sketch that begins with a
flashback to the narrator's past in Russia. Having reflected upon
his contented love affair in St. Petersburg, he observes that as a
writer he must not deafen memories with epithets, as he finds
himself doing in the opening lines of this story. He observes that it
is a peaceful night when even the furniture does not move. In
Nabokov's realistic-symbolic and symbolic stories, furniture moves
when the hero experiences emotional turmoil. Thus this Nabokovian detail emphasizes the tranquillity felt by the narrator. Only
the water gurgles and overflows in the housepipes. The narrator
then wanders from his dark and quiet apartment into the asphalt-
glistening city. He turns to a placid and realistic description of
Berlin. He notes the streets, the vehicles, the buildings, and the
passersby, and he ends up in a tavern where he enjoys watching
happy couples dancing. He philosophizes about fashion trends,
turning specifically to dances, and concludes that this is his own
night:

—a za dver'iu—moia vernaia, moia odinokaia noch', vlazhnye
otbleski, gudki avtomobilei, poryvy vysokogo vetra. (p. 47)

And meanwhile, outside the door, waits my faithful, my
lonely night with its moist reflections, hooting cars, and gusts
of high-blowing wind. (pp. 86-87)

Almost as a postscript, the narrator relates how on the following morning he visited the Orthodox cemetery and saw the crescentlike footprints of an old woman at the foot of her husband's grave cross. She had hanged herself during the narrator's tranquil night. The narrator is able to view this death of a fellow Russian émigŕee as mysterious rather than as dramatic or tragic. Seeing her foot tracks, he suddenly understands that there is a child's smile in death and he wonders if perhaps he has written this letter to his beloved only to tell about this light and gentle death.

In the story's conclusion the hero's final thoughts project into the future. He notes the lasting value of a writer's contentment. Centuries will pass. Schoolboys will be bored with the history of "our perturbations." All of this, however, will pass, save the happiness that the narrator feels and that is reflected in his Berlin night:

> ... v mokrom otrazhenii fonaria, v ostorozhnom povorote kamennykh stupenei, spuskaiushchikhsia v chernye vody kanala, ulybke tantsuiushchei chety, vo vsem, chem Bog okruzhaet tak shchedro chelovecheskoe odinochestvo. (p. 48)

> ... in the moist reflection of a streetlamp, in the cautious bend of stone steps that descend into the canal's black waters, in the smiles of a dancing couple, in everything with which God so generously surrounds human loneliness. (p. 87)

The writer, despite his separation from his homeland, feels happy—unusual for an émigré, particularly one who is an artist and needs his homeland for inspiration. However, this writer implies that it is precisely the peace and absence of uphéavals in Berlin that enable him to be content. Thus the expected tension between émigré and alien land never occurs, as there is no conflict to be resolved.

As early as 1930 Nikolai Andreev aptly noted that this very ability to create abroad was a remarkable facet in Nabokov's work. The historian observed: "[Nabokov's] example destroys with complete distinctness the mistaken and superficial notion that apparently a writer's art, deprived of its native soil, is doomed to perish and wither abroad, remaining at best only a talented and weak reminiscence" (I). Field (p. 115) has observed that this émigré contentment represents an indirect attack by Nabokov on the Soviet Union. I disagree. "Pis'mo v Rossiiu" appears to me to have no political overtones.

Because of the slight, impressionistic plot, the story benefits from its brevity—five pages. Its structure is chronological. The exposition looks to the past. The central portion reflects on the present and observes the three unities. The location is Berlin; the action is the narrator's solitary walk; and the time span is limited to one specific night. The conclusion points to the future.

Although the content of this story is thin, it contains some unique passages of poetic prose, describing the Berlin setting. Nabokov had the gift of catching the beauty of a humdrum, often nocturnal, urban scene. On the broader symbolic level, night is personified and even seems to belong to the narrator, as noted above. There are few "made-strange" adjectives, but images one or two sentences long prevail and lend a serenity to Berlin as the narrator wanders *(stranstvuet)* along its dark and quiet streets. Chiaroscuro is the most significant effect. In the nocturnal setting the streetlamps are reflected on the asphalt. The tram-stop post is lit, as is the firebox, which has a garnet light—not to be associated here with the "low haunts" cited above. An opening door emits a gentle light. The tram and train are illuminated from within, and the giant movie theater is aglow with diamond lights. The shop window is darkly lit. By illuminating the night, the light sets off nocturnal shadows:

. . . ego ten' proxodit u menia pod nogami (pp. 44-45).

. . . its shadow passes me underfoot.

In *Speak, Memory,* Nabokov recalled his early love for just such evening jewels and colored lights: "[Mother] would produce a mass of jewelry for my bedtime amusement. I was very small then, and those flashing tiaras and chokers and rings seemed to me hardly inferior in mystery and enchantment to the illumination in the city during the imperial fêtes, when, in the padded stillness of a frosty night, giant monograms, crowns, and other armorial designs, made of colored electric bulbs—sapphire, emerald, ruby—glowed with a kind of charmed constraint above snow-lined cornices on house-fronts along residential streets" (p. 36). Colors are also found in the night darkness, tending toward brown, yellow, and red.

In this seemingly quiet Berlin there is much motion, often metaphorical: the water overflows in the housepipes, the reflections leak on the asphalt, the firebox is filled *(nalityi)* with yellow light. The tram flies by. The automobile rolls along and its shadow passes the narrator. The door opens and shuts. The cinema wall advertisement swells. A prostitute passes. A mannequin shows off her clothes. A train goes past. Couples dance in the tavern, and finally an old woman hangs herself at her husband's new grave.

Nabokov enhanced the effect of motion in this story by making the images strange. The conductor makes his way "against the current" in the tramcar. A great Dane walks his mistress. The narrator's progress down the street is accented by what passes him, not by what he passes. For instance, the movie star's face on the advertisement grows as the narrator advances. The most striking image in the story is the arrival home of an unseen man:

Sam chelovek ne viden v temnote, da i nikogda nel'zia znat' napered, kakaia imenno paradnaia dver' ozhivet, so skrezhetom primet kliuch, raspakhnetsia, zamret na bloke, zakhlopnetsia; kliuch s vnutrennei storony zaskrezheshchet snova, i v glubine, za dvernym steklom, zasiiaet na odnu udivitel'nuiu minutu miagkii svet. (p. 44)

The man himself is not visible in the darkness, and you never know beforehand which front door will come alive to accept a key with grinding condescension, swing open, pause, retained by the counterweight, slam shut; the key will grind again from the inside, and, in the depths beyond the glass pane of the door, a soft radiance will linger for one marvelous minute. (p. 84)

For all its strangeness, this sentence creates a highly realistic scene. Although the city is peaceful, there are many night noises. Not only does the door close shut, but the train passes with its powerful iron music, and the tram screeches around the curve. The car honks moistly. Parenthetically, note that car honks occur often in Nabokov's stories; for example, in "Zvonok," "Trubnyi rev pros-tuzhennykh taksomotrov . . ." (p. 29) ("The trumpet roar of the chilled taxis . . ."); in "Kartofel'nyi El'f," "Svezho i nezhno propel avtomobil'nyi rozhok" (p. 173) ("The automobile horn sang out freshly and tenderly"). These "made-strange" combinations are even more striking in "Pis'mo v Rossiiu" because of the lengthy sentences, which are frequently expanded with secondary clauses. The cumulative impression is one of very dense imagery in this brief story.

5. "Putevoditel' po Berlinu"

Berlin is the city that is almost always a background theme in Nabokov's early stories. For him Berlin did not have the special, personal, social, or political connotation that Paris had for Balzac or London had for Dickens. It assumed importance because it actually surrounded him as he wrote. Apropos of this, Nabokov said: "I have always been indifferent to social problems, merely using the material that happened to be near, as a voluble diner pencils a street corner on the table cloth or arranges a crumb and two olives in a diagrammatic position between menu and salt cellar." [29] Berlin is the setting for his novels *Mashen'ka* and *Korol' dama valet,* for instance. In *Dar,* Fedor's peregrinations through Berlin are pages long. Berlin is the prominent backdrop in "Blagost' " and "Pis'mo v Rossiiu"; and it is the central theme of one of Nabokov's earliest stories, "Putevoditel' po Berlinu" ("A Guide to Berlin").

Ostensibly this story is a standard guide to Berlin's sights and scenery, but not the type of red guidebook that Nabokov depicted on the old woman's stool in "Blagost'." This is a special guide to some of the "important" sights and aspects of the city: the pipes, [30] the trams, the jobs, the Hotel Eden, the beer hall.

One is struck first by the narrator's opening comment that these disparate and seemingly trifling things are "important" features of Berlin and, secondly, by the odd combination they represent. However, as the narrator describes them, it becomes clear that this is a writer's guide and that this writer has a definite purpose. He has not written it merely for art's sake, nor for a drinking companion, but for future generations:

Mne dumaetsia, chto v etom smysl pisatel'skogo tvorchestva: izobrazhat' obyknovennye veshchi tak, kak oni otraziatsia v laskovykh zerkalakh budushchikh vremen, nakhodit' v nikh tu blagoukhannuiu nezhnost', kotoruiu pochuiut tol'ko nashi potomki v te dalekie dni, kogda vsiakaia meloch' nashego obikhoda stanet sama po sebe prekrasnoi i prazdnichnoi,—v te dni, kodga chelovek, nadevshii samyi prosten'kii segodniashnii pidzhachek, budet uzhe nariazhen dlia izyskannogo mask- arada. (p. 97)

I think that here lies the sense of literary creation: to portray ordinary objects as they will be reflected in the kindly mirrors of future times; to find in the objects around us the fragrant tenderness that only posterity will discern and appreciate in the far-off times when every trifle of our plain everyday life will become exquisite and festive in its own right: the times when a man who might put on the most ordinary jacket of today will be dressed up for an elegant masquerade. (p. 94)

Actually the aspects of Berlin he has chosen are not as disparate as they appear to be initially. They are all facets that particularly interested Nabokov. The Berlin street life, trams, childhood memories that dip into the past or project into the future, and even the fascinating letter combinations considered in this story are recurrent motifs in many of his other works.

The entire story is told in the present tense, and the hero-narrator is the subjective "I." Its tone is marked by the narrator's reiteration of his subjectivity and by his positive reaction to Berlin, which is in turn rejected by the writer's drinking companion in the final frame of this piece. Only then does the narrative move into dialogue. However, this dialogue is onesided. The drinking companion speaks, but the narrator continues his straight narrative. Thus two methods are employed simultaneously.

Seemingly "Putevoditel' po Berlinu" follows a guidebook format and therefore does not have the traditional short-story structure. It does, however, have a compositional design. There is a definite frame. The narrator, after a morning trip to the zoo, goes into a beer hall with a drinking companion. Thus the storyteller and listener are immediately presented. Within the frame are vignettes of various spots in Berlin: I. "Pipes"; II. "Tram"; III. "Jobs"; IV. "Eden"; and V. "Beerhall." The last scene ties the conclusion structurally to the introductory frame. All of these short pieces, although clearly divided by Roman numerals, [31] are intricately linked by subject matter and by the general tone of beauty and philosophy that colors the realistic descriptions. An introductory comment to the effect that the narrator will speak of "pipes and trams" brings the reader to the first sketch, so brief and poetic that it appears to be a poem. The trams, which have left their orange reflection on those pipes, are the subject of the second vignette. Here he speaks of fashions and passing fads. In "Pis'mo v Rossiiu" he had noted modish fluctuations in various dances; now he turns to the fate of diligences and horse trams and sadly reflects that the electric trams will soon be replaced as well. The narrator focuses in particular on the tram conductor, whom Nabokov has already depicted in "Pis'mo v Rossiiu." He observes how nimbly the man goes about his duties:

U tramvainogo konduktora, vydaiushchego bilety, sovsem osobye ruki. Oni tak zhe provorno rabotaiut, kak ruki pianista,—no vmesto togo, chtoby byt' bezkostnymi, potnymi, s miagkimi nogtiami, ruki konduktora—takie zhestkie, chto kogda,—vlivaia emu v ladon' meloch',—sluchaino dotronesh'sia do etoi ladoni, obrosshei slovno grubym, sukhim khitinom, stanovitsia ne khorosho na dushe. Neobychaino lovkie, ladnye ruki,—nesmotria na grubost' ikh i tolshchinu pal'tsev. (p. 96)

The conductor who gives out tickets has very unusual hands. They work as nimbly as those of a pianist, but, instead of being limp, sweaty and soft-nailed, the ticketman's hands are so coarse that when you are pouring change into his palm and happen to touch that palm which seems to have developed a harsh chitinous crust, you feel a kind of moral discomfort. They are extraordinarily agile and efficient hands, despite their roughness and the thickness of the fingers. (pp. 92-93) [32]

In "Putevoditel' po Berlinu," Nabokov's narrator regards the details of Berlin's daily life with sympathy. To him, it seems that in the future this trivial material will be of museum caliber. The rickety yellow tram and the conductor's uniform will be found in display cases and some twenty-first-century writer will see them as curious aspects of the past. This observation brings the narrator to that momentary reflection upon the duty of the writer that I have cited above. For him, however, all of these everyday details are not only valuable for history but are meaningful and beautiful in themselves. For instance, the Christmas trees at the tram stop not only reflect the holiday publication date of this story (24 December 1925) but are poetically shown as a part of the Berlin scene:

... u ostanovki, na kraiu paneli, tolpiatsia rozhdestvenskie elki. (p. 96)

... at the stop, at the edge of the pavement, crowd the Christmas trees.

In Part III, "Jobs," life is—not too surprisingly—described from the tram window. The tram is still the structural link. The observer's field of vision is limited by the window and is perpetually moving. First the narrator sees the asphalt and the street itself. Men are working on it, as in "Vozvrashchenie Chorba." Compare the two following sentences:

Ona staralas' poimat' ego na letu pri pomoshchi lopatki, kotoruiu nashla bliz grudy rozovykh kirpichei, tam, gde chinili ulitsu. Poodal', iz truby rabochego furgona struilsia sizyi dymok, naklonialsia, taial mezhdu vetok, i otdykhavshii kamen'shchik smotrel, podbochenias', na legkuiu, kak bleklyi list, baryshniu, pliasavshuiu s lopatkoi v podniatoi ruke. ("Vozvrashchenie Chorba," p. 11)

She attempted to catch it on the wing by means of a child's spade found near a heap of pink bricks at a spot where the street was under repair. A little way off the funnel of a workers' van emitted gray-blue smoke which drifted aslant and dissolved between the branches—and a resting workman, one hand on his hip, contemplated the young lady, as light as a dead leaf, dancing about with that little spade in her raised hand. (p. 65)

Na perekrestke vdol' rel's razvorochen asfal't: chetvero rabochikh poocheredno b'iut molotami po kotyrge; pervyi udaril, vtoroi uzhe opuskaet razmashistym i tochnym dvizheniem molot; vtoroi molot grianul i opiat' vysoko podnimaetsia, poka rushatsia ravnomerno, odin za drugim, tretii, chetvertyi. ("Putevoditel' po Berlinu," p. 98)

At an intersection the pavement has been torn up next to the track; by turns, four workmen are pounding an iron stake with mallets; the first one strikes, and the second is already lowering his mallet with a sweeping, accurate swing; the second mallet crashes down and is rising skyward as the third and then the fourth bang down in rhythmical succession. (p. 94)

This last image recalls the contented stoking sailors in "Port," for there is a live rhythm and music to their tasks akin to bell chimes:

Ia slushaiu ikh netorpolivyi zvon, chugunnye kuranty, chetyre povtoriaiushchiesia noty. (p. 98)

I listen to their unhurried peal, the cast-iron chiming, four repeating notes.

In *Pnin* Nabokov repeats this image of street repairs: "... workmen came and started to drill holes in the street—Brainpan Street, Pningrad—and patch them up again, and this went on and on, in fits of shivering black zigzags and stunned pauses, for weeks" (p. 63).

In "Putevoditel' po Berlinu" the writer continues to observe other elements of Berlin street life, and with positive adjectives and editorial comments he describes the angelic baker, the emerald bottles on the truck, the graceful larch on the sleigh, the postman with his big black bag, and the most vivid scene, the butcher carrying the meat on his back:

No, byt' mozhet, prekrasnee vsego—blanzhevye, v rozovykh podtekakh i izvilinakh, tushi, navalennye na gruzovik, i chelovek v perednike, v kozhanom kapiushone s dolgim zatylkom, kotoryi beret tiazhkuiu tushu na spinu i, sgorbivshis', neset ee cherez panel' v rumianuiu lavku miasnika. (pp. 98-99)

But perhaps fairest of all are the carcasses, chrome yellow, with pink blotches, and arabesques, piled on a truck, and the man in apron and leather hood with a long neck flap who heaves each carcass onto his back and, hunched over, carries it across the sidewalk into the butcher's red shop. (p. 95)

Having turned his attention thus, the narrator not unexpectedly moves to Part IV, "Eden." In this vignette he becomes increasingly philosophical, reflecting first on the city zoo as an earthly paradise created by man. In the frame to this story, the narrator had noted that he had visited the zoo in the morning. According to him, the zoological gardens tell us about the beginning of the world. Although he laments that all the animals are in cages,[33] he concedes that the lion, if loose, would eat the doe. Nonetheless, it is a paradise to the extent that man can make it so. Appropriately, the Hotel Eden stands opposite the zoo. The writer moves figuratively into the zoo, where now in the winter he finds the amphibians, fish, and insects the most interesting. Jules Verne's Captain Nemo and the mythological submerged continent of Atlantis color his description of his visit to the aquarium. He sees fish and marine flora and focuses on a live, deep red, five-pointed starfish lying on the sandy bottom.

This star evokes one of Nabokov's rare, although oblique, political comments:

Vot, znachit, otkuda vzialas' preslovutaia emblema:—s samogo dna okeana—iz temnoty potoplennykh Atlantid, davnym davno perezhivshikh vsiakie smuty,—opyty glupovatykh utopii,—i vse to, chto trevozhit nas. (p. 99)

This, then, is where the notorious emblem originated—at the very bottom of the ocean, in the murk of sunken Atlantica, which long ago lived through various upheavals while pottering about topical utopias and other inanities that cripple us today. (p. 96)

The upheavals caused by utopian experiments such as Atlantis are still troubling the world today. In "Pis'mo v Rossiiu" these perturbations had been alluded to even more indirectly. Indictments of the Soviet regime by Nabokov are rare. When he focuses on his homeland, it is usually the Russia of his past, not the Soviet Union of his present (1925).

The fifth section of this story, "The Beerhall," represents the other side of the frame but describes the interior, not the exterior, of the beer hall. The narrator notes the bar, the billiard table, the little tavern tables, and presents a scene similar to the restaurant in "Port." However, his description has an interesting twist. It picks out the divan, mirror, and table in the adjoining room belonging to the beer-hall owner. There the narrator observes the owner's child being fed soup and then looking at an illustrated newspaper. Suddenly the narrator inverts the picture and shows what the child sees and how he views the narrator and his fellow drinker. Finally, the writer moves into the future:

—no ia znaiu odno: chto by ni sluchilos' s nim v zhizni, on navsegda zapomnit kartinu, kotoruiu v detstve ezhednevno videl iz komnatki, gde ego kormili supom—. (p. 101)

Yet there is one thing I know. Whatever happens to him in life, he will always remember the picture he saw every day of his childhood from the little room where he was fed his soup. (p. 98)

In this concluding fragment, the drinking companion repeatedly raises questions that indicate he has missed the point of the narrator's guide, thus accentuating and emphasizing by omission what the writer has described. For him the guide and Berlin are boring and dull. For the narrator, on the other hand, all that he has noted is important. Even the future memories of the beer-hall keeper's child hold significance for him. Thus the concluding remarks of the story aptly point to the future:

I kak mne emu vtolkovat', chto ia podgliadel ch'e-to budushchee vospominanie? (p. 102)

How can I demonstrate to him that I have glimpsed somebody's future recollection? (p. 98)

The structure of this story is rather unusual. Not only are the short sections unobtrusively joined, but each section has a realistic description supplemented by a philosophical reflection on some aspect of the scene. Furthermore, the topics enlarge in scope as the story progresses. The reader moves from pipes to trams, to street life in general, to the zoo and animal life, and finally to the child whose life still lies ahead of him. The pervading sense of this story is that life in Berlin is gratifying and meaningful to the artist in all its aspects.

"Putevoditel' po Berlinu" has been compared with Turgenev's *Sportsman's Sketches* by Field. He notes that this story "has some of the air of a carefully arranged 'careless sketch' " (p. 142). These vignettes are in the narrative style and the language is realistic. This realism, as I indicated above, is acknowledged by the narrator. There are only ten or so "made-strange" adjective-noun combinations. Longer metaphoric phrases are more numerous. For example, the street pipes are the iron hoses or intestines *(kishki)* of the street. This image brings to mind Nabokov's later anatomical image in *Dar,* where a poplar resembles the nervous system of a giant. Other extended metaphors deal with the conductor's agile hands, the music of the street workers, and a turtle whose shell is both a bronze cupola and the burden of time. These metaphors are not intended to convey any symbolic dimension in the way that the zoo denotes an earthly paradise. Instead, they serve to revivify ordinary objects that have dulled.

It is crucial here to consider Nabokov's training as a writer. In *Speak, Memory,* he recalled his tutor: "He made me depict from memory, in the greatest possible detail, objects I had certainly seen thousands of times without visualizing them properly: a street lamp, a postbox, the tulip design on the stained glass of our own front door. He tried to teach me to find the geometrical coordinations between the slender twigs of a leafless boulevard tree, a system of visual give-and-takes, requiring a precision of linear expression, which I failed to achieve in my youth, but applied gratefully, in my adult instar . . . to certain camera lucida needs of literary composition" (p. 92).[34]

Nabokov's literary training also owed much to Gogol. Significantly, in his study of Gogol Nabokov cited the following passage from *Dead Souls:* "But a different lot and another fate await the writer who has dared to evoke all such things that are constantly before one's eyes but which idle eyes do not see—the shocking morass of trifles that has tied up our lives, and the essence of cold, crumbling, humdrum characters with whom our earthly way, now bitter, now dull, fairly swarms; has dared to make them prominently and brightly visible to the eyes of all men by means of the vigorous strength of his pitiless chisel" (p. 105).

Nabokov's observations are enlivened not only by metaphoric expressions but by the use of a variety of stylistic devices. Above I have noted his interest in letter shapes and sounds. In the frame of "Putevoditel' po Berlinu" Nabokov focuses on the blue beer-hall sign with white lettering and a picture of a winking lion. Part I concludes on a contemplative note about the letters etched into the snow on the pipes, which read "Otto":

Segodnia na snegovoi polose kto-to pal'tsem napisal "Otto," i ia podumal, chto takoe imia, s dvumia belymi "o" po bokam i chetoi tikhikh soglasnykh poseredke, udivitel'no khorosho podkhodit k etomu snegu, lezhavshemu tikhim sloem, k etoi trube s ee dvumia otverstiiami i tainstvennoi glubinoi. (p. 95)

Today someone wrote "Otto" with his finger on the strip of virgin snow and I thought how beautifully that name, with its two soft o's flanking the pair of gentle consonants, suited the silent layer of snow upon that pipe with its two orifices and its tacit tunnel. (p. 92)

In Part III literary allusions are made not only to Jules Verne and mythology but to the Gospels and the Old Testament. Colors, which quickly convey an impression, occur throughout these sketches, and with particular frequency in the street scene in Part III where realistic vignettes predominate. These are almost fleeting, cinematic shots. Color is singular in its application in Part IV, "Eden." Crimson (*purpurnyi*) is the only color mentioned and qualifies star. This emphasis on the red hue of the star poetically expresses Nabokov's idea of the "notorious emblem," the Red Star of communism.

The grammatical structure of the sentences in "Putevoditel' po Berlinu" is singular. The sentences are very long, with many secondary clauses. Brief sentences are conspicuous by their infrequency. Parts II, III, and IV open with factual statements that give way immediately to sentences a paragraph long. In Part V Nabokov used *v glubine* (in the depths) three times within a single page. I noted this recurrent phrase in "Port"; here it is used strictly with reference to the child whom the narrator sees sitting in the back room. The phrase accentuates not only the writer's spatial detachment from this child but the depth with which the author considers the child and his future memories. It also emphasizes a narrowing or a focusing of Nabokov's artistic lens. Nabokov often coalesced his images. In this instance the mirror, table, divan, and child are brought together linguistically. With the aide of *v glubine,* Nabokov moves from a large image to a small one. I point to the focusing-in found in the following three excerpts. In the final excerpt only the common denominators of the first remain: *v glubine, divan, rebenok* (child). The translation and italics are mine.

(1) *V glubine*—shirokii prokhod, i tam vidna tesnaia komnatka s zelenym *divanom* vdol' steny, pod zerkalom, iz kotorogo vylivaetsia polukruglyi stol, pokrytyi kletchatoi kleenkoi, i prochno stanovitsia pered *divanom.* Eta komnata otnositsia k ubogoi kvartirke khoziaina. Tam zhena, uviadshaia nemka, kormit supom belokurogo *rebenka.* (pp. 100-101)

"In the depths is a wide passageway, and there one can see a cramped little room with a green *divan* along the wall, under a mirror from which flows, a semicircular table covered with a checked oilcloth, and firmly stands in front of the *divan.* This room relates to the squalid little apartment of the owner. There, his wife, a faded German, feeds her towheaded *child* soup.

(2) Iz nashego ugla podle stoiki ochen' otchetlivo vidny *v glubine,* v prokhode,—*divan,* zerkalo, stol. Khoziaika ubiraet so stola posudu. *Rebenok,* opiraias' loktiami, vnimatel'no razgliadyvaet illiustryrovannyi zhurnal. (p. 101)

From our corner, beside the counter, one very clearly sees *in the depths,* in the passageway—the *divan,* the mirror, the table. The mistress clears the dishes off of the table. The *child,* leaning on his elbows, is attentively examining the illustrated magazine.

(3) Tam, *v glubine, rebenok* ostalsia na *divane* odin. (p. 101)

There, *in the depths,* the *child* remained on the *divan* alone.

"Putevoditel' po Berlinu" is thus another contemplative story that focuses on the "important" facets of the hero's surroundings. Once again the narrator is an artist—a writer—who concerns himself with the everyday sights of Berlin. However, this story, like "Pis'mo v Rossiiu," has a philosophical note. Nabokov projected into the future and observed that the child of the beer-hall keeper will someday recall the very minutiae of the present scene.[35] Thus, trivial aspects of daily life not only assume value as past memories but have their place in the creation of new and future ones. The hero concludes that the significance of a writer's creation lies in the depiction of these commonplace things. This was Nabokov's explicit statement of the raison d'être of minutiae in literature.

6. "Passazhir"

The last story of the realistic group is "Passazhir" ("The Passenger"), dealing again with a writer who is absorbed in the details of life. As in "Putevoditel' po Berlinu," he reveals his ideas in conversation rather than in an interior monologue. Like Nabokov's other heroes, he justifies his concern with trifles by claiming that a writer is precisely a man who worries over such trivia. Thus "Passazhir" is a variation of the themes of the preceding realistic stories; but the broader aesthetic question of who is the greater artist, life or man, is also raised. This issue constitutes the crux of "Passazhir." Nabokov considered this problem both abstractly and concretely within the context of the short-story genre. A writer and a critic discuss this issue, and the writer offers an example of life's perfect story.

The entire piece, including the discussion, follows the classic story pattern. It commences with the writer-narrator taking the position that life is more talented than writers are. He points out that a writer plagiarizes life's story, like a film director who distorts a good novel to make a movie entertaining for chambermaids. In contrast, the critic-listener [36] contends that the writer has the tools and the wealth of the "word." For him, the writer has the greater talent. This debate forms the frame of "Passazhir"; unlike "Putevoditel' po Berlinu," it is counterbalanced by a full final frame.

The heart of "Passazhir" is the writer-narrator's argument. To prove his point, he relates a personal experience, recalling how on an express sleeper [37] he once contentedly fell asleep thinking of his projected tale on the life of a train-car chambermaid. Structurally, this fictional subject serves as a clear and banal contrast to the drama that life is about to unfold before the writer. At this point in his narration the writer unobtrusively remarks:

> I tut razreshite mne upotrebit' priem, chasten'ko vstrechaiu-shchiisia v takikh imenno rasskazakh, kakim obeshchaet byt' moi. Vot on,—etot staryi, khorosho vam izvestnyi priem. "Sredi nochi ia vnezapno prosnulsia." Vprochem dal'she sleduet koe-chto posvezhee. Ia prosnulsia i uvidel nogu. (p. 140)

> And here let me use a device cropping up with dreary frequency in the sort of story to which mine promises to belong. Here it is—that old device which you must know so well: "In the middle of the night I woke up suddenly." What follows, however, is something less stale. I woke up and saw a foot. (p. 74)

The writer's editorial aside here signals the start of the rising action that is the essence of the story. The narrator is awakened by a train stop and the arrival of another passenger, who prepares to sleep on the top berth. The lights of the compartment are lit, and the writer sees only a male leg on the ladder to the bunk above. This unexpected mundane detail is emphasized by the critic's interruption: "Vinovat?" (p. 140) ("Excuse me, a what?" [(p. 74]). Here the foot acts as a synecdoche for the man and with the usual Nabokovian twist. Although it is "made-strange," it is a highly realistic figure. Unlike most Nabokov legs, this is a male one and very unpleasant looking. It strikes the writer not only as unattractive but as revolting. The ensuing movement from the leg to the foot, then down to the big toe, and finally to the disgusting toenail that protrudes through a hole in the sock is a fine example of Nabokov's use of a coalescing image. This is a blue mother-of-pearl toenail—a Nabokovian detail that recalls the tram conductor's black square fingernail in "Putevoditel' po Berlinu" (p. 96). In a critical aside, the writer justifies his concern over such trifles as toes, noting that this is not only his artistic prerogative but that a concern for details distinguishes a writer from other men:

Voobshche stranno, konechno, chto takie pustiaki mogli menia volnovat',—no ved' s drugoi storony, ne est' li vsiakii pisatel' imenno chelovek, volnuiushchiisia po pustiakam? (p. 141)

It may seem strange, in a general way, that such trifles should bother me but, per contra, is not every writer precisely a person who bothers about trifles? (p. 75).

This passage echoes the writer's views on the lasting value of details in art expressed in "Putevoditel' po Berlinu."

The foot finally pushes itself up onto the berth and gives way to snorting noises, signaling that the passenger is going to sleep. The lights go out again and the train starts forward. This motion propels the action of the story, for the train furnishes dynamism to an otherwise static scene. It balances not only the darkness of the compartment but the writer's reflective mood, which culminates in the question: Who is the mysterious man above with "the soft, bright-colored, ugly thing" *(pestraia, miagkaia gadina)*? The writer is bothered because he cannot see the passenger's face. In trying to picture the man's appearance, he is frustrated. He can visualize only the wretched toenail and, curiously, his own absurd face. The writer's increasing aversion to his roommate is the essence of this rising action. The negative impression made by the toenail is indirectly emphasized by the weight of the top berth, which creates a low ceiling and acts as a heavy awning for the writer lying below it. In the morning the writer hits his head against this lowered berth—providing still another negative dimension to the writer's thoughts about his fellow traveler. His earlier delight with the privacy of his compartment has obliquely set the mood for his negative attitude toward the intrusion of the second passenger.

With the light out, the visual image is replaced by an aural one— a realistic approach, for in the darkness one's ear becomes sensitized. The writer listens to snorting noises above and wonders if the passenger is falling asleep. He seems to be moaning. The writer raises himself from his pillow and realizes that in fact the man is sobbing desperately. The acceleration of the train and the hammer of the train's wheels encourage the hallucination of hearing. These sounds are abnormal and the sensation of strange noises builds up. It crescendoes. Structurally, this image, like the toe image, is accentuated by the critic-listener's queries: "Kak vy skazali? . . . Rydal?" (p. 142) ("What's that? . . . Sobbing?" [p. 75]). In an evocative and metaphoric passage, the writer turns to the quality of these sobs. They ebb and flow and change in timbre when the man opens his mouth. The rattle of the wheels continues to serve as a basso continuo to this painful music. Although the writer experiences a natural embarrassment at intruding on a fellow man's grief, he feels related to him. Both of them are lying on bunks, one above the other, on a train that is traveling at fifty miles an hour. As the writer notes, only a railroad catastrophe could break their bond. The stress on the motion of the train in this passage is one of the few instances in Nabokov's work when the train, not the passing scene, moves.

The passenger's crying finally culminates in some garbled words spoken in a voice coming from the center of his body. The lengthy description of this pained grief is an expansion of similar passages in "Vozvrashchenie Chorba" and, as will be noted below, in the symbolic stories. Understandably, the writer cannot fall asleep easily. His insomnia contrasts with his easy doze in the exposition. When the passenger's crying subsides to a sniffle, the writer sleeps at last.

The story is thus pushed to its climax by the train's movement and the mysterious negative impression created by the passenger. The climax is further prepared for by a sudden surprising train stop the next morning at a small station to let on the police. The tension is heightened by the explanation that there is a murderer on board. A man who had killed his wife and her lover has gotten on the train during the nighttime stop. The effect of this news is enhanced by the implication that the crying passenger may be the criminal. A search of all the passengers ensues, and the climax reaches its height with the interrogation of the blanket-covered man in the top berth. The narrator turns his back on his fellow passenger while the police investigate. The falling action of "Passazhir" is the negative result of this search. The authorities are satisfied by the passenger's documents. The conclusion is the writer-narrator's "That's all." Because of the full development of the rising action, this succinct falling action and conclusion create an abrupt and startling impression. The expanded rising action had prepared the writer and the reader for a more dramatic resolution to the climactic words: "V poezde nakhodtsia prestup-nik" (p. 144) ("There's a criminal on the train" [p. 78]). The outcome is thus an unexpected reversal. It is, however, a plausible conclusion.

In answer to the story's lingering question of why the passenger was crying, the writer concludes that he will never know. That is art's masterful touch. More standard endings are suggested in this final frame. The writer notes that it would have been fine from a writer's point of view if his fellow passenger had been the murderer. His tears would have been explained. Structurally, it would have been perfect, but not artistic. The intent of this story's author—life—was a hundredfold more subtle and profound than the writer's. The writer-narrator asks the critic whether he assumed the criminal was the crying passenger. The critic reminds him that it is a good detective-story trick to have the most obvious person be the criminal when everyone suspects an obscure character. This story would have been perfect if the criminal were the passenger, but life holds much that is incidental and much that is extraordinary. The "word" has an added dimension in that it can make the incidental unusual and the unusual merely incidental. But the writer still holds that life is a more subtle and deeper artist, for the train incident leaves the lingering question of why the passenger was crying. In the end, the critic takes the pedestrian view that perhaps the passenger was crying over a lost wallet, or merely was given to crying. What neither of them asks is who the criminal was and whether the police ever found him.

Technically, the writer has proved his point within the frame of the story: life is the greater artist. However, as this is a story within a story, the critic has also proved his point. The tenor of the entire piece prompts one to become so absorbed as to lose sight of the fact that it is all Nabokov's fiction. The story "Passazhir" is a masterpiece. Not surprisingly, it is one of the first Nabokov stories translated into English.

The structural frame is unobtrusively woven into the body of the story by the evenly spaced asides and interruptions by the writer and the critic. The main figures—the writer, the critic, and the mute fellow passenger—are distinct despite their anonymity. We know that the writer, the pivotal figure, not only likes night sleepers and late-morning rising but he smokes as well. He begins his story by tapping his cigarette on his cigarette case—a recurrent Nabokovian gesture. In "Port" Nikitin pensively taps his cigarette on his case, which has a golden eagle (Russia's emblem) burned on its surface. In *Podvig* Martin's tutor has a similar case (p. 65). Nabokov uses an identical image in *Dar:* "Never mind, never mind, Fyodor thought rapidly, smiling to himself, looking around and tapping the end of a cigarette against his eagle-emblazoned cigarette case" (p. 77). The cigarette cases here are in a sense variations of Nabokov's treasure-chest images. In "Passazhir" the image is always associated with the writer, but nowhere is he or his manner of smoking described. This image inversion is a favorite artistic technique of Nabokov and recalls the moving lights of the train station in the beginning of this story. That, too, is an image inversion that is found in many of Nabokov's early stories and is discussed more amply below.

The critic is not passive. He is not the obtuse listener of "Putevoditel' po Berlinu." He is described as modest and near-sighted, and it seems that he is also hard of hearing. Despite all of these weaknesses, he is a strong structural device. He not only debates with the writer but accentuates the significant moments of the story with his repeating questions. His long, thin, mobile fingers play and move as he speaks.

The diverse points of view of the writer and the critic reflect their professions. The writer views life in order to create his stories. The critic's métier is to view the stories themselves. The writer's chief concern is life; the critic's is the writer. Thus because of their naturally conflicting values, the remarks of both are well in character.

The passenger is conspicuous by his anonymity, which is credible because he is always obscured from the writer. He is variously described. No one epithet is adequate: *nochnoi sputnik* (nocturnal fellow traveler), *nevedomyi passazhir* (unknown passenger), *rydaiushchii passazhir* (sobbing passenger), *figura v odeiale* (figure in the blanket). The most important point about him is that he does not match the description of the wanted criminal.

I have noted the coalescing image of the toenail and the expanding and contracting image of the cry that is expressively set against the constant hum of the train in the rising action. These images occur at night. In the falling action, in the early morning, the image of the passing scenery is also notable. The gradual, subtle details of the locale reflect the braking of the train as it approaches its destination. Here is another of Nabokov's inverted images. The scenery, not the hero, moves, acts, and responds. This is a neutral image, reflecting nothing of the hero observing the scenery. It is *l'art pour l'art*. Bent shadows recur and the ubiquitous advertisement poster attracts the hero's attention as the train moves toward its destination.

The language of this brief eight-page story is highly poetic. Its "made-strange" combinations and many metaphors and personifications yield graphic, true-to-life scenes. Finally, passages, paragraphs long, support the critic's contention that the writer, with the tools given him by the "word," has defeated his own argument. He has not only re-created a "slice of life" but, as a true realist, has revivified the "word."

A Great
Jewel-Bright Advertisement

THE REALISTIC-SYMBOLIC STORIES

The symbolic outlook in literature seeks to express something
beyond what is directly visible and real. This view invests
mundane aspects of life with a broader and sometimes an
allegorical meaning in order to express an intangible or spiritual
side of life. The symbolic perspective can present man's hidden and
more extreme states of mind and emotion—joy, sorrow, fear,
horror. Further, it can express man's fluctuation between reality
and fantasy, waking and sleeping, consciousness and unconsciousness. Clearly the symbolic modus operandi permits a variety of
views, in contrast to that of realism, which allows for only one
direct view.

Nabokov melded his realistic method with the symbolic within
the framework of the short-story genre in "Groza," "Zvonok,"
"Sluchainost'," "Britva," "Rozhdestvenskii rasskaz," "Skazka,"
"Podlets," and "Kartofel'nyi El'f." These stories have very realistic
and tangible settings, and their heroes are often depicted in
excessive detail. However, each of the stories is complex in nature

and a symbolic level lies below the surface. The simple images from daily life that are recurrent motifs in Nabokov's purely realistic stories here have additional meaning. Plot themes familiar from the preceding chapter—confrontation of memories, love stories, poetic Berlin vignettes—recur, but with a twist. The ambiguity between reality and fantasy that is obliquely hinted at in Nikitin's reaction in "Port" figures importantly in the portrayal of the heroes of "Groza" and "Podlets," for instance. In "Zvonok," "Sluchainost'," and "Britva" Nabokov's émigré heroes still search for memories and face their past, but this confrontation does not yield satisfaction, tranquillity, and peace. The artist-hero in "Rozhdestvenskii rasskaz" is not a vibrant young man but an old Russian who derives little or no deep satisfaction from his vocation. Here Nabokov's parodistic and ironic talents surface, and a sophisticated knowledge of Russian literature is required to understand what he wrote below the text. "Podlets" is an open parody on a romantic literary theme. In "Skazka" he toyed with the children's tale. In these last three stories Nabokov turned from his realistic approach and played not only with themes but with literary styles.

In the realistic stories none of the love affairs is genuinely consummated or fulfilled, yet the measured and balanced tone conveys a sense of satisfaction and even happiness on the part of the hero and consequently to the reader. The love stories of "Podlets" and "Kartofel'nyi El'f," on the other hand, despite their very lifelike German or English setting, are both absurd and abnormal, and the characters see their world as disjointed and unreal.

Whereas the realistic stories are cohesive because of the author's consistent fascination with realia in form and content, the stories considered in this chapter are more individualized. This is due partially to the fact that the proportion of realism to symbolism in the author's technique varies with each story. In his realistic-symbolic approach to literature, Nabokov was doing his most serious experimentation.

1. "Groza"

The clearest example of Nabokov's combined realistic-symbolic outlook is "Groza" ("The Thunderstorm"; in his English translation Nabokov explained that "thunder is *grom* in Russian, storm is *burya*, and thunderstorm is *groza*, a grand little word, with that blue zigzag in the middle" [p. 118]). Despite the violence implicit literally and figuratively in the title, this story is reminiscent of "Blagost'." It is a fine poetic sketch that reflects the hero-narrator's placid mood. Nabokov's controlled style reinforces this sense of contentment. In "Groza," however, he moved a step beyond the impressionistic level of "Blagost'." The rainstorm that figures in the latter not only becomes the central event of "Groza" but also assumes symbolic proportions. The biblical Prophet Elijah personifies the storm. For all of Elijah's legendary quality, he is graphically portrayed. To the reader and the narrator alike, Elijah is as vivid and lifelike as the red geraniums on the courtyard windowsills.

"Groza" is Nabokov's briefest early story—it is five pages in length—but it contains all of the elements of a well-balanced short story. In the exposition a young man comes from a city street into a small courtyard. As a storm gathers, he goes up to his room overlooking this court. He falls asleep, dreaming happily of his beloved. As in "Port" and "Skazka," sleep acts as a structural transition. It marks the end of the introduction in which the hero and his surrounding world are presented.

Thunder and lightning, which rouse the young man, signal the rising action. In characteristic Nabokovian fashion, the hero looks out of his window. As he breathes in an unearthly air, the equally unearthly Prophet Elijah appears in a flaming chariot drawn by fiery steeds. The story climaxes with the Prophet's crash landing on a nearby roof. As the horses touch the metal of the roof, the Prophet is thrown out of his chariot and one of the flaming wheels falls off and tumbles into the courtyard below. To judge by the annoyed expression of Elijah, this is not the first time that this has occurred. The hero rushes down to the courtyard to help the old man, who casually refers to him as his faithful biblical follower Elisha.[1] The Prophet directs young Elisha to help in the search for the missing wheel.

The falling action begins when the two uncover the chariot wheel—a rusty wheel from a child's carriage. Thereupon a happier Elijah mysteriously scrambles up onto the roof. He climbs dawn's clouds in his chariot and disappears into the morning sky. In the

concluding section of "Groza," the young man rushes out to tell his
beloved how the Prophet dropped down into his small world. As in
much of Nabokov's fiction, the beginning and the end of the story
are linked. The matching mental and physical actions of the
narrator bind the frames of "Groza." In both the hero is thinking
of his loved one. In the introductory frame he enters the courtyard,
and in the concluding frame he leaves it. In this manner the hero
leads the reader in and out of his microcosm.

It is not clear whether the narrator's adventure is a dream.
Nabokov has prepared the reader for this interpretation by
stressing that the hero has fallen asleep:

> V etoi tishine ia zasnul, oslabev ot schast'ia, o kotorom pisat'
> ne umeiu,—i son moi byl polon toboi. (p. 77)

> In this silence I fell asleep, exhausted by the happiness of my
> day, a happiness I cannot describe in writing, and my dream
> was full of you. (p. 120)

If this is a fantasy or dream, then the narrator never awakens and
the story is a figment of his imagination right through to the
conclusion. There is no abrupt switch to reality, nor is there an
oblique explanation of what has actually occurred. On the other
hand, the lack of distinction between fantasy and reality does not
in any way detract from the story's charm.

The major figure, the first-person narrator of the incident, is, as
implied in the above cited passage, someone who is writing or
preparing to tell this story to his beloved. In this regard he is
similar to the heroes of "Blagost' " and "Pis'mo v Rossiiu." As the
story progresses, the narrator takes part in the fantasy-drama of the
story: he becomes Elisha. In the final scene, still in his bedroom
slippers and bathrobe, he rushes out to the tram. This concluding
detail indicates that the story has not returned to normalcy. The
scene still appears to be unrealistic, and the ending is not
altogether conclusive.

Elijah, the second character of the story, is the storm. His
presence is prepared for in the exposition. The wind of the
approaching storm is repeatedly personified:

Tumannye gromady podnimalis' po nochnomu nebu, i kogda pogloshchen byl poslednii zvezdnyi prosvet, slepoi veter, zakryv litso rukavami, nizko pronessia vdol' opustevshei ulitsy. (p. 76)

Masses of mist were ascending in the night sky and, when the last star-filled hollow had been absorbed, the wind, a blind · phantom, covering his face with his sleeves, swept low through the deserted street. (p. 119)

The narrator who witnesses the incident from the window admits to himself that he is weak from love and drunk from the heady atmosphere, thus allowing for all manner of unexpected events or hallucinations.

Elijah's dramatic and fantastic entrance is accepted by the narrator without surprise. He first identifies the apparition on the rooftop as the Prophet and then as Elijah. Nabokov has taken liberties with the biblical Elijah of 2 Kings, merging him with the thunderer *(gromoverzhets)* of Russian folklore and perhaps the roof-landing Saint Nick. The old man is a likable fellow despite his extraordinary power and overwhelming size. He is disheveled and runs agitatedly around in his pointed slippers and long ecclesiastical robe. Even though Elijah seems to be supernatural and an element of the storm, he too is affected by its force. His beard and hair are all tangled. His nose drips with rain, and his robe and slippers are soaked. His face is expressive. He winks and blinks and knits his brows. He grunts, breathes hotly, clicks his tongue, and mumbles. He scrambles about on rooftops and amid lilacs [2] searching for his wheel. His amiability is reflected in his easygoing conversation with the narrator. Nabokov maintains a certain sense of reality by masking Elijah's descent from the roof and his equally mysterious ascent back onto it. The first occurs when the narrator is hurrying downstairs and the second when Elisha, as requested, has turned his back on the scene.

In "Groza," as in "Port" and "Skazka," there is a sympathetic and companionable dog who stands beside the narrator quietly observing the scene. Although he is old, gray, and scruffy, he resembles a human as he looks up at Elijah with frightened brown eyes. When Elijah leaves, the dog finally lets out a characteristic bark.

The storm scene is limited to the courtyard, which provides not merely a poetic backdrop for the story but a specific atmosphere. In its confines there is much vertical motion, and the focus is on its depths. The storm is seen from it and reflected in it, and it whirls within this microcosm. In the exposition the yard is described from the height of the narrator's window. During the day it is a noisy and busy place, frequented by ragmen collecting empty bottles and by itinerant singers. The effect of the rising wind is conveyed by the sound of slamming doors and creaking shutters. Gradually this small world fills with an oppressive haze—in a sense, the calm before the storm. The advent of the rainstorm is accentuated by the vertical motion of the characters. The narrator "awakens" to see the distressed Prophet and his chariot wheel dropping into the courtyard below. The narrator then makes his own descent down the deep stairwell of the building. The end of the storm is marked by Elijah's ascent from this yard, which now reflects the clearing weather. The bushes, gate, and doghouse swim in the "sleepy blue air." The yellow, orange, and fiery-red sky and clouds, into which Elijah has ascended, are mirrored in the courtyard rain puddles. The crimson geraniums on the balconies begin to flutter in the light wind. The windows, which had dozed off, now awaken, and the narrator chases after a sleepy tram.

The language of "Groza" is its strength. The personification of the wind and the symbolic Elijah metaphorically express the storm. The courtyard and the sky, particularly the cloud effects, poetically reflect the storm. Many of Nabokov's typical "made-strange" metaphoric passages occur, most of them quite lengthy. Images of color, light, and dark are employed. In the climax of the story, when Elijah appears, the metaphor is of course weakened by the fantastic element. Hyperbole and symbol take over. There is a high proportion of alliterations in "Groza," summoning up the rattling and thundering of the storm. Consider the repeating sound patterns in the following phrases: *buinym taiushchim tumanom; s konchika krupnogo kostistogo nosa.* Repetitions also produce a sense of rhythmic and rumbling thunder as seen in the repeating phrases: *grokhotom za grokhotom; vse blizhe, vse velikolepnee.* Fog, haze, twilight, dimness, and shadows form images that contrast with those of light, fire, brilliance, sparkle, and gold. This effect is a variation of Nabokov's frequently employed chiaroscuro technique.

The contrasting images of brilliance and fog alternate and can be mapped in a metaphorical analysis of the story. Fog occurs prior to Elijah's arrival, a visual as well as tactile effect. Elijah brings lightning and brightness. When he loses his wheel, dimness and fog set in once again, and are even reflected in Elijah's features, his darkened face and swarthy bald spot. Light and fire return with the discovery of the wheel and Elijah's flaming departure coincides with the morning sunlight:

Solntse strel'nulo v ego koleso, i ono srazu stalo zolotym, gromadnym,—da i sam Il'ia kazalsia teper' oblachennym v plamia, slivaias' s toi raiskoi tuchei, po kotoroi on shel vse vyshe, vse vyshe, poka ne ischez v pylaiushchem vozdushnom ushchel'e. (p. 80)

Sunlight shot through his wheel whereupon it became at once huge and golden, and Elijah himself now seemed robed in flame, blending with the paradisal cloud along which he walked higher and higher until he disappeared in a glorious gorge of the sky. (p. 123)

In "Groza" the hero's wavering between waking and sleeping is an ambiguous yet crucial aspect of the story. It is not clear whether the storm is a figment of his imagination or whether it is all a dream. This symbolic ellipsis is complemented by the fantastic figure of Elijah, who embodies nature's storm. Despite this double-pronged symbolism, the old man is presented with realistic details. The rusty carriage wheel, doghouse, red geraniums, and creaking windows are aspects of the scene that evoke real life. As the hero rushes to catch Nabokov's ubiquitous tram, he gathers up the hem of his robe, implicitly so that he will not trip. With this last crucial detail, the symbolic dimension of "Groza" obtrudes: Is the hero still dreaming or imagining? The question of reality and fantasy is raised here. This vacillation is never explicitly stated and it is never resolved.

2. "Zvonok"

In moving from "Groza" to Nabokov's longer story "Zvonok" ("The Doorbell"), I find that his realistic-symbolic approach acquires greater complexity. The remembrance of things past that thematically dominates so many of Nabokov's realistic pieces also figures in this remarkable story. However, this theme is no longer exclusively treated directly and realistically. Nabokov's addition of the symbolic perspective gives a twist to the familiar Proustian motif. In "Zvonok" an émigré hero searches for a link not only with his Russian past but with his personal past. A son seeks and finds his parent. The meeting is not clear-cut. It is distorted. The peace and tranquillity of the confrontations in "Port" and "Blagost' " are absent. The bittersweet satisfaction experienced by Chorb is denied this hero.

The plot line of "Zvonok" is a symmetrical rising and falling of the action. The page-long exposition presents the departure of a man from a woman at a St. Petersburg railroad station—a scene that recalls the opening pages of *Korol' dama valet* and the concluding scene in *Mashen'ka*. This opening passage indicates the time as well. Through grammatical sleight of hand, a symbolic device, the hero and the reader are transferred from the present to the past. Seven years earlier becomes for the moment the present tense:

Sem' let proshlo s tekh por kak on s neiu rasstalsia. Gospodi, kakaia sutoloka na Nikolaevskom vokzale! Ne stoi tak blizko, seichas poezd tronetsia. Nu vot,—proshchai, moia khoroshaia. . . . Ona poshla riadom, vysokaia, khudoshchavaia, v makintoshe, s cherno-belym sharfom vokrug shei,—i medlennym techeniem ee unosilo nazad. (p. 27)

Seven years had passed since he and she had parted in Petersburg. God, what a crush there had been at the Nikolaevsky Station! Don't stand so close—the train is about to start. Well, here we go, good-bye, dearest. . . . She walked alongside, tall, thin, wearing a raincoat, with a black-and-white scarf around her neck, and a slow current carried her off backwards. (p. 101)

This transition from the Russian past tense to the historical present produces a subtle realistic flashback in time, an effect in turn enhanced by the parallel motion of the train. In leaving the station, the train is not described as moving forward. Instead, in a "made-strange" image, the hero in the train sees the woman on the platform as being carried backward. Thus motion in time and space move back seven years. Then with a steady series of *zatem* (after that; then; next), the hero begins to step forward to his climactic reunion.

These first sentences also raise the questions needed for the beginning of an effective story: Who is he? Who is the loved one—a fiancée, a relative, or a mother? These informational gaps anticipate the more drastic ones in Nabokov's purely symbolic stories. In this story Nabokov's world is not confined to the small Berlin courtyard of "Groza." Rather, this story has the pattern of some of Nabokov's other stories in which the hero finds himself alone, sometimes on the loose, in a very wide world. Gradually this hero is brought to a special spot where he faces a critical situation which then may enable his future life to take shape, even direction. Therefore the brief introduction to "Zvonok" describes the hero Galatov's "stupendous roaming around the world" following the station farewell. His solitary journey, so typical of that of many Russian émigrés, is full of far-flung stops, chance meetings, and bits of valuable news. However, for Galatov, this aimless wandering is not a trial. It satisfies his childhood dream for freedom. This wanderlust is complemented by his easygoing and happy personality, which is stressed throughout "Zvonok." His travels lead him from St. Petersburg to Yalta in the Crimea. There, by chance, he meets a Moscow uncle and learns that his loved one has obtained a passport and is off to Germany. His peregrinations take him to Africa, Italy, the Canary Islands, and back to Africa. (In the English version Nabokov changed the order of these exotic stops.) Along the way the hero hears that the loved one's second husband has died, leaving her some Berlin real estate. The implication is that she is now free for him. While in Italy he spots a Russian-language Berlin newspaper and places an advertisement searching for her. But this is in vain. In Cairo while continuing his adventures Galatov meets the elderly journalist Grushevskii [3] who is off to Berlin, and so he asks him to inquire for him. This source brings no news either. Subtly, his search for his loved one has intensified.

The rising action of the story begins with Galatov's decision to drop everything and find this mysterious woman himself. This quest takes him from southern Africa to the north and, with fate's help, up the stairs of No. 59 Plannerstrasse in Berlin. His search is thus a rising action that is reflected in the crescendo of the hero's emotions and the question: What will this woman be like after so many years? Galatov conjures up his image of her as she seemed to him in the past and as she should be now. As he hunts, it emerges that the woman is Galatov's mother.

Galatov's evening arrival in Berlin echoes Chorb's nocturnal arrival in the German town. Like Chorb, he notes a poster and spends a restless night in a shabby hotel:

V zheltom pal'to s bol'shimi pugovitsami, v kletchatom kartuze, korotkii i shirokoplechii, s trubkoi v zubakh i s chemodanom v ruke, on vyshel na ploshchad' pered vokzalom, usmekhnulsia, poliubovalsia brilliantovoi reklamoi, proedaiushchei temnotu. Noch' v zatkhlom nomere deshevoi gostinitsy on provel plokho. (p. 29)

Wearing a trenchcoat and a checked cap, short and broad-shouldered, with a pipe between his teeth and a battered valise in his good hand, he exited onto the square in front of the station. There he stopped to admire a great jewel-bright advertisement that inched its way through the darkness, then vanished and started again from another point. He spent a bad night in a stuffy room in a cheap hotel, trying to think of ways to begin the search. (p. 103)

Thoughts of his mother increase as he approaches her. Galatov's emotional anticipation of being in the same city with her and the hope of seeing her color his impression of his urban surroundings. The following morning, Galatov senses that Berlin's streets are full of Russian talk, and he feels that he is in a lost Russian province where perhaps he can locate his mother precisely.

Unexpectedly, Galatov comes upon the dental office of Dr.

Weiner from St. Petersburg, a name from his own past. He rings the doorbell and learns that though this is not the dentist of his childhood, this new Dr. Weiner has treated his mother. This coincidence is not so farfetched, as Russian émigrés knew one another well in the small, tight expatriate community in Berlin. In *Podvig* Nabokov mentioned precisely this: "But perhaps the most unexpected thing about this new, much expanded, postwar Berlin so peaceful, rustic and bumbling, compared to the compact and elegant city of Martin's childhood, was the free-mannered, loud-voiced Russia that chattered everywhere, in the trams, in the shops, on the street corners, on the balconies of apartment houses" (p. 135). In speaking of Berlin as a lost Russian province, Galatov thus anticipates this image in *Podvig*. Dr. Weiner gives Galatov his mother's address. Here the hero notes that fate has helped him as if by a card trick. And Berlin appears to reflect his good fortune:

Prekrasnyi gorod, prekrasnyi dozhd'! (Bisernyi osennii dozhd' morosil kak by shopotom, i na ulitsakh bylo temno). (p. 32)

Beautiful city, beautiful rain! (the pearly autumn drizzle seemed to fall in a whisper and the streets were dark). (p. 106)

Structurally, this meeting with Dr. Weiner is an important episode in Galatov's search. It foretells his confrontation with his mother. At Plannerstrasse he will again go upstairs; again he will ring the bell; and again he will expect to meet someone from his past. As with Dr. Weiner, so with his mother, Galatov will discover that this is not the same person that he knew in St. Petersburg. The only difference in these episodes is that Dr. Weiner is quick to help Galatov, while his mother will offer none.

The momentum of the story accelerates to its climax as Galatov nears his mother's apartment. His memories of her, although emotional, become sharper:

Teper' on staralsia voobrazit' ee litso, no mysli uporno ne okrashivalis', i on nikak ne mog sobrat' v zhivoi zritel'nyi obraz to, chto znal umom: ee khuduiu vysokuiu, kak by nekrepko svinchennuiu figuru, temnye volosy s naletom sediny u viskov, bol'shoi blednyi rot, potrepannyi makintosh, v kotorom ona byla v poslednii raz, i ustaloe, gorkoe, uzhe starcheskoe vyrazhenie, kotoroe poiavilos' na ee uviadshem litse v te bedstvennye gody. (pp. 32–33)

Now he tried to to picture her face, but his thoughts obstinately refused to take on color, and he simply could not gather in a living optical image what he knew in his mind: her tall, thin figure with that loosely-assembled look about it; her dark hair with streaks of gray at the temples; her large, pale mouth; the old raincoat she had on the last time he saw her; and the tired, bitter expression of an aging woman, that seemed to have always been on her face. (p. 106)

His nervous anticipation is seen in his need to pull out his pipe for a smoke. Almost blind with emotion, he stumbles, trips, burns his finger, and agitatedly makes his way up the stairs. This agitation is reinforced by the darkness caused by an electrical blackout. Here, an emotional heightening coincides with the physical ascent of the hero. Galatov's ringing of the doorbell on the dark upper landing and his blind reunion with his mother are the climax of the story. This key scene in a camera obscura is, of course, a technique that is central to Nabokov's later novel *Kamera obskura.*

In this darkness Galatov's memories are fulfilled first by the sound of his mother's voice:

... iz etoi temnoty k nemu vyletel zvuchnyi i veselyi golos. "U nas vo vsem dome pogaslo elektrichestvo,–priamo uzhas,"–i on mgnovenno uznal eto dolgoe, tiaguchee "u" v "uzhase" i mgnovenno po etomu zvuku vosstanovil do maleishikh chert tu, kotoraia, skrytaia t'moi, stala v dveriakh. (p. 34)

... and out of that darkness floated a vibrant joyful voice. "The lights are out in the whole building—*eto oozhas*, its appalling"—and Nikolay recognized at once that long emphatic "oo" and on its basis instantly reconstructed down to the most minute feature the person who now stood, still concealed by darkness, in the doorway. (p. 107)

Galatov, unlike Chorb, in completing his mnemonic image will destroy, not immortalize, his loved one. In the darkness, as Galatov gropes to kiss his mother, her perfume evokes a response, but it is an ambiguous reaction. On the one hand, this fragrance captures the past for Galatov.[4] On the other hand, this Proustian response simultaneously raises the questions: Why is she youthful now? It hints that his mother may no longer be the faded, dark-haired woman he left at the railroad station. The perfume thus acquires a broader connotation in "Zvonok." It is a two-faceted image:

—i tol'ko odno bylo v nei novoe (no i eto novoe neozhidanno napomnilo samuiu glubinu detstva,—kogda ona igrala na roiale)—sil'nyi, nariadnyi zapakh dukhov—slovno ne bylo tekh promezhutochnykh let . . . i on iz dalekogo izgnaniia popal priamo v detstvo. . . . (pp. 34–35)

. . . and only one thing about her had changed (and even this novelty unexpectedly made him recall his earliest childhood, when she used to play the piano): the strong, elegant smell of perfume—as if those intervening years had not existed . . . and he had passed straight from distant exile into childhood. . . . (p. 108)

Here again, as in the opening passage, the hero mnemonically shifts from the present to the past and from the past to the present.

The falling action balances the rising action. The rising action is six pages long; the falling action, eight pages. It entails the gradual revelation that Galatov's mother is "youthful," a stark contrast to his memory of her. She is not the young woman of his childhood, nor is she the fading woman of his youth. In moving from the darkness, Galatov sees his mother by candlelight:

"Nu, pokazhis' . . . ," skazal on, vkhodia v oranzhevoe mertsanie svech' i zhadno vzglianul na mat'. U nee volosy byli sovsem svetlye, vykrashennye v tsvet solomy. (p. 36)

"Well, let me look at you," he said, entering the flickering
aura of candlelight and gazing avidly at his mother. Her dark
hair had been bleached a very light strawlike shade. (p. 108)

When the electricity comes back on, it breaks through like the sun
coming from behind a cloud. In this full light, Galatov's mother
emerges as an aged courtesan. Her déclassé situation is more
pronounced in Nabokov's English rendering, where she is described as having been born *Countess* Karski. Nabokov also changes
her married name from Nellis to Kind in the English version.

A direct progression from darkness to light has thus served as a
poetic vehicle to unmask a central figure of "Zvonok." [5] Now
Galatov realizes that his mother is exactly what he imagined her
not to be. He is quick to observe the *poshlost'* of her apartment,
which reflects her degradation. Small details do not escape
Galatov's eye. First, of course, is the screen behind which stands the
bed. Only its footboard is visible, with its decoration of Frederick
playing the flute.[6] Then there is the plush pussycat on the
mantelpiece that is probably a lover's souvenir, and finally the
little vases standing on a shelf. The table set for an intimate dinner
for two keeps attracting Galatov's attention. Not surprisingly, his
mother tries to hide it from him. As if to compound his distaste,
Galatov notices a gift box with a cheap cigarette case—Nabokov's
mini-treasure chest—and a cake with twenty-five unlit candles.
This detail not only indicates that the paramour is three years
younger than Galatov but brings forth a childhood memory of his
tenth birthday, when his mother had placed only nine candles on
his cake. This finely tuned comment on his mother's personality
subtly verifies Galatov's feeling that even during his childhood his
mother's life had no place for him.

Although Galatov seems to take this nightmarish situation in his
stride, his nervous pipe smoking reveals his uneasiness. As he
approached his mother's flat, he had lit the pipe almost in an
attempt to fill himself with courage. Now he uses the pipe again as
a support. He tries to force himself to hug her, but he is repelled by
her brightly dyed hair. Her sleazy blue dress strikes Galatov as a
vivid contrast to her former drab mackintosh. Her shiny stockings
and her mannerisms convey the uneasy feeling that her maternal

love is unwittingly colored by her seductive love. Nabokov succinctly imparted this affectation. Though Galatov's mother acts like a young woman, the full glare of the electricity reveals that she has the face of the aging woman that Galatov had expected to meet.

The uneasy mood of this reunion is threatened by the arrival of Galatov's mother's admirer. Her emotional and familiar greeting can now in retrospect be understood as a greeting intended for her suitor. The arrival of the latter while her son is still with her seems inevitable. The presence of her son, who is older than her patron, can destroy her livelihood. She is distracted and disturbed and nervously watches the clock. At last five strident doorbell rings by the paramour punctuate the reversal in Galatov's "fortunes." They push the mother's emotions to a crescendo, but she will not allow her son to answer the bell. She bursts into tears. Implicitly she is torn between her natural love for her son and her unnatural love for her paramour.

Galatov tries to comfort his mother gently and then prepares to go. He knows now that her present way of life has no place for him. This turn of events has not been entirely unprepared for: Galatov had recalled earlier that when he grew older he felt he was of little use to her. When the doorbell ceases to ring, the mother realizes that her son is leaving to roll on to Norway. Momentarily her maternal instinct comes to the fore. She hugs and caresses him, but withdraws when she self-consciously senses that her son is mocking her tear-stained makeup. Galatov promises to return in a year and leaves to resume his footloose wandering, making the separation absolute.

The conclusion is a short objective paragraph:

I kak tol'ko dver' za nim zakhlopnulas, ona, shumia sinim plat'em, kinulas' k telefonu. (p. 42)

And no sooner had the door shut after him than she flew, her blue dress rustling, to the telephone. (p. 115)

For the mother, her life also continues as before.

Surprise, an integral part of a fast-moving short story, plays a substantial role in "Zvonok." I have noted that the reader does not immediately know who the central characters are. Unlike "Vozvrashchenie Chorba," the hero's identity is gradually revealed. Nikolai Stepanych Galatov is a twenty-eight-year-old likable Russian expatriate. The woman in the mackintosh is first identified as "she"; next by her surname Nellis; and then by her name and patronymic, Ol'ga Kirillovna. Four pages into the story she is revealed to be Galatov's mother. Surprise is crucial in the reunion in the dark. His mother greets Galatov familiarly as her paramour. Only when she hears her son's voice does she understand her mistake. She confesses her surprise by pointing out that Galatov has descended on her from out of the blue. This meeting continues to yield surprises. When the lights come on, Galatov discovers that this woman is not the person whom he had left on the station platform. Suspense further complicates the tense atmosphere of this story. The mother fears a second meeting, one between her son and paramour. However, this threatening confrontation is not allowed to occur. The doorbell repeatedly rings, but unlike the case with Chorb, the door is never opened.

Save for the final objective observation concerning the mother's rush to the telephone, the entire story follows Galatov's stream of experience. At times this treatment slips into a complete stream of consciousness:

Neozhidannoe vospominanie tak i osharilo ego. Etot milostivyi gosudar' podgnil, pridetsia udalit'. V okne—priamo protiv kresla pytok—stekliannye snimki, shveitsarskie vidy. . . . Okno vykhodilo na Moiku. Teper' propoloshchite. I doktor Vainer, tolstyi, spokoinyi starik v belom khalate, v pronitsaltel'nykh ochkakh, perebiral instrumentiki. (p. 30)

An unexpected recollection virtually scalded him. This fine friend of ours is pretty well decayed and must go. In the window, right in front of the torture seat, inset glass photographs displayed Swiss landscapes. . . . The window gave on Moika Street. Rinse, please. And Dr. Weiner, a fat, placid, white-gowned old man in perspicacious glasses, sorted his tinkling instruments. (p. 104)

This elliptic passage exemplifies Nabokov's modernistic style. Galatov's interior monologues, and his dialogues with his uncle from Moscow, with Dr. Weiner, and with his mother form a substantial part of "Zvonok." They lend a spontaneity and momentum to the story that make it more vivid and immediate. These passages are full of interjections and colloquialisms, which lend veracity to the personality of the characters. Diminutives are used, particularly with reference to Galatov's mother and, as in "Vozvrashchenie Chorba," point to the *poshlost'* of the parent. The high emotional pitch of Galatov, his mother, and Dr. Weiner is underscored by the constant repetition of words, especially adverbs or imperatives. Devices of punctuation—e.g., suspension and exclamation points and dashes—impart a sense of urgency and excitement. In short, the literary style is more expressionistic.

In the shorter narrative sections of "Zvonok," Nabokov's poetic language in its characteristic "made-strange" form has a significant place. The primary image is personified Russia:

Rossiia dolgo derzhala ego, on medlenno soskal'zyval vniz s severa na iug, i Rossiia vse staralas' uderzhat' ego,—Tver'iu, Kharkovom, Belgorodom,—i vsiakimi zanimatel'nymi derevushkami . . . ne pomoglo. (p. 27)

And at last Russia let go of him—a permanent leave, according to some. Russia had held him for a long time; he had slowly slithered down from north to south, and Russia kept trying to keep him in her grasp, with the taking of Tver, Kharkov, Belgorod, and various interesting little villages, but it was no use. (p. 101)

Secondary adjective-noun and verb-noun images are evenly threaded through this story. These metaphorical expressions are brief, generally a clause long, and not as concentrated as in "Port," for example. Their brevity in no way diminishes their impact, as the following colorful fragment testifies:

Uzhe vecherelo, i ocharovatel'nym mandarinovym svetom nalilis' v sumerkakh stekliannye iarusy ogromnogo universal'nogo magazina. (p. 30)

It was already evening, and, in the twilight, a beautiful
tangerine light had filled the glassed tiers of a huge depart-
ment store. (p. 104)

Nabokov's ever-present colors are for the most part attributive and
tend to yellow-orange-red hues and the blue and purple shades.
Polilovet' (to turn purple) is the only verbal chromatic expression.
The colors of gems and minerals provide linguistic effects: diamond, gold, mercury, silver—elements that are used in "Port" as
well.

The titular symbol of the doorbell resounds through this story.
First Galatov rings at Dr. Weiner's office and then at his mother's
apartment. His reunion with her is interrupted by the five doorbell
rings of her lover. These bells produce a great deal of noise. They
crack, drill, stop short, and ring out. Often they are followed by the
resounding clang or windlike crash, bang, or slam of the doors.
Finally, these doorbells announce the arrival of the unexpected
and expected guests at No. 59 Plannerstrasse.

The central action of "Zvonok," like "Groza," is set in a realistic
Berlin locale. The trivia of Frau Nellis's attire and apartment are
described with abundant details in the spirit of the portrayal of the
Kellers in "Vozvrashchenie Chorba." However, the minutiae of
Frau Nellis's appearance serve an ironic purpose. They are exactly
what the hero is not seeking. They lend a bizarre twist to his
confrontation with his memories. On meeting his mother, Galatov
gradually realizes that she is first a mistress and only second a
mother. The horror of the encounter goes beyond even this
realization. For now Galatov senses that Frau Nellis may never
have been the mother that her son had imagined her to be, even in
his childhood. They are once again parted, each to live his life as
before—Frau Nellis with her paramour and Galatov with his happy
travels—but each has, in his own way, confronted their mutual
past. The story's structural symmetry is therefore rendered perfect.
It is not surprising, then, that "Zvonok" was one of Nabokov's
favorite stories.[7]

3. "Sluchainost' "

"Sluchainost' " ("A Matter of Chance") is another poignant
story of a Russian seeking a loved one abroad after a long

separation. In a variation on "Vozvrashchenie Chorba" and "Zvonok," both hero and heroine are looking for one another. However, fate does not intercede to bring about a reunion as it does in "Zvonok." Instead, chance prevents it; and in the end death takes the hero, leaving the heroine engaged in a hopeless search.

The main plot line is Aleksei Ivanovich Luzhin's [8] story. In a clear, short introduction, the young hero's background is given in a flashback. Luzhin, like so many of Nabokov's early heroes, has been torn from his loved one by the Russian Revolution. In the intervening five years, he, like Galatov, has been in far-flung places as a jack-of-all-trades: "a farm laborer in Turkey, a messenger in Vienna, a housepainter, a sales clerk, and so forth." Now he is a waiter with two Germans on a train, and his life has become an iron seesaw as this train shuttles to and from Berlin. Luzhin's life has been a seesaw in other ways also. The reality of his daily chores in the dining car has been balanced by the fantasy of his free hours at night in his smelly nook, during which he is absorbed with his past. These recollections have centered on his comfortable St. Petersburg study and his wife Elena—neither of which are a part of his present déclassé existence.

Thus Luzhin is a typical Nabokov hero, wavering between the reality of his present and the dreams of his past life. However, in "Sluchainost' " the theme acquires greater complexity. Luzhin is not able to balance the two halves of his existence, and his personality has degenerated. The ultimate horror is that he realizes this. He is quick to admit that his frequent doses of cocaine, although initially enchanting, have begun to ravage not just his nostrils but his mind. His nocturnal recollections are intoxicated dreams in which all trivia become miraculous, as he jots down elaborate plans to find his wife. The sobriety of the day, however, shows these notes to be meaningless. Further, the aftereffect of the drug makes Luzhin ill, and more than ever he realizes that his life is wasting away. As the introduction concludes, Luzhin's rising and falling fear—his sense of the worthlessness of his life—supplants his remembrance of this past, and particularly his efforts to find his wife. And the familiar bittersweet theme of *recherche du temps perdu* is twisted into a tragic death theme. For now Luzhin elaborately plans not to find his wife but to die. It is the fanciful plans, particularly their Nabokovian details, that now occupy him, but even these pale by day. Only a realization that there is no use in continuing life remains. To ease his task Luzhin has set the night between August 1 and 2 as the date of his death.

The exposition has provided the needed background for Luzhin's story; and the rising action, designated by a break in the text, [9] aptly focuses in:

A pervogo avgusta, v polovine sed'mogo vechera, v prostornom, polutemnom bufete berlinskogo vokzala . . . (p. 7)

The first day of August ran its course. At six-thirty in the evening . . . in the buffet of the Berlin station . . . (p. 145)

Here the story shifts to a seemingly extraneous figure who links the main plot to the secondary one. Mar'ia Pavlovna Ukhtomskaia, [10] an old lady, is installed on a train with three bags—all her worldly belongings:

U reshetki ee zhdal nosil'shchik. Podavali poezd. Mrachnye, zheleznogo tsveta, vagony tiazhelo piatilis', prokhodili odin za drugim. Na fanere mezhdunarodnogo, pod srednimi oknami, belela vyveska: Berlin-Parizh; mezhdunarodnyi, da eshche restoran, gde v okne mel'knuli vystavlennye lokti i golova ryzhego lakeia,—odni napomnili sderzhannuiu roskosh' dovoennogo Nord ekspressa. (p. 7)

A porter was waiting for her at the gate. The train was backing into the station. One after another, the lugubrious iron-colored German carriages moved past. The varnished brown teak of one sleeping car bore under the center window a sign or the inscription BERLIN-PARIS; that international car, as well as the teak-lined diner, in a window of which she glimpsed the protruding elbows and head of a carroty-haired waiter, were alone reminiscent of the severely elegant prewar Nord-Express. (p. 145)

This near-photographic passage is a fine example of Nabokov's approach, as the highly detailed surface reality of the description of the teak train has a secondary level. For the old woman it yields a remembrance of the past, while on a purely structural level the select detail of the carroty-haired waiter indicates that this is Luzhin's fellow waiter, Max, and therefore this is his train.

In her compartment, Ukhtomskaia is joined by a fellow émigrée, a young woman who is overheard giving Russian farewells. A switch is made here to the contrapuntal theme as Ukhtomskaia learns that this is Elena Nikolaevna Luzhina, who is seeking her lost husband. Complex suspense thus figures in the rising action: none of the characters is aware that by chance both husband and wife are on the train. The reader alone anticipates the climactic reunion. This central section of the story stands apart from the exposition and the conclusion, not merely because of the use of dialogue, but because of the shifting authorial camera. The omniscient narrator continually moves from Luzhin in the dining car to Elena in the compartment, creating a dramatic acceleration and suspense.

In this rising action, Luzhin's regression moves from pure fantasy to drugged euphoria and finally toward his death. This disintegration is poetically expressed in Luzhin's repeated sense that his body will sneeze up his soul. His imbalance reaches such proportions that he takes some cocaine while he is on the job, in the light of day, his last day. Well into the story the calculated details of Luzhin's suicide are revealed: on this day he will place his head between the buffers of two train cars, and as they clash, his bowed head will "burst like a soap bubble and turn into iridescent air."

Simultaneously the second story unravels in the nearby compartment as Elena converses with Ukhtomskaia, who had known the Luzhin family many years before. Her recollections paint a picture of opulence and high society that is in stark contrast to the plight of these émigrés. In recalling the Luzhin family, Ukhtomskaia conjures up Luzhin's past while he himself is planning his imminent, fatal future. Ironically, the old woman remembers the connection between herself and Luzhin; whereas Luzhin himself, although he sees her when he announces dinner, cannot place her. The drugging effect of the cocaine on his memory is expressed with an image which combines past life and future death:

> Chuvstvo, chto, vot-vot, chikhnet telo—teper' stalo opredelen-nee: vot-vot, seichas vspomniu. No chem bol'she on napriagal mysli, tem razdrazhitel'nee uskol'zalo vospominan'e. Ver-nulsia v stolovuiu khmuryi. Razduval nozdri. Gorlo szhimala spazma. Ne mog pereglotnut'. (p. 8)

> The sensation that his body would sneeze up his soul any instant now became more concrete—any moment now I'll remember whom that old woman resembled. But the more he strained his mind, the more irritatingly the recollection would slip away. He was morose when he returned to the diner, with his nostrils dilating and a spasm in his throat would not let him swallow. (pp. 151–52)

The cocaine does not work its accustomed miracle, and for once Luzhin's memory cannot surface. The link between the two plots remains broken.

Elena's tale of separation and emigration complements Luzhin's, giving both poignancy and drama. Her search elaborates Luzhin's story and acts as an interlocking puzzle piece. Elena has heard that Luzhin is alive and has put an advertisement in a Russian-language newspaper in Berlin.[11] Her smile reflects her crescendo-ing emotions as she listens to Ukhtomskaia reminisce. After Luzhin, unseen, makes the call for dinner, Elena sets off for what will surely be a joyful reunion. Her movement toward the story's crisis is thwarted, however, on the platform of the dining car. The foreigner who has been eyeing her in the compartment accosts her. The extent to which chance and Ukhtomskaia have aided the reunion is offset by this man. Elena makes a sudden about-face, and the falling action of this story is punctuated by the observation that she felt unbearably hurt. She forgoes dinner in the dining car and returns to take a nap.

In "Sluchainost'" the falling action, often the weaker section of a story, is as gripping as what has gone before. Elena awakens later to realize that in her scuffle she has lost her wedding ring, and the emotional level again increases as she searches for it. But her quest proves futile; the dining car has been uncoupled during her nap. She has lost her wedding ring for good, and unknown to her, she has also lost her husband. Elena's plot line has not intersected Luzhin's doomed line. This lack of contact is underscored by the open-ended train car with Elena's limitless view:

... skvoz' zadniuiu dver' uvidela—prosto—vozdukh, pustotu, nochnoe nebo, chernym klinom ubegaiushchii put'. (p. 8)

She . . . saw nothing but air, emptiness, the night sky, the dark wedge of the roadbed disappearing into the distance. (p. 154)

The final detail of the charwoman with her pail and brush standing at the toilet where Luzhin perhaps had his last sniff of cocaine seems to underscore Elena's tragedy.

A space in the text indicates the beginning of the conclusion of Luzhin's story, which directly matches that of Elena. Like his wife, Luzhin is at the open-ended platform of the dining car, gazing at the tracks from inside the frame of the door. This is the typical pose of a Nabokovian hero at a window or door frame before death. Only Ukhtomskaia's face has left a disturbing gap in Luzhin's planned suicide.

Behind his back his marital drama continues to unfold. By chance Max finds Elena's gold ring as he sweeps the train platform. Stealthily he reads the inscription, but it is indecipherable to him: "Must be Chinese." The omniscient narrator adds matter-of-factly:

A na samom dele bylo: 1 Avgusta 1915 g. Aleksei. (p. 8)

Actually, the inscription read "1-VIII-1915. Aleksey." (p. 155) [12]

Max returns the ring to his pocket. This incident lends an electrifying dimension to the conclusion, for had Luzhin found the ring, he would have been saved. Instead, he moves off the car to his end. This concluding suicide is only suggested as Luzhin calmly

jumps down onto the cinders of the railbed. *Pokoino* (calmly) here
echoes *pokoinyi* (the deceased). The thundering, hungry bound of
the through train signals the catastrophe. It passes unnoticed in the
final laconic sentence:

Maks, *ne ponimaia,* videl izali, kak promakhnuli sploshnoi
polosoi osveshchennye okna. (p. 8)

Max, *totally unaware of what happened,* watched from a distance
as the lighted windows flew past in one continuous stripe. (p.
155) [13]

This conclusion, however, contains an implied reversal: Luzhin has
been killed, not according to his well-calculated plans, but by a
sudden instinctive move.

Much of the strength of this story is found in the limitless
possibilities of what might have happened if any of the missed
chances had coincided; for example, if Luzhin had handed out the
meal tickets, as he offered to do; if he had not taken the drug and
had recognized Ukhtomskaia, or noticed his wife beside her; if the
dining car had not been uncoupled early; or if he had found the
lost wedding ring. In Elena's simpler story there is only one missed
chance—her failure to reach the dining car.

Nabokov's characterizations in "Sluchainost'" are superb.
There are the two main characters, the Luzhins, and two linking
figures, Ukhtomskaia and the foreigner; and there are five minor
German characters. The distinctive external features of each are
given and then repeated in various shortened configurations. This
method of recurring spot characterizations ties the two plots
together. Nabokov assigned unusual traits to his characters.
Luzhin's close-cropped head and tense forehead are accented by
his bushy eyebrows, which resemble an inverted mustache: *chernye,
gustye brovi, podobnie perevernutym usam* (black, thick eyebrows, comparable to an inverted mustache); *s chernymi broviami, vrode perever-
nutykh usov* (with black eyebrows, similar to an inverted mustache).[14] His wide, ivory-white smile becomes synecdochic for his
personality. Luzhin's fellow waiters love him precisely because of
his smile, but as he loses hope he smiles less often. He flashes a

flustered smile when he thinks of the cocaine, which gives him temporary bliss. He smiles after he sniffs it and has a frightened smile when Max calls him from his drugged reverie. In his sober moments, however, his smile is replaced by a weary look, an expression that he shares with his wife.

Elena is described as a "young woman with a big painted mouth and a tight toque that covered her forehead." Her lips recur as a characteristic detail; for instance, she wonders if the foreigner has not chased her because she uses lipstick. Later, when she awakens, she licks her lips, which are dry from sleep, and wearily rubs her forehead.

Ukhtomskaia is colorful in appearance, and her mannerisms and conversation are gentle and sympathetic. A dowager with a big-knobbed man's cane, she is the first of Nabokov's long line of stout matrons. Her most distinguishing traits are her obesity and a sallow face that is likened to a eunuch's. The foreigner who shares the compartment and prevents so many chances is described in a manner that underlines his sinister role. First he is the man in the beige suit, and then he becomes the "olive and beige man" *(olivkovyi chelovek)*. (This progressive synecdoche recalls the image of the "brown, old woman" in "Blagost' " [See above, p. 49.].) His eyes are most revealing. He peers at Elena and tries to catch her glance. For Elena they are "nasty, glassy protuberant eyes that seemed filled with dark iodine." Her suspicions are confirmed when he chases after her through the train and grabs her with "rough tenderness," saying, "My precious." His accented German is also a negative touch. In character, he imperturbably returns to the compartment and hides his head behind the flap of his overcoat to take a nap.[15] As if to underline his perversion, Nabokov noted that "his legs are grotesquely spread."

The remaining minor characters are Germans. The waiter Hugo, "a thickset, fair-haired Berliner," is not as prominent as the "quick, red-haired, sharp-nosed Max, who resembled a fox." The stress on Max's carroty hair is a curious detail, because Russians tend to be superstitious about redheads. The manner in which Max slithers between tables like a fox foreshadows his sly acquisition of the gold ring. The final concise indictment is that Max cannot differentiate between Cyrillic and Chinese characters.

This indicates that he is not only dishonest but illiterate. Nabokov's generally negative portrayal of the Germans provides a sharp contrast to his highly sensitive and sympathetic depiction of the Russian characters.

In spite of its structural complexity, "Sluchainost' " is an extraordinarily cohesive story. Recurring motifs and interrelated temporal and spatial devices pull the two plots together, making the double drama flow. Repeated minute, unrelated details and situational echoes tie this piece together. For instance, the arrival of the train in Berlin is signaled "with a clang of bumpers"; later, Luzhin plans to use the bumper plates as the instrument of his suicide. The gold rim running around Ukhtomskaia's dinner plates reflects Elena's wedding ring. Ukhtomskaia's gesture of firmly wiping "her nose, left to right and back again," echoes Luzhin's greedy application to each of his nostrils. Finally, the scene in which Luzhin cannot clear his throat is repeated directly in the succeeding paragraph when the foreigner clears his throat as he pursues Elena.

The clear-cut use of time also gives this story a sense of unity and pushes the action forward. In the exposition, time passes in a grand sweep of five years, from 1919 until the "present." The central action of the story is then confined to the fateful evening of August 1. Here the story temporally expands. Timetables, actual train arrivals, departures, lurching gilt-handed station clocks all push the immediate drama ahead. In Nabokov's poetic passages, sunset and twilight are followed by night. Implicitly time rushes on as the question lingers of whether Elena will reach the dining car before it is uncoupled. The eventual suicide pushes the story toward an effective and predetermined conclusion. The date of 1 August 1915, inscribed in the wedding ring, that is revealed in the conclusion, pushes the story back to the period in which it opened. A perfect temporal balance is thus achieved.

The story's setting also provides dynamic unity and equilibrium. In the introduction the spatial element, like the temporal, is diffuse. It is worldwide, as Luzhin wanders during his early emigration. The rising and falling actions are limited essentially to the Berlin-Paris express—to the compartment and dining car, in particular. As the train itself moves back and forth, so do the characters. Thus a sense of perpetual motion is produced. At the heart of the story Elena enters Luzhin's microcosm. For a brief period they are within reach of one another, but at the conclusion they are once again flung apart. There is an exchange of roles as Elena continues traveling on the train, and Luzhin steps off it forever.

In "Sluchainost' " the train is more than a setting and accelerating device. It is a source of poetic images. Nabokov's love for trains is apparent both in the realistic passages and in his lyrical descriptions of the express. The train is personified. It moves lugubriously into the station and halts with "a long sibilant sigh of brakes"; later the car stops, "with a prolonged sigh of relief." The speed of this train is indicated by descriptions of the passing locales. These passages act as structural devices that inconspicuously shift the scenes. They also provide both poetic relief and a structural braking to the highly charged drama on the train. Most important, they are examples of Nabokov's "made-strange" style. For example, the passing telephone poles provide refreshing images. First they are telegraph wires (strings in Russian), then these wires are likened to flags, and finally they are simply harp strings.

(1) V okno, skvoz' stekliannuiu dver' v prokhod, vidat' bylo, kak vzmyvaiut rovnym riadom telegrafnye struni. (p. 7)

Through the corridor window . . . the even row of telegraph wires could be seen swooping upward. (p. 147)

(2) Chernyi telegrafnyi stolb proletel, perebil plavnyi vzmakh provolok. Oni opustilis', kak flag, kogda spadaet veter. I vkradchivo stali podnimat'sia opiat'. (p. 7)

A telegraph pole, black against the sunset, flew past, interrupting the smooth ascent of the wires. They dropped as a flag drops when the wind stops blowing. Then furtively they began rising again. (pp. 147–48)

(3) Vdol' okon otchaianno vzmyvali piat' otchetlivykh strun. (p. 7)

Five distinct harp strings swooped desperately upward alongside the windows. (p. 149)

In these passages the emphasis is not on the movement of the train but on the scene through which it passes. This method is used also in the following excerpts:

Mimo okna plyli zadnie kirpichnye steny domov; na odnoi byla reklama: ispolinskaia papirosa, slovno nabitaia zolotoi solomoi. V luchakh nizkogo solntsa goreli kryshi, mokrye ot dozhdia. (p. 7)

The brick rear walls of houses went gliding past; one of them displayed the painted advertisement of a colossal cigarette, stuffed with what looked like golden straw. The roofs, wet from a rainstorm, glistened under the rays of the low sun. (p. 146)

Poezd shel bystro mezhdu vozdushnykh sten shirokogo, zolotistogo vechera. (p. 7)

The express was traveling swiftly between the airy walls of a spacious fire-bright evening. (p. 148)

This "made-strange" image of the train is fully inverted and therefore neutralized in the final sentence, as if pinpointing that the onrushing train is acting as it kills the more passive Luzhin: "Max . . . watched from a distance as the lighted windows flew past in one continuous stripe."
In "Sluchainost' " there are many refreshingly original similes:

Luzhin zhil, kak na zheleznykh kacheliakh. (p. 7)

Luzhin lived on a kind of steel seesaw. (p. 143)

... kak rozovyi iazyk, torchal kusok vetchiny. (p. 8)

A piece of ham stuck out like a pink tongue.

Raschityval kazhduiu meloch', slovno reshal shakhmatnuiu zadachu. (p. 8)

He calculated every little detail, as if he were composing a chess problem. (p. 151)

The central image in "Sluchainost' " is the wedding ring. As a symbol of the Luzhin marriage, it is the figurative and literal link between the husband's and wife's stories. Its loss brings horror and grief to Elena and represents the complete break of the marriage. This image is threaded through the story, at times appearing metaphorically as a "golden ray" (*zolotoi luch*). The tragedy is foreshadowed when the wedding ring falls off Elena's hand as she settles in the compartment. Here she notes that she keeps losing her ring because her fingers seem to have grown thinner. This little detail also suggests the deprivations Elena has endured without Luzhin. For Elena the ring actively symbolizes her husband. The fact that for a while she had thought him dead and had worn her ring on the chain of her cross is full of prophetic meaning. She explains that she was afraid that it would be taken from her by the German authorities. Here the implication is that in the 1920s the gold ring is of particular material value, an aspect recalled later when Max pockets it for this reason. Ironically, Elena loses the ring in repulsing the advances of the foreigner and is unaware of her loss until it is too late. She grieves openly when she discovers what has happened. Unknowingly, she is also grieving for her dead Luzhin. The ring has by chance followed Luzhin, but he never finds it.

This symbolic ring provides an element of suspense and surprise that gives "Sluchainost' " a highly effective conclusion. It holds the answer to the question unobtrusively raised in the introduction: Why has Luzhin chosen to die on the night between August 1 and 2? The ring's inscription indicates that this is the anniversary of

Luzhin's wedding night, and in all his drugged weariness and hopelessness he has never forgotten his marriage to Elena. However, in reliving his wedding night, Luzhin, unlike Chorb, seeks not rebirth but death.

4. "Britva"

In Nabokov's story "Britva" ("The Razor"), the Russian hero's attempted confrontation with his past, as in "Zvonok" and "Sluchainost'," takes on a deeper and therefore a more symbolic meaning. This familiar theme is amplified by a second motif, that of human vengeance. Superfluous, trivial details recede into the background. A sense of economy pervades. A few tangible, concrete objects assume complex significance. The razor of the title symbolizes the passion of the revenger, and a clock and a Greek statue epitomize the object of his revenge.

The plot of "Britva" is tightly constructed, and the story unfolds quickly and credibly. The exposition describes an émigré, Colonel Ivanov, who is now a barber in Berlin; and his associates in the barbershop are presented. As in "Groza," the locality of the story is confined. The opening scene of "Port" becomes the exclusive setting of "Britva." [16] In the opening passages, Ivanov's past and his growing need for revenge are set forth. His ruling passion stems from a deep-seated grudge against the Red officer who had condemned him to death six years before. Ivanov's reaction is human and natural; the officer embodies all that had destroyed Ivanov's homeland.

The rising action is marked by the phrase, "One very hot, blue-gray summer morning," and is confined to one specific day. Ivanov is alone in the shop when by coincidence the detested Red officer walks in for a shave. The protagonists confront one another. As Ivanov shaves his customer, they tacitly recognize each other. The rising action mounts with the increasing threat of Ivanov's revenge. This accelerating tension is unbroken by flashbacks. What previously occurred between these two Russians is only intimated by the statement that the original incident had been recounted by Ivanov to his officer and that the story frightened his listener. Here the questions are only implied: Was the original confrontation horrifying? Was Ivanov's rendition frightening? These questions are never answered. The situation is ambiguous, thus allowing for one or all of these interpretations.

The climax of "Britva" is signaled by Ivanov's completion of the shave and his surprising remark: "That's enough out of you . . . I'm satisfied, you may go." In contrast to the lengthy rising action, the brief falling action, just over a paragraph long, depicts a passive, frightened customer. He has to be pulled out of the chair by Ivanov, who claps his bowler on his head, thrusts his briefcase under his arm, and pushes him across the threshold into the sunlit street.

No conclusion is needed. The climax and the falling action speak for Ivanov. His revenge has been achieved. Although "Britva" is not classically balanced—that is, the exposition and the rising action predominate—the plot and the tone of the story recall Silvio's delayed revenge in Pushkin's classic tale, "The Shot." In "Britva," however, the reversal occurs in the climax, not in the conclusion. On the other hand, in both stories psychological revenge proves to be more effective than bloody reprisal.

It could be argued that "Britva" is a classic story. In that event, the opening paragraph, which describes the hero, would be considered the exposition. The rising action would consist of his growing desire for vengeance. The climax would be his confrontation with and recognition of his customer. The falling action would be the gradual satisfaction of his revenge. The conclusion would be a reversal—his release of his unharmed victim. This version, however, is not as interesting as the one Nabokov chose.

Ivanov, who is known as "Razor," is the central figure of the story. The first sentence notes that his nickname is derived not from his profession alone. Physically, his profile resembles a razor:

—i etot profil' byl zamechatel'nyi: nos ostryi, kak ugol chertezhnogo treugol'nika, krepkii, kak lokot', podborodok, dlinnye nezhnye resnitsy, kakie byvaiut u ochen' upriamykh i zhestokikh liudei. (p. 2)

—and this profile was marvelous: a sharp nose, like the corner of a drafting triangle, a chin as firm as an elbow, long, kindly eyelashes, which very stubborn and cruel people are apt to have.

The appelation "Razor" also characterizes his personality. His features reflect a stubborn and cruel temperament.

The exposition of the story is a justification of his lingering hatred and sets the scene for his eventual revenge. The difficulties of forced emigration form the essence of Ivanov's predicament. He describes his emigration as an epic flight and his adjustment in Berlin as a series of minor trials. Although he has finally found work in Germany, he remains very Russian. He is unable to communicate in German save by *nicht, was,* and gestures. Despite his German training as a barber, he cuts hair like a Russian. His natural tie to his homeland lingers in his personality and feeds his growing desire for revenge. This feeling is likened to a wound-up spring by Nabokov, with the implication that the spring need only be released once.

The intensity of the story is strengthened by being narrated from Ivanov's point of view. This perspective is clearly and poetically indicated in the shaving image:

Ivanov . . . zavernul ego v prostiniu, vzbil teplovatuiu penu v farforovoi chashechke, kistochkoi stal mazat' gospodinu shcheki, kruglyi podborodok, nadgub'e, ostorozhno oboshel rodimyi pryshch, ukazatel'nym pal'tsem stal vtirat' penu. (p. 2)

Ivanov . . . wrapped him up in a towel, whipped up a warmish foam in a little porcelain cup, with a brush he started to lather the gentleman's cheeks, round chin, upper lip, he carefully avoided the mole and with his index finger he started to rub in the foam.

You will recall that in "Port" this image is reversed—the hero is the customer, not the barber.

The release of the metaphorical spring is the major event of "Britva." When Ivanov recognizes his customer as the very person he holds responsible for his forced emigration, he is stunned. Ironically, he is too surprised to adjust to the very opportunity of which he has dreamed—a highly realistic reaction that lends credibility to the story. In a fog of amazement, he prepares to shave the officer. Mechanically he lathers the man's face. (This mechanical action is expressed by the officer in a transfer of emotions later when he exits.) Ivanov recovers from his amazement only when he sharpens his razor and realizes its possibilities. But again, ironically, he does not use it as the weapon it represents in his belligerent imagination. Instead he gently, carefully, and slowly shaves his trapped customer.

What Ivanov tells the officer, however, is quite a different matter. By his remarks and, even more, by implication he begins to terrorize him. He reminds his customer of their former dealings and observes that despite the sentence dealt him six years before he is still very much alive. He then proceeds to shave and chat, interspersing his conversation with pointed references to blood and to arteries. He keeps repeating that the two of them are alone and asks rhetorically: How can one expiate a death sentence? What can match the sharp end of a sword? The unanswered response, of course, is the razor that he holds in his hand. Ivanov proceeds to note that both the dead and the condemned are shaved and points out that he too is shaving an individual. Implicitly Ivanov's treatment of his customer is the inversion of their previous confrontation. In this case Ivanov grants life. He does not take it. Calmly and matter-of-factly, he releases his victim. Technically both men are released: Ivanov from his overwhelming desire for vengeance and the officer from torture.

The former officer is nameless, and the reason for his presence in Berlin remains unexplained. He is, after all, a Red officer. His black suit, bowler, and briefcase have a certain bourgeois aspect that is not in keeping with communist militarism and that is in sharp contrast to that of Ivanov, a lowly barber. His face is not immediately visible, even though it is the center of all of the action. The glare of the sun blinds Ivanov as the customer pushes his way into the barbershop. The many mirrors reflect the newcomer:

Togda voshedshii otrazilsia vo vsekh zerkalakh srazu,—v profil', v poloborota, potom voskovoi lysinoi, s kotoroi podnialsia, chtoby zatsepit'sia za kriuk, chernyi kotelok. (p. 2)

Then the one who had entered became reflected in all the
mirrors at once—in profile, in half-turn, then by the waxy bald
pate, from which a black bowler arose to get caught on a
hook.

In typical Nabokovian "made-strange" fashion, his face is seen last,
and then Ivanov recognizes only the features that confirm him as
his former tormentor. Nabokov's use of suffixes and the repeating p
sound underscore the derogatory impression:

Ivanov mgnovenno uznal eto podvizhnoe, pukhliavoe litso s
pronzitel'nymi glazkami i tolstym rodimym pryshchom u
pravogo kryla nosa. (p. 2)

Ivanov instantly recognized this mobile, plumpish face with
its penetrating little eyes and the fat mole on the right wing of
the nostril.

The officer's eyes reflect the entire horrifying experience. They
are piercing when he first sits in the barber's chair. Then they are
likened to a clock mechanism—an image that forecasts his subsequent condition. When the officer recognizes the barber, the little
piercing wheels begin to go even faster; then the eyes tightly close,
like those of a savage who believes himself invisible if he shuts his
eyes. The officer's eyes never really open again. As the torture
progresses, he comes to resemble a corpse with bulging eyelids. His
pale full face is now described as eyeless. This repeated stress on his
eyes serves to underline the shock that he experiences.

The metaphor of death is also threaded through this passage.
The warm lather of the soap creates a mask, implicitly a death
mask. The white sheet is likened to a shroud. The officer is sapped
of life and resembles an automaton. When he leaves, he moves
with a mechanical gait and holds his briefcase with an arm that
has become wooden. This picture culminates in a more poetic
classical image. His eyes are likened to those of a Greek statue. The
deadened eyes reflect his deadened soul. The entire portrayal of
this officer has been figurative, indicating Nabokov's symbolic
approach in this story.

The titular symbol of the razor has many facets, and all are associated with Ivanov. Physically and temperamentally he resembles a razor. He is nicknamed "Razor," and his profession as a barber in turn provides him with the potential instruments for his revenge—the scissors and the razor. Thus in the end he is able to choose between his real razor and his razorlike personality to accomplish his task.

The multileveled symbol of the razor and the story's compressed structure are matched by a rich poetic language. The tropes are predominantly similes, metaphors, and hyperboles, brought together in a single passage, with "made-strange" adjectives added as well. The combined effect is a very dense poetic style. The Nabokovian shadow image occurs in a new and refreshing combination:

Mimo mel'kali liudi v soprovozhdenii svoikh sinikh tenei, kotorye lomalis' po kraiu paneli i besstrashno skol'zili pod sverkaiushchie kolesa avtomobilei, ostavliavshikh na zharkom asfal'te lentochnye otpechatki, podobnye uzorchatym shnurkam zmei. (p. 2)

People were glimpsed fleetingly being escorted by their dark-blue shadows, which were breaking at the edge of the pavement and fearlessly sliding under the gleaming wheels of the automobiles, which were leaving on the hot asphalt, ribbonlike prints, similar to the patterned cords of snakes.

Here the shadows are personified as they break and fearlessly slip under automobile wheels. Of all of the tropes found in Nabokov's early prose, the personification predominates. His use of this device was almost excessive and here is comparable to a pathetic fallacy. However, even in his personifications Nabokov exhibited verbal dexterity. In this passage there is a verbal personification: *liudi v soprovozhdenii svoikh tenei, kotorye lomalis'* (People . . . being escorted by their shadows, which were breaking); followed by an adverbial personification: *tenei, kotorye . . . besstrashno skol'zili* (shadows, which . . . fearlessly slid). The richness of this excerpt is marked not only by this double personification but by the concluding snake simile.

In another passage of "Britva," Nabokov used still a third variety, the adjectival personification. The ring is personified, as in *etot shchegol'skii zvon* (this foppish ringing). There is very little color in "Britva." The emphasis is on sultriness, haze, and transparency.

Even though the backdrop of "Britva" resembles the realistic scene in "Port," the plot line is essentially symbolic in tone. Field has gone so far as to remark that: *"The Razor* is a cleverly serious adaptation of Gogol's *The Nose* (Adamovich once declared: 'Granted Russian literature came out of *The Overcoat,* but Sirin came out of Gogol's *Nose')* put to a political use" (p. 114). Field seems to me too extreme in his interpretation. Perhaps Gogol's story "The Nose" does lie below the text of "Britva," adding to the value of this early story. This parallel would be most obvious in the character of Ivanov. However, the essence of "Britva" lies more in its tragic confrontation with the past.[17] Ivanov clearly faces his Russian past when he confronts the officer. Their meeting is colored and distorted by the multifaceted symbol of the razor. These devices endow this story with a definite symbolic aspect.

5. "Rozhdestvenskii rasskaz"

Nabokov's anti-Soviet tone, which is only intimated in "Britva," becomes more prominent in "Rozhdestvenskii rasskaz" ("The Christmas Story"). Here Nabokov obliquely indicted the Soviet literary scene. The setting is highly unusual for Nabokov: it is the Soviet Union. As if to accentuate this fact, the story takes place on Christmas Eve, when an old writer, a young writer, and a critic meet, thus producing an immediate conflict of two generations and of two worlds: the old Russia and the new Soviet Union.

The *siuzhet* is structurally weak and does not lend itself to the traditional analysis. The story can be only roughly diagrammed. The exposition is the opening paragraph, which sets the scene and describes the three central characters. Background details about the hero, Dmitrii Dmitrievich Novodvortsev, are also given.[18] This grand old man of letters is visited by a critic from the journal *Krasnaia Iav'* and his protégé Anton Golyi. As Golyi reads his new work for Novodvortsev's approval, the older man becomes sad. Golyi, like others before him, has made use of Novodvortsev's own literary themes [19]—this one taken from Novodvortsev's novelette published the preceding year. Novodvortsev says nothing other than that it is a fine piece; he makes some suggestions and invites the young author to come again. Novodvortsev hopes that the critic will catch the plagiarism, but the latter does not.

The rising action consists of this discussion. As the critic and the young author prepare to leave Novodvortsev, the critic remarks: "Today, by the way, is Christmas Eve." This climactic observation is followed by the critic's suggestion that Novodvortsev write a Christmas story—a new one—implying that it should be within the context of the Soviet scene. The young author adds that it should be a story of a Christmas tree with the Red Star atop it. The critic, however, offers a stronger theme—a war of the worlds against a snowy Christmas background. Novodvortsev cautions that one must be careful with the symbolic level. However, after the others go he sits down to write a story, the greatest ever.

The falling action—the remaining half of "Rozhdestvenskii rasskaz"—consists of Novodvortsev's reflections, past, present, and future, on the Christmas theme. In the quiet of his room he ponders at his desk. He notes a squarish glass in its holder, which has survived all life's storms and is still in one piece. He finally settles on the Christmas theme, and it brings a flood of memories. He recalls the trees that used to be sold in the shadows of St. Isaac's Cathedral. He remembers that he has already touched upon the Christmas theme in his hero Tumanov's dream in the work "Gran'," the one that had been plagiarized. Novodvortsev then recollects a Christmas he had spent in a merchant's home with a woman he had loved some twenty years before. He recalls how the eyes of his beloved reflected the festive scene:

... vse ogni elki khrustal'nym drozhaniem otrazhalis' v ee shiroko raskrytykh glazakh. (p. 3)

... all of the lights of the Christmas tree were reflected with a crystal shiver in her wide-open eyes.

This "made-strange" device may well have been influenced by Nabokov's favorite writer Flaubert. The same image occurs in expanded form in *Madame Bovary:* "Seen thus closely, her eyes seemed to him enlarged, especially when she opened and shut them several times quickly on waking. Black in the shade, dark blue in the full daylight, they had depths of different colors, which, darker in the center, grew paler toward the surface of the eye. *His own eyes lost themselves in these depths; he saw himself in miniature down to his shoulders, with his handkerchief around his head and the top of his shirt open.* "[20]

In "Rozhdestvenskii rasskaz," once again, Nabokov focused on the significance of trivial moments of the past. Novodvortsev muses about present-day Christmases. He imagines the sickly Christmas trees that are being set up in secret in homes around him, and then shifts to the thought of Russian émigrés crying beside their trees in the West. He sees them squeezing into their full-dress coats, weeping for the homeland. The implicit problem that Nabokov presented in this passage may be comparable to one stated by the Russian émigré author Merezhkovskii in Paris when he asked his poetess-wife Zinaida Gippius which was better, Russia without freedom or freedom without Russia.

In the end of his musings, Novodvortsev only manages to achieve an impotent vision of Christmas. His creative urge, his excitement, reflections, and memories yield a miserable capitalist Christmas scene with a poor worker, the victim of a lockout, gazing into festive Christmas windows.

The conclusion of "Rozhdestvenskii rasskaz" is Novodvortsev's self-contradicting text:

Naglaia elka . . . perelivalas' vsemi ogniami radugi. (p. 3)

The insolent Christmas tree . . . was iridescent with all of the lights of the rainbow.

The conclusion represents a reversal. The tone of Novodvortsev's fragment in no way matches his original inspiration. It is banal and confined within the traditions of Soviet literature. This approach has stifled Novodvortsev's basically artistic personality.

The three central characters of the story are portrayed in physical detail. Anton Golyi, usually nervously coughing, is briefly shown: ". . . young, fat-faced, in a Russian shirt under a black jacket." His sponsor, the critic, is more fully drawn. He sits at the edge of the sofa like a large sad bird. Later he is compared to an ox:

Eto byl kostliavy, raskhliabannyi, ryzhii chelovek, stra da iu shchii, po slukham, chakhotkoi, no na samom dele, veroiatno, zdorovyi kak byk. (p. 2)

This was a bony, tottering, red-haired man, who, according to hearsay, was suffering from tuberculosis, but who actually probably was as strong as an ox.

Novodvortsev is the most fully described:

V krupnom pensne, chrezvychaino lobastyi, s dvumia polos-kami redkikh volos natianutykh poperek lysiny i s sedinoi na podstrizhennykh viskakh, on sidel prikryv glaza, slovno pro-dolzhal slushat', skrestiv tolstye nogi, zashchemiv ruku mezhdu kolenom odnoi nogi i podkolennoi kostochkoi drugoi. (p. 2)

Wearing a large pince-nez, having an extraordinarily large forehead, with two streaks of sparse hair pulled across his bald spot and with gray hair on his shaven temples, he sat with shaded eyes, as if continuing to listen, having crossed his fat legs and having jammed a hand between the knee of one leg and the popliteal bone of the other.

The prevailing mood of this story is one of melancholy and sadness. Novodvortsev speaks quietly and evenly, in a manner that immediately sets a subdued and understated tone. He is sympathetic and kindly. The story is related by an omniscient narrator who brings out Novodvortsev's positive qualities. Novodvortsev has been writing for twenty-five years; a six-volume collection of his works has been published, and he assumes that he will be feted on his anniversary. He is paid homage by all the young writers. The fact that he can be readily plagiarized indicates the extent to which he is famous. Novodvortsev is eager for praise and proudly enlists himself in the ranks of Gorky and Chirikov a minor émigré writer. He is overjoyed when an obscure critic calls his hero's malady a *tumanovshchina*, a clear play on the Russian term *oblomovshchina* (oblomovism).[21] However, Novodvortsev is wise enough to realize that his is false fame and that the praise is not genuine. In the future others will take credit for his work. Nevertheless, Novodvortsev still tries to create a masterwork.

For all of Novodvortsev's sensitivity and introspection, he produces an impoverished and even hypocritical version of Christmas as a matter of class warfare. His story, written in the Soviet Union, in no way matches the symbolic and inspiring Christmas image created by Nabokov himself in early emigration that is entitled "Rozhdestvo." (See below, p. 193 bottom.)

However, bitter as this Christmas story may appear, it had literary precursors to whom Novodvortsev and Nabokov himself were clearly heir. Many of Charles Dickens's Christmas stories were published, like Nabokov's,[22] in the Christmas issues of journals and newspapers. More often than not, they portrayed the unfortunate of the lower classes gazing wistfully into wealthy homes at Christmas. More direct forerunners were Dostoevsky's Christmas stories: "The Christmas Tree and the Wedding" and "The Boy at Christ's Christmas Party." In the last piece a starving child is pictured looking into three separate windows where expensive decorations, Christmas trees, and parties are visible. However, in Dostoevsky's story the expiring child's plight is tempered by his Christmas party with Christ after his death. In Novodvortsev's vision, the ending is abrupt and stark.

"Rozhdestvenskii rasskaz" combines the Christmas theme with the Soviet theme; the result, like Novodvortsev's creation, is lackluster. Its redeeming feature is that Novodvortsev's creative urge and its weak result can be viewed as Nabokov's Aesopian condemnation of Socialist realism. To catch this subtle point, the reader has to be well versed in Soviet literature. Oblique yet functional details give the story a Soviet slant. *Krasnaia Iav'* recalls the Soviet journal *Krasnaia Nov'*. Anton Golyi recalls such early Soviet authors as Artem Veselyi and Mikhail Golodnyi. The serious discussion of Golyi's—that is, Novodvortsev's—work concerning the conflict of classes, and the use of traditional Soviet heroic names like Petr and Aniuta verge on parody. The scene is never specifically identified as the Soviet Union, but details confirm the locale. *Das Kapital* stands on Novodvortsev's shelf, and an active party member lives next door. The suggestion of the Red Star as a Christmas decoration confirms the Soviet setting.

The language of "Rozhdestvenskii rasskaz" is direct and neutral, save for one typically Nabokovian passage describing a view from the hero's window:

Luny ne bylo vidno . . . net, vprochem, von tam, siianie iz za temnoi truby. Vo dvore byli slozheny drova, pokrytye svetiashchimsia kovrom snega. V odnom okne gorel zelenyi kolpak lampy, kto-to rabotal u stola; kak biser, blesteli shchety. S kraiu kryshi vdrug upali, sovershenno bezzvuchno, neskol'ko snezhnykh kom'ev. I opiat',—otsepenenie. (p. 3)

The moon was not visible . . . no, on second thought, there was a radiance from behind the dark smokestack. In the yard logs were stacked which were covered with a luminescent carpet of snow. In one window a green lampshade was glowing, someone was working at a table; the abacus glistened like beads. Suddenly several snowy clumps fell absolutely sound-lessly from the edge of the roof. And once again all was frozen to the spot.

Despite the stark Soviet backdrop, Slavonicisms color this story. Perhaps reflecting his ties with the pre-Revolutionary world, Novodvortsev thinks and speaks in archaic and obsolete terms: *pestun* (mentor), *istovyi* (proper, devout), *ibo* (for). The critic's comment to Novodvortsev emphasizes this point and even indicates a certain contempt for the older man's heritage:

Vo vremia ono, v sei den', vasha bratiia strochila rozh dest venskie fel'etonchiki. (p. 2)

In days of yore, on this day you people dashed off short Christmas feuilletons.

Once more the artist and his creations form Nabokov's basic theme. In "Rozhdestvenskii rasskaz," as in "Putevoditel' po Berlinu," "Passazhir," and "Uzhas," the hero is a writer. Although the problem of creativity is considered in this story, it is impotent. This is reflected in the fact that there is only one lyrical passage in the story. It is of stillness, moonlight, and snow-covered logs, which curiously recalls the snow-covered pipes in "Putevoditel' po Berlinu." Novodvortsev's sense of inspiration is described:

On pochuvstvoval tu shchekochushchuiu pustotu, kotoraia vsegda u nego soprovozhdala zhelan'e pisat. (p. 3)

He sensed that tickling emptiness, which always accompanied his desire to write.

It is interesting that the urge of the hero to sculpt in "Blagost' " is a strikingly similar tickling sensation.

The dearth here of the lyricism and artistic devices that are the hallmark of Nabokov's work may be due to the theme: the "creative spirit" underlying Soviet literature. As such "Rozhdestvenskii rasskaz" could be said to represent Nabokov's reaction to the sterility of the Soviet arts. The subtle details that evoke the Soviet world enhance this story. These elements are strengthened by Nabokov's use of Soviet literary jargon and by Novodvortsev's Dostoevskian version of Christmas. These disparate devices all lend symbolic dimension to the story. The reader has to probe below the surface of Novodvortsev's experience to understand fully Nabokov's "Rozhdestvenskii rasskaz." Even so, this is one of Nabokov's least satisfying stories.

6. "Skazka"

Nabokov's "Skazka" ("A Nursery Tale") is no more appropriate to a nursery than "Rozhdestvenskii rasskaz" is to Christmas. Once again Nabokov's simple story has a hidden meaning. In "Skazka" he played with the short-story form. His English translation of the title emphasizes precisely this point. Rather than choosing the traditional translation for "Skazka," "A Fairy Tale," Nabokov picked the unusual and limiting title "A Nursery Tale." [23] As the hero's amorous exploits unfold, the story takes on a tone that is clearly not intended for a nursery audience. It is primarily this parody of genres that gives "Skazka" its second, more symbolic dimension.

The word *skazka* implies a specific short-story category. A *skazka* is a verbal work of a narrative character that is almost exclusively prosaic. Sometimes it is a form of entertainment; sometimes it has a didactic purpose. Often it has a whimsical character and contains "supernatural or obviously improbable events, scenes, and personages." [24] Nabokov's "Skazka" adheres to all of these accepted tenets, and it is these generic qualities that set it apart from his other stories. Tsetlin, in reviewing the *Vozvrashchenie Chorba* collection in 1930, felt that this story could have been omitted. Evidently, he considered that "Skazka" did not deal with the deeply human experiences of life that all the other Nabokov stories handle so well.

It is true that life is not earnest in "Skazka." There is no serious ambivalence between reality and fantasy, as in many of Nabokov's more symbolic pieces. The prevailing mood is one of entertainment and humor, and therefore all magical elements and mysterious "missing links" are implicitly justified. Fantasy pervades the story. The opening, incomplete sentence apostrophizes "Fantaziia, trepet, vostorg fantazii ..." (p. 49) ("Fantasy, the flutter, the rapture of fantasy!" [p. 41]). This line is repeated twice, once on the second page, and then on the penultimate page, thus acting as a shorthand reminder that "Skazka" is pure fantasy. The hero's conscious awareness of this fantasy and his own imaginative powers ("Ervin khorosho eto znal" ["Erwin knew these things well"]) are complemented by the purely fantastic figure of the sorceress Frau Ott. The story takes place in an appropriate locale, primarily at night, the time of witches, devils, and fairies. Not unexpectedly, it is set in Berlin, where all of the action leads up to a villa beyond the Kaiserdamm at No. 13 Hoffmannstrasse. This location is a clear literary allusion to E. T. A. Hoffmann and his fantastic tales. The numeral also has a superstitious connotation. For all of these apparent marks of unreality, the theme is remarkably real: man's lust after woman. This is Nabokov's first effort at the theme that culminated in *Lolita* with man's lust after a nymphet.

"Skazka" is a clever and imaginative story. The short-story pattern is standard, and the *fabula* and *siuzhet* coalesce. "Skazka" is of medium length, seventeen pages, and a six-page exposition sets the scene. Erwin, a young German, is too shy to approach any young woman. Having once been rebuffed, he passes his time mentally collecting a harem behind the safety of a tram window. One evening, while enjoying watching the girls go by his café table, he is joined by a matron, Frau Ott. She proceeds to read his mind and proposes that she will give him all the girls for his delectation that he can mentally round up from midday to midnight. She matter-of-factly explains that she is the devil, and her one condition is that the number of girls must be uneven. The stage has been set for action.

The rising action, Erwin's accumulation of desirable women, is the predominating section of this story. The following day he does not quite believe what has transpired, but he finds himself consciously and accidentally acquiring the women. Each of them acknowledges his secret desire, and in a different manner. By the time that he has five, he decides to stop. At this point the action halts. The ubiquitous Frau Ott reappears and arranges the final details concerning the midnight rendezvous at No. 13 Hoffmannstrasse, when the women will become Erwin's.[25] Frau Ott reminds him that the number must be odd and urges him to stop with the five he already has.

Erwin returns home for a satisfying nap, reminiscent of Nikitin's in "Port." This break in the momentum marks a structural division in the unusually long rising action of "Skazka." Both halves are evenly balanced, or at least complement one another. Before his rest Erwin clearheadedly considers his harem choices. After his nap he concludes that five are not enough and proceeds to rush about indiscriminately gathering six more. By eleven in the evening he has acquired the needed odd number. But unexpectedly he spots a fourteen-year-old lass, and, without consciously willing it, he has her. Now with twelve, Erwin needs an additional girl.

Throughout this portion of the rising action Erwin's values deteriorate, and now they are at their lowest point. When he finds a thirteenth woman, the magic number, Erwin runs after her. He judges her by her back alone, a criterion that he himself has earlier dismissed as inadequate. This proves to be Erwin's undoing. The physical chase after Number Thirteen and his rising emotions as time runs out push the action to the climax. Under the lamplight—Nabokov's signal of a revealing moment—the mysterious woman turns around and Erwin sees her face: she is Number One and all is lost. He has gathered an even, not an odd, number of women. The suspense of the scene is increased by the fact that all of the action takes place at a villa gate. Erwin has unwittingly been led to the villa at midnight. The gate acts like a barrier to Erwin's harem of twelve lovely women.

The falling action requires less than a page.[26] As Erwin realizes that he is indeed at Hoffmannstrasse, he is greeted by Frau Ott, who is waiting in a car. She agrees with Erwin that it is a pity that he missed his chance. He bids her good-bye and heads homeward. The irony of the falling action lies in the fact that his harem is all gathered for him but is not for his having. He has been unable to honor the one condition. The ending is a single sentence:

On shagal tiazhelo, nyli ustavshie nogi, ugnetala mysl', chto zavtra ponedel'nik, i chto vstavat' budet trudno. (p. 66)

He walked with a heavy step, his legs ached, he was oppressed by the thought that tomorrow was Monday and it would be hard to get up. (p. 58)

There are many characters in "Skazka." The primary ones are Erwin and Frau Ott. Erwin, the hero, is not fully described physically. His pale nose with an indented tip is his only distinctive facial feature. He wears bright yellow, almost orange, shoes. He prides himself that when he sets forth on the second half of his quest, he is in clean clothes, implying that this is not always the case. He is shy, and with reason, for the one time that he had approached a woman he had been rebuffed with: "Kak vam ne stydno . . . Podite proch' " (p. 49) ("You ought to be ashamed of yourself. Leave me alone" [p. 41]). Ever since then, he has contented himself with gathering an imaginary harem. His characteristic mannerism is his repeated lip-biting, which signals another captive. When Erwin meets Frau Ott, he is understandably incredulous but accepts her offer. Now he can still collect his ladies, but the outcome will be real, not imagined. It is precisely his temperament, his timidity and imagination, that have attracted the devil to him.

In the rising action there is a certain element of character development, which is unusual for a short story. In this instance it is successful, because there is motion and movement in time and space. Erwin's rising emotions carry the tempo of the story. At the thought of a harem, his fertile imagination evokes joy, lightness, satisfaction, and desire. Throughout the rising action, these emotions accelerate, and they climax with his final chase. He feels a sweet sensation under his ribs:

> ... on ne mog by ob"iasnit', chto imenno tak vzvolnovalo ego, otchego s takoi muchitel'noi zhadnost'iu emu zakhotelos' ee obognat', zaglianut' ei v litso. (p. 63)

> He ... could not have explained why he yearned so poignantly to overtake precisely *her* and have a look at her face. (p. 55)

Erwin knows that he must look at her face, yet he is too timid. Unlike the men in "Port" and "Pis'mo v Rossiiu," he dares not look the woman in the eyes. Everything, including the trees, seems to join in his pursuit. The chase makes him drunk. Erwin's escalating emotions set the pace:

> Ne pokhodka, ne oblik ee ... Chto to drugoe, ocharovatel'noe i vlastnoe, kakoe-to napriazhennoe mertsanie vozdukha vokrug nee,—byt' mozhet, tol'ko fantaziia, trepet, vostorg fantazii,—a, byt' mozhet, to, chto meniaet odnim bozhestvennym vzmakhom vsiu zhizn' cheloveka,—Ervin nichego ne znal,—tol'ko shel po trotuaru. (p. 64)

> Not her gait, not her shape, but something else, bewitching and overwhelming, as if a tense shimmer surrounded her: mere fantasy, maybe, the flutter, the rapture of fantasy, or

maybe it was that which changes a man's entire life with one divine stroke—Erwin knew nothing, he just sped after her over asphalt and stone. (p. 56)

Suddenly the woman stops and faces him. He smiles painfully when he recognizes her. Ironically, she is the first to respond to him directly. The ensuing deflating moment is made painful by her remark, which exactly echoes the rebuff uttered by the woman in the exposition: "You ought to be ashamed of yourself." This is followed by the realization that he has reached his rendezvous. Frau Ott's matter-of-fact remarks and Erwin's equally casual replies are accentuated by his nervous fidgeting. The pace of the story has been broken. Erwin has missed his chance. In contrast to his lightfooted arrival, his departure is heavy and deliberate. Although Erwin's portrait is not intended to be a deep one, in comparison with that of Frau Ott his has dimension.

There is no development in Frau Ott's personality following her revelation that she is the devil. Her name, Ott, is as strange as her background.[27] She appears three times; in the exposition, midway through the rising action, and in the conclusion. She is a fantastic figure, and structurally considered, she is the sole bearer of the fantasy theme. Everything else is relatively normal.

To all appearances Frau Ott, who is fully described, is a stately matron who moves with the authority of her age. She sits down at Erwin's café table for lack of a seat elsewhere. She is conservatively dressed in a dark gray suit and has a large suitcaselike handbag, which she places on the table with great aplomb. Her large hand in a shining black glove is noted first when she grasps the chair at the café and later when Erwin kisses it in farewell. Her fingernails are long, convex, and beautiful. Her flickering eyes are variously described. In the exposition they are likened to showy false jewels (*iarkie poddel'nye kamni*), an image that recalls the eyes of Chorb's wife, which resembled beach pebbles. Her eyes are also reflecting in the Flaubertian manner:

Gospozha Ott sidela ochen' priamo ... i v ee tverdykh blestiashchikh glazakh mel'kali nochnye ogni goroda. (p. 54)

Frau Monde sat erect . . . and the city lights flashed in her
gemlike eyes. (p. 47)

Frau Ott appears completely nonchalant about her supernatural
powers. She acknowledges them with a blasé yawn and observes
that she is usually imagined as a man with horns and a tail. She
has taken that form only once and cannot comprehend how this
image persists. She explains that she is born three times every two
hundred years. Last time she was a kinglet in the African
hinterland. (This is the first appearance of a Nabokov rex.) She
notes that this regal incarnation was a respite from more responsible ones. Now she reflects that she has done a fair share of mischief
as Frau Ott and is getting bored. In fact, she has done so much
mischief of late that she has to get out of life quickly. Monday at
dawn she plans to be born elsewhere. Her last bit of magic in her
present guise will be performed as an innocent amusement. She
thereupon proves her diabolic powers to Erwin by correctly
predicting that a man across the street will be hit by a tram. She
sardonically adds that she could have forecast his death, thus
intimating that she not only predicts, but controls, events. In her
proposal to Erwin she does not require his soul as payment, but
instead kindly drives Erwin home for a good night's sleep.

Frau Ott reappears midway through Erwin's search, when he is
mistakenly attracted to her. This amuses her no end. However, her
appearance is, indeed, surprisingly provocative:

... sleva ot prokhoda sidit, obernuvshis' k nemu chernoi
barkhatnoi shliapoi, dama v legkom plat'e, razrisovannom
zheltymi tsvetami, perepletaiushchimisia po lilovatomu polu-
prozrachnomu fonu, skvoz' kotoryi prostupali svetlye pere-
khvaty lifa. (p. 58)

She wore a black velvet hat, and a light frock patterned with
intertwined chrysanthemums against a semitransparent
mauve background through which showed the shoulder straps
of her slip. (p. 50)

In the final passage of the story, in her chauffeur-driven car, her soft, hoarse voice resounds as she greets Erwin. She placidly adds that she is lonely because she is waiting for a friend. They intend to poison themselves at dawn, as planned. She remarks indifferently to Erwin, "Pity."

The secondary characters are the ladies of Erwin's harem, each portrayed differently. Each woman is a distinct feminine type, by age and in moral fiber. The harem thus represents the complete gamut of womanhood. Most of them are accompanied by at least one man. These portrayals are enhanced by the ingenious ways that Erwin learns that they are his. All are nameless and are described from Erwin's lustful viewpoint. This is effected by an emphasis on the naked parts of these women; their legs, arms, chests, necks, shoulders, bent backs, and lips.

Excluding the first girl who had rebuffed Erwin in the introductory section, there are twelve women who attract him. The first and last is a girl in a white dress playing with her dog. She answers Erwin's desire originally by turning around on the run and flashing a smile to her dog, who follows. Numbers Two and Three are two thin sisters who are slightly painted, with lively eyes. Like the unseen beloved in "Blagost'," they are in black silk, waiting at the glass trampost where the schedule is posted. Erwin quickly asks for both sisters, and one answers, in response to her sister: "Yes, of course." Thus she also acknowledges Erwin's thoughts. The fourth woman is coming down the steps of one of the best hotels. Her dark hair is boyishly bobbed. The bright red rose on her lapel is reflected in an affirming cigarette advertisement:

Ervin zametil ... papirosnuiu reklamu—svetlousyi turok v feske i krupnoe slovo: Da!—a pod nim pomel'che: "ia kuriu tol'ko Rozu Vostoka." (p. 57)

Erwin remarked ... the advertisement on a billboard: a blond-mustached Turk and, in large letters, the word "Yes!" under which it said in smaller characters: "I smoke only the Rose of the Orient." (p. 49)

Here Nabokov's recurrent use of signs and lettering has a functional purpose in the plot. Next, in a restaurant Erwin spots a woman, but she is too old. A pretty waitress is more to his liking. A man at a nearby phone agitatedly answers: "Yes! Yes! Yes!" The sixth is cleverly presented by Nabokov. Erwin notes that a lady is speaking to her companion in an unfamiliar tongue, Polish or Russian. (This detail recalls the linguistic play with languages in "Port.") In this manner Nabokov imaginatively reminds the Russian reader that Erwin is German. This girl with gray slanting eyes confirms Erwin's desire when she accidentally interjects a German phrase in her Slavic conversation. The next woman, Number Seven, is spotted at the gates of the amusement park. She is a voluptuous creature, and her answer to her boyfriends is for Erwin's benefit as well: "All right,—I'm willing!" In this amusement park Erwin picks up four other women at once. They are performing cyclists in red, blue, green, and yellow pants and are brightly made up. The twelfth girl is a fourteen-year-old accompanied by a frail old man, "a famous poet, a senile swan." This child is alluring in a festive dark dress that is very décolleté:

—chto-to bylo v etom litse strannoe, stranno skol'znuli ee slishkom blestiashchie glaza—i esli b eto byla ne devochka . . . mozhno bylo podumat', chto ee guby tronuty karminom. (p. 62)

. . . there was something odd about that face, odd was the flitting glance of her much too shiny eyes, and if she were not just a little girl . . . one might suspect that her lips were touched up with rouge. (p. 55)

Nabokov observed that while translating "Skazka" into English he "was eerily startled to meet a somewhat decrepit but unmistakable Humbert escorting his nymphet in the story" (p. 40). Here is the earliest sketch of Lolita.

The time element is very distinctly conveyed in "Skazka." The exposition opens on a Saturday evening in May. Erwin's search is limited by Frau Ott to the period between midday Sunday and midnight Sunday. Time passes unobtrusively at first as Erwin collects his harem. It is pinpointed only during the last three hours, at nine, and at eleven in the evening, thus pushing the story to its midnight climax. Frau Ott's remark that, just as planned, she is going to poison herself at daybreak brings the action to a fitting conclusion. This fantastic character will disappear at her Monday-morning deadline.

There is no symbolic imagery in this story. The imaginary harem is the only metaphor of any breadth, and that is all Erwin's *fantaziia*. Lesser motifs recur within the story and extend to motifs in Nabokov's other stories: the nymphet, the kinglet, and the lettering. His familiar tram also moves in and out of the tale. The story's action begins on a tram. At the café Frau Ott predicts a tram calamity. Later she completes the arrangements on a tram. Her taxi whisks around the city like many of Nabokov's taxis. Berlin, so often the background of his stories, is obliquely identified by the tram system and by the references to the Kaiserdamm and Hoffmannstrasse.

The language in this story is particularly poetic and lyrical, especially in the many brief but evocative descriptions of the metropolis. They serve no structural or characterizing purpose. Lyrical asides can be seen in the following fragment:

Nebo bylo splosh' rozovatoe, i v sumerkakh kakim to nezem-nym ognem goreli fonari, lampochki vyvesok. (p. 50)

The entire sky was tinged with pink and the street-lamps and shop-sign bulbs glowed with a kind of unearthly light in the gathering dusk. (p. 43)

Here Andreev's comments about Nabokov's style are appropriate: "At times we hear Gogol: his running start into lyrical digressions about Berlin at eventide" (II).

In "Skazka" Nabokov's prose has poetic elements. Many "made-strange" adjectives are found, generally in the context of longer unusual images. Often these metaphors and personifications describe in lifelike detail Nabokov's favorite urban features: shadows of leaves and trees (one of which bends on the wall as in "Port"); signs and lampposts; shiny, reflecting asphalt streets and sidewalks.

Moving trams and cars all shade the urban scene in unusual poetic combinations. Similes are numerous and in general refer only to characters in the story. They describe the tertiary characters succinctly. The features and feelings of Erwin and the traits of Frau Ott are often depicted with similes as well.

"Skazka" is true to its genre. It is humorous, frothy, and a fantastic tale related in realistic terms. Although it is highly doubtful that Nabokov intended any moral message in his "Skazka," it is curious that its frivolous mood is balanced by an underlying lesson, foreshadowing perhaps Humbert's drama in *Lolita*. Here, man, even in the fantastic world, must not be avaricious. Erwin's character, experience, and failure are the outcome of greed and lust, two ancient vices. They are universal qualities and cannot be forgotten even in the supernatural world of Frau Ott. The presence of this secondary, but universal, theme in "Skazka" places the story in the realistic-symbolic category.

7. "Podlets"

Nabokov again focused on literature per se in "Podlets" ("The Scoundrel" or "The Cur," but entitled by Nabokov "An Affair of Honor"). However, this short story is not a commentary on Soviet or émigré literary practices, nor a subtle parody of literary styles. In a rare instance of direct authorial intrusion, Nabokov explicitly defined his artistic approach in "Podlets." In the foreword to the English translation, he wrote that "Podlets" "renders ... the degradation of a romantic theme whose decline had started with Chehov's [sic] magnificent story THE DUEL (1891." [28] Here Nabokov indicated that he was parodying the romantic literary theme of the duel, and he pointed specifically to Chekhov, "one of the few Russian prose writers whom [he] unconditionally admired." [29] Thus Nabokov clarified the imitative aspect of "Podlets" for his English readers who might not catch his literary innuendos.

Nabokov centered the duel theme in a traditional manner, within a love triangle. Themes with this configuration are the crux of Nabokov's earliest novels: *Mashen'ka, Korol' dama valet,* and *Kamera obskura.* In "Podlets" the duel theme is denigrated, first by the cowardice of the dishonored husband, and second, as in Chekhov's story, by the nature of the challenge. At this point the similarity with Chekhov's long story ends.

As opposed to the reflective stories that have been considered to this point, "Podlets" has a strong external *fabula.* Tsetlin noted this very aspect in his review (p. 531). All the elements of a classic short story are developed in "Podlets." Because of its length—thirty-five pages—reality prevails over metaphor. The language is not compressed or poetic. It is straightforward. The action is clear. There are no substantial flashbacks, withheld bits of information, or reversals in time sequences. There is nothing elliptical. If anything, there is some literary padding.

Nabokov divided "Podlets" into two parts. Part I consists of the eleven-page exposition. It depicts the three central figures of the love triangle and shows how and when they come into conflict. Anton Petrovich, the husband, returns early from a business trip and finds his friend Berg in his bedroom and his wife in a nearby bathtub. For the sake of his honor and for the love of his wife, Anton Petrovich challenges Berg to a duel and orders the lovers out. In the heat of the moment, Anton Petrovich asks two drunken Russians to be his seconds.

Part II contains the rising action, the climax, the falling action, and the conclusion. The rising action is the moment when Anton Petrovich awakens to a new day. He then realizes that he has thrown down the gauntlet and must see his predicament through to its conclusion. Berg is a marksman, whereas Anton Petrovich does not even know how to shoot. In this second part Anton Petrovich feels so doomed that he progressively becomes more cowardly. En route to duel he is overcome with fear, and at the climax he turns and flees this affair of honor.

His return to Berlin is the conclusion. Technically this is the strongest section of "Podlets." It has minor elements of surprise, summing up, and reversal. As Anton Petrovich tries to hide, he hears "Good day" in his ear. This surprise proves to be, as the hero notes, a false alarm. It is only an acquaintance, Leont'ev. Having shaken him off, Anton Petrovich retreats into the solitude of a hotel and considers the implications of what he has done.

Unobtrusively, a sudden reversal in his fortunes occurs. Anton Petrovich's stream of consciousness slips into reverie with the pivotal sentence:

Mozhet byt, est' kakoi-nibud' vykhod? (p. 137)

Perhaps there was a way out? (p. 114)

He imagines that he leaves the hotel and returns home to collect his belongings. He finds Tania and his seconds waiting with the happy news that Berg has proved to be a greater coward. They add:

I ty vyshel s chest'iu, a on opozoren navsegda. (p. 138)

And you came out honorably, while he is disgraced forever. (p. 115)

The conflict appears resolved until the penultimate paragraph, when the reversal is in turn reversed. Fantasy shifts back to reality:

Anton Petrovich, shiroko ulybnuvshis', vstal, zaigral lentochkoi monoklia. I medlenno ischezla ulybka. Takikh veshchei v zhizni ne byvaet. (p. 138)

Anton Petrovich smiled broadly, got up and started fiddling with the ribbon of his monocle. His smile slowly faded away. Such things don't happen in real life. (p. 115)

Only now does the reader fully understand Nabokov's stylistic tour de force. Such conclusions do not occur in real life, and Anton Petrovich knows this. He has lost everyone's respect, including his own. He is no longer an honorable man. This return to reality is underlined by his wolfish devouring of a sandwich—the final view we have of him.

The characters in "Podlets" are nearly all Russian expatriates living in Berlin in the 1920s. The Russian title points to the importance of characterization in this story. The scoundrel (*podlets*) at first is clearly Berg. The word is used twice to refer to him. The lover is fully described: he is broad-shouldered, well built, and clean-shaven; and he compares himself to an athletic angel. He likes to crack jokes and is gregarious. He brags of his heroic exploits; and his little black book, listing the men he has killed, epitomizes his bravery and daring. At Luna Park, Berg's crack shots evoke Tania's premonitory comment that Anton Petrovich later recalls:

A s vami nepriiatno bylo by drat'sia na dueli. (p. 120)

It wouldn't be pleasant to duel with you. (p. 99)

Anton Petrovich, as the cuckolded husband, is the central figure of "Podlets." The entire story is related from his point of view, either by the stream-of-experience or the stream-of-consciousness method. Like Berg, he has been successful as an émigré. He is a banker and buys everything that is in fashion; for instance, the latest rainbow-colored tie and handkerchief. Throughout the story his accouterments give evidence, not only of his propriety, but of his *poshlost'*. His shiny fountain pen, his monocle, his shoes and socks, [30] and his gloves are such images. Anton Petrovich's physique is hardly heroic, and after he learns of his wife's infidelity he becomes progressively more absurd-looking. His second, Mitiushin, observes that "his mug is as white as chalk." The mirror in his apartment reflects him on three occasions and shows his deterioration. On the train en route to the duel, his appearance is so strange that it evokes the surprise of the passengers.

Anton Petrovich's distinctive virtues have been his honor and his love for Tania, both of which he has lost at the conclusion of the story. His jealousy has been understandably roused during Berg's visits by his boasting. On the fateful night he approaches his illuminated apartment with warm anticipation. He hears "noisy water" and lovingly thinks that his "Tan'ka" is bathing. Nabokov's use of an affectionate, even emotional diminutive hints that the hero is aroused as he hears his wife. Thus he is nonplussed when he finds Berg in his bedroom. The water image is critical here. In "Podlets" Nabokov's motif of running water for the first time acquires a secondary and veiled meaning, not only of love-making, but of illicit love-making.[31] In *Kamera obskura* (pp. 204-5) and *Ada* (pp. 13, 22) the running tub water again masks unlawful love. On the other hand, in the realistic story "Pis'mo v Rossiiu" the image of water has no symbolic meaning:

> Izredka za stenoi v vodoprovode vskhlipyvaet, perelivaetsia voda, podstupaia kak by k gorlu doma. (p. 44)

> Occasionally, behind the wall the water slurps and overflows in the pipe, rising as if to the throat of the house.

Also in *Pnin* (p. 63) and *Lolita* (pp. 134, 296) the crashing bathroom waterfalls and toilet cascades have no secondary meaning. Nabokov was content to use this theme at both the realistic and the symbolic levels throughout his work.

Anton Petrovich's love comes to the fore after he chases the guilty pair out of the apartment, and he tries to write a note to Tania. At Mitiushin's he breaks down, saying, "I so loved her." He tries to forget her, but with little success. Although she precipitates the conflict, Tania does not act directly in it. She figures primarily in the memories that she evokes in Anton Petrovich. Thus she is impressionistically drawn. The following excerpt of Anton Petrovich's memory of her is critical in both content and form. It exemplifies Nabokov's symbolic method; note particularly the shifting narrator that foreshadows "Sogliadatai":

> —golos u nee byl tsyganskogo poshiba, milyi golos, schast'e, letnii vecher, gitara . . . ona poet, shchurias', na podushke posredi komnaty . . . i Anton Petrovich so vcherashnego dnia zhenikh, schast'e, letnii vecher, nochnaia babochka na potolke, ia tebia bezkonechno liubliu, dlia tebia ia otdam svoiu dushu. . . . (p. 108)

> She had a gypsy kind of voice, a bewitching voice . . . happiness, a summer night, a guitar . . . she sang that night seated on a cushion in the middle of the floor, and slitted her smiling eyes as she sang. . . . He had just proposed to her . . .

yes, happiness, a summer night, a moth bumping against the ceiling, "my soul I surrender to you, I love you with infinite passion. . . ." (p. 87)

Like Mashen'ka and Chorb's wife, Tania is portrayed as the embodiment of love; hence Anton Petrovich's predicament is made poignant.

The characterization of Anton Petrovich shows the beginning of the double theme that Nabokov employed extensively in nearly all of his later work. The split between Anton Petrovich's honor and cowardice is noted:

"Pustiaki!" slabo pisknula kakaia to malen'kaia chast' dushi Antona Petrovicha, ta chast' ego dushi, kotoraia zastavila ego brosit' perchatku, khlopnut' dver'iu, nazvat' Berga podletsom. (p. 121)

"Nonsense," faintly sqeaked some little particle of Anton Petrovich's soul, the same particle that had made him throw the glove, slam the door, and call Berg a scoundrel. (p. 100)

The three mirror images that catch Anton Petrovich's eye emphasize a certain bifurcation of his personality. They are not exclusively photographic descriptions. Furthermore, Berg is pointedly described as everything that Anton Petrovich is not. Thus Anton Petrovich has no surname and Berg has no Christian name or patronymic: the two figures are complementary.

The central event of "Podlets," the duel, never occurs. The circumstances leading up to it and its nonoccurrence are best seen against the deterioration of Anton Petrovich's personality. The basic conflict of the story is not so much between the central figures as between Anton Petrovich's sense of honor and his cowardice. Although the story is told from his point of view, it is not a psychological or introspective portrait. The element of absurdity has too great a role in "Podlets" for Anton Petrovich to be seen as a tragic figure.

The overtone of ridiculousness degrades the romantic theme, as is noted eight times by Anton Petrovich himself. His sister-in-law says that the situation is a terrible mess. The basic absurdity of this affair of honor is that Anton Petrovich has challenged his rival in the 1920s. As he observes: "In our time nobody fights duels." Moreover, the confrontation is ridiculous: a weak-kneed coward has challenged the blasé personification of bravery. Consequently, in attempting to defend his honor as a husband, Anton Petrovich is unwittingly drawn into a series of ever more absurd and irrevocable situations. The new glove that he casts down will at first not slip off his hand. When it finally does, it flips against the wall and drops into a water pitcher. At this point the lover emits a hearty laugh. The seconds are ridiculous drunkards. The culminating absurdity is Anton Petrovich's flight from the duel itself. His pretext is that he must go to the men's room in a tavern. From there he makes a mad and unromantic dash, slipping and sliding, his legs outspread. His concluding grunting, greedy munching on a sandwich is the final touch of absurdity in the tale.

The secondary figures are sketched portraits with no clear character development. Leont'ev has an ill-shaven, yellowish long face. Nabokov noted that all of him looks clumsily emaciated and lugubrious, as if nature had suffered from a toothache when creating him. He is a pessimist and a ridiculously unobservant man. Gnushke, one of the seconds, is a very long-faced man in a tall collar who resembles a dachshund. Although his name implies that he too is a scoundrel, in the end he is far less of one than Anton Petrovich. He performs his duty as a second honorably. The other second, Mitiushin, is identified only by his drunken, rosy face. The Berliners who surround Anton Petrovich at the conclusion of the story are vividly portrayed in colorful epithets.

The setting for "Podlets" is presented with exactitude in the opening paragraphs—the Russian émigré circle in Berlin during the 1920s. The Kurdiumov's home on St. Mark Strasse in the Moabit district, the fifth-floor apartment of Anton Petrovich, and Mitiushin's dim-lit room serve as the background for the story, particularly for the exposition. Even though Nabokov described this locale as a "drab expatriate setting,"[32] it has definite color, especially in relation to the central figure. The milieu often reflects Anton Petrovich's mood. The furniture becomes animate and is often metaphorically presented. Berg is introduced into Anton

Petrovich's purview as emerging out of nonbeing and lowering back down into a chair. The furnishings and chessboard in Mitiushin's home move, glide, and collide before Anton Petrovich's eyes after he has had too much vodka. Whenever Anton Petrovich loses his sense of balance, this optical illusion recurs. The furniture seems to die when he is told that the duel has been set. It reflects and metaphorically conveys his thoughts of doom. In the concluding hotel scene it is the furniture that metaphorically observes his solitude:

> Mebel', postel', umyval'nik prosnulis', posmotreli na nego ispodlob'ia i zadremali opiat'. V etom sonnom, nichem neprimetnom nomere Anton Petrovich byl, nakonets, odin. (pp. 135-36)

> The furniture, the bed, the washstand seemed to awake, to give him a frowning look, and go back to sleep. In this drowsy, totally unremarkable hotel room, Anton Petrovich was at last alone. (p. 113)

Andreev accurately assessed Nabokov's descriptions of material objects: "The world of things is animated and breathes (the description of rooms and furniture is an entire poem) and in connection with this a particularly saturated and speeding dynamism is reached, giving once again a newness and unexpectedness" (II).[33]

The external Berlin setting with its Nabokovian street repairs also has a life of its own and is in step with Anton Petrovich's trauma. The urban backdrop reflects his exhaustion and mental disorientation after he learns that Tania has been unfaithful. The poplars are shadows. The bar from which he telephones Mitiushin arises before him as in a dream and then recedes into the distance like the taillight of one of Nabokov's favorite trains. Even the taxi that drives him is drowsy and falls asleep at Anton Petrovich's. (This sleeping taxi is a variation of the sleepy tram in "Groza.") Not surprisingly, on the morning of his duel, when life is running short, he is struck by its natural beauty. In Nabokovian fashion, he implicitly views it from his window. This beautiful morning becomes progressively marvelous as Anton Petrovich rides out to the duel. The woods, the pines, and the gleam of the lakes all appear touching and poetically fragile to him. The sun is warm and welcoming as he steps off the ubiquitous train. A Nabokovian splash of sunlight pinpoints the moment when Anton Petrovich takes flight to save his life. Berlin suburbia hides Anton Petrovich as he slips through the thickets and elder bushes to the Wannsee. Once again, the conclusion is reached in Berlin proper, with the familiar square, the newspaperman, the flower vendor, the shoeshine man, the little old lady, and even the ever-present Russian émigré. A wretched little hotel—Nabokov's recurrent edifice—is where he finally finds refuge.

"Podlets" is Nabokov's longest early story. However, its momentum is maintained by an unobtrusive use of motion in space and time. In Part I the action is dynamic. Characters leave, return, come, go. They move up and down stairs, whisk across Berlin, and revolve in drunken vertigo. Doors slam. Furniture shifts and even chess figures move and checkmate. In Part II Elspeth, the maid; Natasha, the sister-in-law; Gnushke and Mitiushin come to and go from Anton Petrovich's home. This perpetual motion pushes the action to the point where Anton Petrovich is left alone to ponder his problem. For five pages there is limited action, as he paces back and forth, gazes at himself in the mirror, or merely reflects on duels—particularly that of Eugene Onegin. The motion in this interval is primarily emotional. The action resumes when the seconds appear the next morning. The speeding taxi, the jerk and subsequent "u-boi, u-boi, u-boi" [34] of the train, and the passing firs push Anton Petrovich closer to the duel. At the rear door of the tavern his motion is unexpectedly reversed. Anton Petrovich then descends, slipping and sliding toward the Wannsee. This flight is linguistically accentuated by the repetition of *mimo* (past) and the verbs *proiti* (to pass by) and *doiti* (to come to, to reach). These are complemented by a compressed use of verbs of motion with the alliterative prefix *s* that alludes to the slipping and sliding action. I note these sounds in the following verbs: *sbezhat'*, *skol'zit'*, *spuskat'sia*, *s"ezzhat'*. Later he himself admits that this physical descent was a moral descent as well.

Motion in space is underscored and complemented by a subtle

but definite motion in time. Throughout "Podlets" the passage of time is closely indicated. As in "Zvonok," it appears in the first sentence:

Prokliatyi den', v kotoryi Anton Petrovich poznakomilsia s Bergom, sushchestvoval tol'ko teoreticheski: pamiat' ne prilepila k nemu vo vremia kalendarnoi nakleiki, i teper' naiti etot den' bylo nevozmozhno. (p. 103)

The accursed day when Anton Petrovich made the acquaintance of Berg existed only in theory, for his memory had not affixed to it a date label at that time, and now it was impossible to identify that day. (p. 83)

Although the date is pointedly vague in this opening passage, it becomes progressively more exact. On Saturday evening at ten, in late July, Anton Petrovich returns from Kassel to find his wife with Berg. Time is repeatedly mentioned during the following thirty-six hours as the action proceeds. In Part II, when Anton Petrovich is at home and the action is relatively static, the element of time acquires importance. As the hours pass before his duel, Anton Petrovich becomes highly aware of them. He notes that it is eleven o'clock when he awakens in the morning. Natasha comes at around four; Gnushke and Mitiushin, at around seven. They leave when it is already growing dark. Inconspicuously, time maintains the tempo: ten, midnight, four, five, and at six-thirty the doorbell. Thus motion in time and in space combine to retain the story's intensity, to grip the reader's interest, to push "Podlets" to an effective conclusion.

Poetic prose, particularly in the noun-verb configuration, occurs in long sections of "Podlets." Primarily it is related to Anton Petrovich. His monocle, which is like a glistening eye on his chest; his tie, colored like a setting sun; his gentle fountain pen; the enlivened shoes; and his widowed glove—all are metaphorically (in the broad sense) depicted. As I noted above, furniture is personified in numerous images, mirroring Anton Petrovich's physical and mental state. Nature is lyrically described and reflects his mood on the morning of his duel:

V vysokoi lipe, pod oknom, besnovalis' vorob'i. Golubaia barkhatnaia ten' splosh' pokryvala ulitsu, a kryshi tam i siam zagoralis' serebrom. (p. 126)

The sparrows twittered like mad in the tall linden tree under the window. A pale-blue, velvet shadow covered the street, and here and there a roof would flash silver. (p. 104)

Colors have essentially no part in "Podlets." There are many colloquialisms, as Anton Petrovich's dialogues form a significant portion of the story. Curiously, some of them are also tropes—clichéd hyperboles: "Chut' ne zaekhal v zuby" (p. 117) ("I nearly punched him in the teeth" [p. 96]); "Vse ravno tam ni psa net" (p. 119) ("There isn't a damn soul [dog] to be seen out there anyway" [p. 98]); "Polozhis' na Gospoda Boga i akhni" (p. 120) ("Put your trust in God" [p. 99]). Others are metaphorical clichés: "On uronil . . . : 'U menia s nim duel' ' " (p. 116) ("He let it drop casually . . . 'I'm having a duel with him' " [p. 95]); "vyigrat' vremia" ("to win time"); "Leont'ev prilip" ("I'm stuck with Leont'ev").

There is a linguistic play with names in "Podlets." Anton Petrovich remarks that Gnushke is a strange name, much the way that Galatov remarks that Bab is a funny name in "Zvonok." Berg's seconds have amusing names. Mitiushin remarks that they are Malinin and Burenin. The wordplay here is clear. Malinin and Burenin authored the standard arithmetic textbook in Russian pre-Revolutionary schools, an object of much mockery. In the English version of "Podlets," Nabokov changed them to Marx and Engels, which go just as well together.

When Gnushke corrects Mitiushin with *Magerovskii* and Burenin, Nabokov may well have been continuing his literary joke. Magerovsky is the name of a real (and fairly prominent) émigré whom Nabokov might have known in Prague where the former played an important role in the Russian Historical Archive.[35] In the English version this wordplay is obviously perpetuated when Gnushke says that the seconds are not Marx and Engels but Markov and Colonel Arkhangelski (Archangel). These linguistic games point to Nabokov's more indirect approach to his craft in

"Podlets." The reader has to look more closely at names in the symbolic-realistic stories that in the purely realistic ones.

This wordplay and the enrichment of the realistic images—of running water and shifting furniture—indicate Nabokov's increasing use of the symbolic method in "Podlets." This view is, of course, most explicit in his intentional downgrading of the romantic duel theme that is the basis of "Podlets." He has taken the chivalric situation of love and honor and the traditional love triangle and debunked it. He has transposed it from the romantic nineteenth-century scene to the very real everyday setting of Berlin in the 1920s. An element of absurdity is introduced by such comic details as Anton Petrovich's glove landing in a pitcher and Anton Petrovich sitting on his hat. The degeneration of the hero is graphically portrayed. His final lapse into the wishful thinking of his subconscious and his subsequent animalism verify the degree of his deterioration. This final scene of "Podlets" points toward the double theme that is highly developed in Nabokov's purely symbolic stories.

8. "Kartofel'nyi El'f"

"Kartofel'nyi El'f" ("The Potato Elf") is like "Podlets" in that the major theme is a love story with the traditional Nabokovian triangular configuration. As in *Mashen'ka* and *Korol' dama valet,* and unlike "Podlets," the hero is the lover, not the husband. The story also has an unromantic, even grotesque twist: the lover is a dwarf and the husband is a magician with the soul of a poet.[36] It is not surprising that this is one of the first early stories to be translated into English. Its London background is unique among the early stories. Nabokov noted: "[An] aspect separating 'The Potato Elf' from the rest of my short stories is its British setting. One cannot rule out thematic automatism in such cases, yet on the other hand this curious exoticism (as being different from the more familiar Berlin background of my other stories) gives the thing an artificial brightness which is none too displeasing; but all in all it is not my favorite piece." [37]

Tsetlin observed that "Kartofel'nyi El'f," like "Podlets," had a

strong external *fabula*. Despite its length, the structure of "Kartofel'nyi El'f" is cohesive and tight. It has all of the balance and
measure of the classic story as exemplified by Bunin's "The
Gentleman from San Francisco" and Chekhov's "The Lady with
the Dog." Nabokov divided this story into seven parts. (It was
originally published in four installments.) The exposition com-
prises Parts I, II, and III. In Part I, Fred Dobson, the circus-dwarf
hero, is introduced and his past, as well as his association with
Shock [38] the magician, are presented. Part II shows the force
motivating Dobson—his longing for a woman's love. Part III tells
of Nora, Shock's wife, her background and her life with Shock.
Part IV is the rising action. The three principals confront each
other. Shock brings Dobson home in his arms so that he may be
cared for by his wife. Dobson has been abused by some female
acrobats. Nora, being childless, babies Dobson. The following
morning her maternal attention becomes a mistress' caresses. This
section concludes with the climactic love scene between Dobson
and Nora:

I vnezapno kakim to nelepym i upoitel'nym obrazom vse
prishlo v dvizhenie. (p. 174)

And all at once, in some absurd and intoxicating way,
everything came into motion. (p. 230)

This central event of the story is presumed, not depicted; Victorian
understatement was sufficient for the Russian readers of the 1920s.
Such a structural "missing link" is characteristic of the modernist
approach in Nabokov's craft. Although all the laws of short-story
structure are observed, certain gaps in the action exist that force
the reader to make his own interpretation. In this story the climax
is implied, not explicit.

Part V reflects the effect of the climax on the hero. Dobson
leaves Nora to wander happily in London. He dreams that he is a
romantic hero who has saved her. Once again Nabokov degraded
the romantic theme in this symbolic slant. Structurally, the
opening paragraphs of this part have remarkable internal balance.
The first paragraph describes the poetic beauty of an August day;

the second notes that each individual has his day; the third states that this is Dobson's day; and the fourth adds that Dobson knows that it is his day. Thus the chapter increasingly focuses on Dobson, moving from the general situation to the particular, recalling Nabokov's coalescing technique in "Putevoditel' po Berlinu." The remainder of Part V follows the rest of Dobson's joyful day. He ends up exhausted at a London restaurant frequented by the circus troupe. Shock is there, and Dobson tries to explain honestly to Shock that he has seduced his wife. Shock appears disinterested and leaves the restaurant quietly. Dobson is relieved and elated; he decides to leave the circus and run away with Nora. Thus Part V concludes on a high note; at this turning point in his life, Dobson's options begin to dwindle.

Part VI is not strictly a falling action. Rather it is an intermezzo. In a sense this section matches Part III, which was given over to Nora. It confirms what has already been implied in Part IV, that Nora has no intention of following Dobson. A minor theme is introduced as well. This is unusual for a short story, where the strength of the genre lies in its economy and single plot line. Fully aware of her infidelity, Shock returns home to Nora. He pulls his final trick; he commits a horrible suicide, but is magically restored. Nora is so frightened by this act that she recognizes that she loves Shock after all. This supernatural component distorts the credible grotesquerie of the major theme. For all of his strangeness, Dobson can be accepted as believable and then as tragic. Shock is fantastic and as such enhances the unreal aspects of the story. Structurally, this part is important only in that it breaks the temporal pace of the action.

Part VII, the denouement, begins years later. This hiatus is another example of the "missing link" that characterizes the twentieth-century symbolic method. The reader is forced to puzzle out what actually has happened during this interval. Gradually the important details are revealed: Dobson has indeed quit the circus; Nora did not follow him; and he is now secluded in the town of Drowse, never to come out into the light of day.

The brief four-page conclusion is marked by a sudden temporal shift: "Proshlo vosem' let. Bylo voskresnoe utro" (p. 188) ("Eight years elapsed. It was Sunday morning" [p. 245]). The passage of time here is halted and accentuated, as in "Zvonok": "Sem' let proshlo s tekh por kak. . . ." ("Seven years had elapsed since. . . ."). As in so many of Nabokov's earliest stories, Sunday is the critical day here; it is a nice summery one, recalling Dobson's earlier August day. Nora's unexpected arrival balances Dobson's earlier unexpected arrival at her home. Her news of a son seems to resolve the question raised at the climax. Dobson gains a new lease on life and experiences joy:

> J mgnovenno on ponial vse, ves' smysl zhizni, dolgoi toski svoei, blika na chashke. (p. 191)

> And all at once he understood everything, all the meaning of life, of his long anguish, of the little bright window upon the cup. (p. 248)

Even that minute detail now has significance for him. Dobson runs after Nora when she leaves so that he can see the boy. Nora's unexplained, deepening grief, and Dobson's growing happiness and palpitating heart, are balanced by the running motion of all of Drowse's citizens, who are following the dwarf. The story is propelled to a height. At this point the classical reversal occurs, and in this instance it is compounded. Dobson drops dead at Nora's feet, never to glimpse his child. When approached, Nora implies that she does not know the dwarf lying at her feet. Her final muttered comment that her son has recently died is the story's startling finis. Again Nabokov unlocked a secret at the end of his piece.

This compound conclusion is an excellent example of the surprise that is a critical element in "Kartofel'nyi El'f." Suspense, ambiguity, and surprise are traditional short-story techniques and, in a story as long as this one, are needed to retain the reader's attention. All three of these elements figure in "Kartofel'nyi El'f." Suspense arises from the questions raised in the opening paragraphs: What precisely is wrong with Dobson? Is Dobson the Potato Elf of the title? Ambiguity and resultant suspense color the climax: Was Dobson's love-making real or imagined? The ubiquitous three points are full of meaning and are translated in the conclusion by Nora's remark: "U menia ved' byl syn ot vas . . ." (p. 191) ("The fact is I had a son from you" [p. 248]). Something still remains unsaid. These ellipses leave room for surprise.

The secondary theme of Nora and Shock has a component of surprise that is tinged with the supernatural. Shock's magical powers change alarm clocks to nickel pocket watches, and then to gold wristwatches; they rearrange food, pull circus tricks. Perhaps it is because Shock's tricks cease to work—for example, with Dobson in the restaurant—that Shock learns of Nora's infidelity. He takes poison and lies dying. When Nora asserts her love, he inexplicably comes to life. Nabokov did not make clear whether it is her love or Shock's supernatural powers that resurrect him. If Shock can bring back life, why can he not conjure up a child for Nora, or save the child she has by Dobson? Perhaps this is intended as just an authorial trick. Both the reader and Nora are surprised by what Nora sees when she returns to the bedroom.

Fokusnik, svetlyi i gladkii, v belom zhelete, v chernykh chekannykh shtanakh, stoial pered triumo i ˌrasstaviv lokti, ostorozhno zaviazyval galstuk. (p. 184)

The conjuror, bright-faced and sleek, in white waistcoat and impeccably pressed black trousers, stood before the pier glass and elbows parted, was meticulously working upon his tie. (p. 240)

This scene parallels the one that Anton Petrovich unexpectedly came upon in his bedroom: "In the bedroom, Berg was standing before the wardrobe mirror, putting on his tie" (p. 85).

There are essentially only three characters in "Kartofel'nyi El'f": Dobson, who is grotesque in appearance but normal in his human emotions; Shock, the magician, who is normal in appearance but grotesque in his actions; Nora, the object of the attention of these freaks, who is normal but ugly. They form the love triangle. They are initially described with a wealth of details that recalls the elaborate descriptions of the realistic stories. Subsequent characterizations are epithetical, reflecting the original portrayal.

Field is incorrect in writing: "In a sense the one criticism that could be made of this short story in which every detail and proportion are perfect . . . is that it has perhaps been inadequately titled: Dobson, Shock, and Nora all lay equal claim to the reader's attention and interest" (p. 252). The title indicates that this is Frederic Dobson's story. It begins with his tale, covers his entire life, and ends with his death. Five of the seven parts are told from his point of view. Sometimes the narrative dips into his interior monologue. Dobson is not simply a dwarf; he is an elf, and thus there is a supernatural or mythical overtone to his personality. *El'f* is not strictly a Russian word, and it is used concurrently with the Russian *karlik,* thus stressing his pixielike qualities as well as his non-Russianness. Every detail of his personality is given: his parentage, the reasons for his elfin stature, his habit of sneezing and snorting, the precise details of his clothing, his way of life, and his desires and ideals. Dobson is exactly twenty years old and weighs sixty-five pounds. A bulbous "potato nose" *(nos kartoshkoi)* has prompted his nickname Potato Elf. His nose, his round shiny forehead, and later his whole head recur as salient features. His flaxen hair is carefully parted; and his eyes have a slightly strange appearance, as if he were trying to stunt his growth. Unlike most dwarfs, he is well proportioned and resembles an eight-year-old boy. (This detail structurally foretells the age of his son.) Only the furrows in his forehead reveal his age. Dobson is always nattily dressed and sports a bowler, like many of Nabokov's heroes. He wears striped trousers, a jacket, and yellow gloves. His dapperness is not unlikely; his father was a children's tailor. He is repeatedly depicted wearing spats. His little figure never walks. It dances and minces along. Most often it rolls into a little ball. Dobson has traveled widely with circuses and has always evoked applause by his strange appearance alone. For all of the excitement of the big top, Dobson has seen it only as the uneventful perpetual circle of a circus horse. The culminating feat of his act is to be locked by Shock into a black box and escape through a trapdoor—a bit of Shock's fake magic. Although Dobson's appearance is abnormal, his emotions are human. He becomes readily attached to ponies, to giants, and finally to Nora. Dobson's normal but obsesseive desire for a woman sets the story in motion. He is a romantic at heart, and his life acquires meaning only when he becomes Nora's self-appointed Lilliputian knight. This is the crux of the story.

Nora, Dobson's lady love, is the daughter of a respected artist who met Shock in bohemian circles. She is singularly unattractive—a slovenly woman of uncertain age, with dark dry hair, parchment skin, and a mustache. She is in a bathrobe when she entertains Dobson—a situation reversed in the conclusion of the story. Her seduction of a willing Dobson is marked by her cigarette smoking, her bared elbows, her half-closed eyes, her pompom-slippers, and her lounging pose on the plush sofa. These mannerisms, which she shares with Tania and Leont'ev's wife, tag her as a woman of loose morals and frustrated desires. Her maternal emotions are her only worthwhile trait. She nearly cries when she thinks that Shock has brought her a child. When she recognizes Dobson, she feels compassion and tenderness. He becomes her son, and she comforts him and listens to the story of his life. Later as she searches in Dobson's face for the features of her lost child her grief is genuine. The other dimension of Nora's personality has contradictory elements. Her motives for making love to Dobson stem from curiosity, compassion, and a desire for vengeance on Shock. Dobson is first her baby, then her lover, and finally a worm. By totally rejecting him in the end, she indicates her blindness to the fact that it is Dobson who had given her a son. Her view of Shock is also ambivalent. She loves him and hates him. She does not comprehend his magic. After her love-making with Dobson, when Nora sees Shock he strikes her as strange. (This appears to be a parodic echo of *Anna Karenina,* where in Part I, Chapter 30, Anna returns home to Karenin and finds him strange.) In "Kartofel'nyi El'f" Nora is neither a real nor a symbolic figure. Her mixed motives and her inconsistent portrayal make her an unsuccessful short-story character.

Although Nabokov's description of Shock is sketchy and one-dimensional, he is clearly supernatural. His traits combine to lend him a magical quality. His appearance is strange: his chestnut forelock; his thin, almost ethereal hands; his transparent fingertips. His singing voice, dreamy glance, and spectral eyes convey a sense of unreality. He is a "rubber ghost," not a human being. His portrait anticipates the pale hero, Smurov, in "Sogliadatai." Nora sees him as a mirage, a walking trick, a deception of all five senses. His brief stroke is his final trick. If Nora has any aesthetic role in "Kartofel'nyi El'f," it is to bring into question and emphasize Shock's unreality. In sum, Nabokov's characterization of Shock represents a stage in his development of the symbolic outlook. Here, the combination of illusion and reality appears in a nascent form.

Nabokov's portrayal of Shock dovetails with the magic, masks, and grotesque tonality of "Kartofel'nyi El'f." Circus figures, reminiscent of Belyi and Leonid Andreev, are drawn. Save for a giant, they are all normal individuals hiding behind circus paint. Only Dobson is naturally strange. The tertiary characters lend a distinct masquerade atmosphere to this story; for example:

> . . . poiavliaiutsia i akrobaty, reiushchie v zveniashchem trepete trapetsii, i inostrannyi tenor (neudachnik na rodine) s narodnymi pesniami, i chrevoveshchatel' v morskoi forme, i velosipedisty, i neizmennyi, miagko sharkaiushchii po stsene kloun-ekstsentrik v kroshechnom kotelke i v zhilete do polu. (p. 168)

> . . . there are acrobats soaring in the tinkle and shiver of the trapezes, and a foreign tenor (a failure in his own country) singing barcaroles, and a ventriloquist in naval uniform, and bicyclists, and the inevitable clown-eccentric shuffling about in a minuscule hat and a waistcoat coming down to his knees. (p. 223)

This atmosphere of unreality and masks serves as an appropriate background for the metaphoric aspect of Dobson's story—namely, the intricate confusion between child and man.

Images and themes form a balanced pattern in "Kartofel'nyi El'f." The epithets describing the major figures are repeated like musical themes: Shock's transparent fingers and chestnut hair; Nora's goldfish bowl, eau de cologne, and green pompom-slippers; Dobson's bulbous nose, which metaphorically extends to his ball-like form and bowler hat. It is tempting to view recurrent images symbolically. However, whatever their oblique meaning, the salient images have a beauty of their own without any possible overtones. In *Nabokov's Deceptive World* Rowe has explored Nabokov's more suggestive images. He has correctly shown that Dobson's attraction to the pompoms on Nora's slippers "strangely interechoes" with the crimson pompom-slippers that represent sexual intercourse in *Korol' dama valet,* which I add was written during this same period.[39] In reviewing Rowe's study, Nabokov heatedly denied this type of interpretation.[40] Nevertheless, in defense of Rowe, I would observe that in these early stories pompom-slippers, like legs and feet *(nogi),* and shoes, recur often. The red slippers in "Vozvrashchenie Chorba" and the green slippers in "Kartofel'nyi El'f" both precede love scenes. Certainly Nora's slippers attract Dobson in the same way that the prostitute's legs and shoes attract Nikitin, and that Madame Nellis's stockings and shoes attract the attention of Galatov.

Unlike the aforementioned images, the image of the Spanish dancer does not recur in the same configuration each time. It is a progressive image. Dobson first notices the legs of the Spanish dancer beneath the orange flounces of her dress as she dances. Later Dobson catches sight of her, now shamefully referred to as *pliasulia* ("dancer" with a derogatory suffix), as she crosses her legs in the restaurant. She is sitting alone. Finally Dobson sees her leave on the arm of a blue-eyed fellow. This unobtrusive image gathers meaning as it is repeated and underscores, although subtly, Dobson's lust. Structurally viewed, this composite image, like the coalescing image, is a means of making recurring images strange and refreshing.

In the final scene, Dobson loses his slippers. Clearly this is another example of Nabokov's recurring shoe image. Here it adds an absurd dimension to Dobson, who is already wigless and scurrying for cover in a black bathrobe. It produces a comically sad effect. The related glove image is also repeated. If these gloves stand for anything, it is for dignity or honor. (Recall the gloves in "Podlets," which, like these, are crumpled and ball-like.) Dobson at the height of his joy parades around London in yellow gloves. When Nora visits him, she is gloved. First she takes off the dark glossy gloves and crumples them. They fall off her lap in much the same way that Dobson's slippers fall off his feet. She later picks up the sticky black balls these gloves have become. At the conclusion Dobson's collapsed body in the black bathrobe lies at Nora's feet: "... pokhozhee na chernyi komok perchatki" (p. 195) ("... resembling a crumpled black glove" [p. 321]). Rowe sees these gloves as symbolic of death,[41] but this interpretation does not take Dobson's yellow gloves into account.

The realistic image of food, which has its Russian literary roots in Gogol and Tolstoy, is recurrent in "Kartofel'nyi El'f." The most obvious example is the metaphoric potato in the title. Food figures in the German and Spanish theaters. Magically, and not so magically, food appears at Shock's home. Food is also eaten in the restaurant scene and prepared at Dobson's breakfast table:

Na stole, nakrytyi kolpakom vvide golovy popugaia, zhdal Freda kuvshin kakao. (p. 118)

A jug of cocoa under a cozy in the guise of a parrot's head was awaiting Fred on the breakfast table. (p. 245)

The fragrance of bacon, grass, and leaves and the transparency of these leaves, and of ears and fingers, are all examples of the sensual images that are characteristic of many of Nabokov's early stories. Taxis, buses, trams, and asphalt streets are found in "Kartofel'nyi El'f" as in so many other stories. The taxi image is a prize example of Nabokov's poetic prose:

Veselyi shofer zvonkim udarom sognul zheleznyi flazhok taksometra, mimo polilas' ulitsa, i Fred to i delo soskal'zyval s kozhanogo siden'ia i vse smeialsia, vorkoval sam s soboiu. (p. 175)

A cheerful taxi driver turned down with a resounding blow the iron flag of his meter; the street started to flow past, and Fred kept slipping off the leathern seat, while chuckling and cooing under breath. (p. 232)

This poetic image recalls the picture of the departing train in "Zvonok" and *Mashen'ka,* and the moving trams in "Skazka" and

"Blagost'." In all these examples, the vehicle is stationary; it is streets, station platforms, and sidewalks that move.

Dobson's happy day is metaphorically expressed as God's gift to the dwarf:

Chelovek ne mozhet providet', kakoi imenno den' dostanetsia emu, kakuiu meloch' budet vospominat' on vechno,— svetovuiu li riab' na stene vdol' vody ili kruzhashchiisia list, da i chasto byvaet tak, chto uznaet on den' svoi tol'ko sredi dnei proshedshikh, tol'ko togda, kogda davno uzhe sorvan, i skomkan, i broshen pod stol kalendarnyi listok s zabytoi tsifroi. (p. 175)

A person cannot foreknow which day exactly will fall to his lot, what trifle he will remember forever: the ripple of reflected sunlight on the wall bordering water or the revolving fall of a maple leaf; and it often happens that he recognizes *his* day only in retrospection, long after he has plucked, and crumbled, and chucked under his desk the calendar leaf with the forgotten figure. (p. 231)

Like Anton Petrovich's accursed day, this one is symbolically pinpointed by the large numeral on the peculiarly Russian rip-off calendar. This slip of paper conveying the date thus becomes a metaphor of time.

Lengthy passages of poetic prose are found in the paragraphs describing Dobson's day. Despite their urban setting, they are lyricized by the poetic-sounding words for grass (*murava*) and leaves (*listva*). This concentration of poetic prose in the climactic section of the story accentuates the joy of the miniature hero. Later Drowse, an obvious metaphor in itself, epitomizes Dobson's withdrawal and then mirrors his final revival. When he chases after Nora, the entire town comes to life:

... gde-to zvonko prolilis' kuranty, sonnyi gorodok ozhival i vdrug razrazilsia bezuderzhanym, davno taimym smekhom. (p. 194)

Somewhere afar church chimes rang forth: the drowsy town was coming to life—and all of a sudden it burst into uncontrollable, long-restrained laughter. (p. 250)

The tropes employed in the story are usually the metaphor and, to a lesser extent, the simile. Often they refer to the animal world: whale, Japanese dog, bulldog, worm, parrot, monkey. There is one significant alliteration on the hard *g* sound—*grubym, gortannym golosom;* and two examples of synesthesia—*vkusno pakhlo* (tastefully smelled), *teplyi zapakh* (warm whiffs). The adverb *mgnovenno* (instantly) and its related noun, *mgnovenie* (instant), often signal critical revelations in Nabokov's early stories. In "Zvonok" Galatov sees his mother for what she really is when instantly (*mgnovenno*) the electric power is restored. In "Rozhdestvo" this word will signal another revelation. (See below, p. 193.) The italics are mine.

... i na *mgnovenie* emu pokazalos', chto do kontsa poniatna, do kontsa obnazhena zemnaia zhizn' ... I v to zhe *mgnovenie* shchelknulo chto-to. (p. 74)

... for an *instant,* it seemed to him that earthly life was completely understandable ... and in that very *instant,* something cracked!

In "Kartofel'nyi El'f" these words introduce two culminating moments in Dobson's story. The italics are mine.

(1) ... v to zhe *mgnovenie,* po neponiatnomu sochetaniiu myslei, ei [Nora] pomereshchilos' drugoe, mstitel'noe i liubopytnoe. (p. 174)

... at that *instant,* by an enigmatic association of thought, she called forth something else, a curious, vindictive vision. (p. 230 with my translation)

(2) I *mgnovenno* on ponial vse, ves' smysl' zhizni, dolgoi toski svoei, blika na chashke. (p. 191)

And *instantly* he understood everything, all the meaning of life, of his long anguish, of the little bright window upon the cup. (p. 248 with my translation)

Understandably, diminutives are used liberally in reference to Dobson to emphasize his size. The play of light and shadows also figures in Nabokov's effects. Happy sunny moments contrast with Dobson's dark closeted life in the theater, in Shock's black case, and in the confines of his darkened home. Many colors recur in the attributive function, but no real pattern is apparent. Here I quote Nabokov's prefatory consideration of aspects that made "Kartofel'nyi El'f" a unique story for him:

Although I never intended the story to suggest a screenplay or to fire a script writer's fancy, its structure and recurrent pictorial details do have a cinematic slant. Its deliberate introduction results in certain conventional rhythms—or in a pastiche of such rhythms. I do not believe, however, that my little man can move even the most lachrymose human-interest fiend, and this redeems the matter (p. 220).

In "Kartofel'nyi El'f" Nabokov moved still closer to a purely symbolic outlook. This story, with its high cinematic potential, manifests Nabokov's fragmented view of the world.[42] The story contains significant structural ellipses. Unusual images such as the pompom-slippers and the gloves are ambiguous, even suggestive in their connotation. The description of Dobson's day is a fine extended metaphor. Nabokov even nodded to Tolstoy's *Anna Karenina*. This parodic element will develop to become the crux of *Ada*, which opens: " 'All happy families are more or less alike,' says a great Russian writer in the beginning of a famous novel" (p. 13). In "Kartofel'nyi El'f" Nabokov once again mocked a romantic theme. The chivalric love affair is that of a frustrated dwarf. The entire tone of "Kartofel'nyi El'f" is one of strangeness and distortion. Monstrous and sorcerous elements are central to the *fabula*. In Dobson's story, human emotions reach extremes. Joy and happiness are readily transformed into despair and sadness. There is no moderation. The heroines are heartless and, in the case of

Nora, downright ugly. The abnormality and the normality of the characters is unclear and at times masked. However, many photographic features of their person, and of their English milieu, recur, producing a bizarre montage of the circus world. This realistic-symbolic story is dominated, therefore, by the warped and dislocated impression so characteristic of Nabokov's symbolic tales.

IV

Those Temples Suspended
on High

THE SYMBOLIC STORIES

Nabokov's artistic pendulum swings completely away from the unilinear world of his realistic method to a multilinear world in five of his early stories. These symbolic pieces—"Bakhman," "Draka," "Uzhas," "Katastrofa," and "Rozhdestvo"—form a cohesive unit. In them the love tale, Berlin vignette, and personal confrontation themes are present, but as points of departure for the hero's own cataclysmic internal experiences. These internal events are more critical than the external ones. The everyday world that provides a prominent and solid locus for Nabokov's realistic hero is therefore found in the background, and Nabokov's central characters are not guided by the tangibles of life. Instead, they move through disconnected scenes. Details are not extraneous. If anything, there are not enough of them, thus creating gaps that the reader must bridge for himself. Random occasions and momentary confrontations with life's trivia are not the clear sources of consolation or inspiration for Nabokov's symbolic hero. Objects and souvenirs are far less important than the memories and trials that they evoke. The human reactions that they release are rich and extreme. The tears intimated or restrained in "Vozvrashchenie Chorba" and "Zvonok," for instance, are explicitly shed in "Bakhman," "Katastrofa," "Uzhas," and "Rozhdestvo." The hero's vacillation between reality and unreality is not the result of poetic and contented musing as in "Port" and "Groza." Nor is it confined to dreams and nightmares alone. The hero's personality is unsettled, disjointed, and at times abnormal in this group of stories. In "Bakhman" he wavers between sanity and genial insanity; in "Draka" between reality and fantasy; in "Uzhas" between rationality and madness; in "Katastrofa" between physical life and death; and in "Rozhdestvo" between spiritual death and rebirth.

Complementing this portrayal of a disintegrating world is the discontinuous, interrupted temporal element of these symbolic stories. Periods of time do not pass logically. Years, months, even weeks are condensed, telescoped, or deleted. Salient hours and minutes replace them. In "Bakhman," "Uzhas," "Katastrofa," and "Rozhdestvo," a single moment is valuable, even critical, for the hero as he attempts to come to grips with himself and the life around him.

Similarly, narrative is not direct and unbroken. Discourse shifts and is blurred. It is not always clear who is talking or thinking. In addition, it may be uncertain whether the shifting voice is conscious, semiconscious, subconscious, or, for that matter, coming from the grave. The gamut of human expression is covered as Nabokov's man endures deepest grief or supreme joy. Metaphors and images are not simple in Nabokov's short symbolic stories. For example, in "Uzhas," a heretofore real, photographic mirror is distorted, revealing a shattered mind. In "Rozhdestvo" a butterfly is not netted, nor is it a poetic metaphor; it is the symbol of birth. Structural omissions and unusual or repeating linguistic and punctuating elements mark the emotionalism of these five stories. Finally, the subtle parodic and ironic elements that are introduced in the realistic-symbolic stories are absent here, almost as if even the use of literary allusions is too prosaic for these exquisite creations.

1. "Bakhman"

The theme of "Bakhman," as that of the two preceding stories, is man's love for a woman. In this symbolic piece, however, genius and madness create a world for two older lovers.

The love story is straightforward: the principals meet and love, and when one dies the other goes insane. The structure of "Bakhman," on the other hand, is complex, particularly as the *fabula* and *siuzhet* are not synchronized.[1] The opening paragraph is the conclusion of the story, announcing the death of the titular figure, Bachmann, a pianist-composer. In the exposition that follows, the narrator tells of Bachmann's love for a married woman. The couple is portrayed, and their meeting is fully described.

The rising action is their romance, as it is woven into Bachmann's artistry. In keeping with the symbolic device of the missing structural link, the lovers' trysts are only suggested, never portrayed:

Kogda i gde Perova soshlas' s nim,—etogo nikto ne znaet. No posle vechera u priiatel'nitsy Perova stala byvat' na vsekh kontsertakh Bakhmana, v kakom by gorode oni ni davalis'. (p. 85)

When and where they became lovers, nobody knows. But after the soirée at her friend's house she began to attend all of Bachmann's concerts, no matter in what city they took place. (p. 174)

The climax of "Bakhman" is expanded. It singles out the critical evening in the couple's affair. Bachmann disappears on a customary drinking binge before his concert. While trying to find him, Perova becomes gravely ill. When Bachmann is finally found he refuses to play, for he has spotted Perova's empty seat. Structurally, there is a parallel within this climax. Bachmann quits the stage to search for Perova at her hotel room; in a reverse action Perova, fatally ill, leaves the hotel to go to the theater to encourage

Bachmann to play. They miss each other. Perova arrives at the hall too late. When she returns to her room, she finds Bachmann awaiting her. A few hours have made a critical difference. Now Perova is dying, and Bachmann is verging on madness. But they are united for a final night of exalted happiness.

The falling action, like the rising action, is abbreviated. The next day Perova is dead and Bachmann vanishes after her funeral. Some years later Zak, his manager, sees Bachmann at a railroad station. He is demented and surrounded by curious onlookers. The manager does not come up to him because he is in the company of a woman. There is no conclusion, as the opening paragraph has already stated that Bachmann has died in a Swiss asylum.

This structural analysis is based on Bachmann's story, but there is another possible interpretation, one that assumes this is the manager's tale. The opening paragraph announcing Bachmann's death and introducing Zak's story constitutes a frame. The final scene at the station would properly be the end of Zak's narrative. However, there is no frame at the conclusion. Structurally, this represents a weakness in the classic pattern. The story is thus unbalanced. On the other hand, it can be viewed as a very modern conclusion, in which the absence of the frame emphasizes the callousness of Zak's account.

This intricate *siuzhet* is enhanced by shifts of time. The story begins at its end. As in *Lolita* and *Ada,* the principals are announced as dead. The recollection of the story is prompted by news of the death of the hero. The action spans a decade, which is unusually long for a short story. It begins ten years earlier, and the romance lasts three years. The story is brought up to the present with the news of Bachmann's death. Thus it is implied that Bachmann was mad for seven years. Despite its temporal breadth, the action of the story is limited. It is confined, first, to the evening of the meeting (the exposition); second, to the evening of the reunion and Perova's death (the climax); third, to the moment at the railroad station; and fourth, to the news of Bachmann's death (the conclusion). The location of the action is diffuse. It vaguely follows Bachmann on his concert tours through the cities of Europe. It climaxes in Munich and concludes in the Swiss town of

Marivale. The actors move in Russian-German circles, if one judges by the names Perova and Bachmann. (Nabokov germanized the latter with a double *n* in the English version.)

Intricately linked with structure is the role of the narrator, his viewpoint, and his manner of expression. Among these early Nabokov stories "Bakhman" is unique in that it bears a certain resemblance to the narrative structure of Lermontov's *A Hero of Our Time*. There are two narrators of Bachmann's story: Zak and (I) *ia*. The latter will be referred to here as the narrator. As Bachmann's manager, Zak witnesses the romance; the narrator does not see the romance and apparently does not know the central figures. He is forced to rely on Zak's version and on the album that the manager shows him. These two points of view (Zak's and the narrator's) are interlaced through the story and become quite confusing, particularly when Zak also expresses himself in the first person. This confusion is, to a certain degree, compensated for by the fact that the two versions are at odds. Thus the characterization of the two central figures is bifurcated—sympathetic and antipathetic.

The distinctive feature of Zak's firsthand story is that it is told in the dialogue form. More accurately, it is a monologue, because the narrator never replies to him—recalling Nabokov's technique in "Groza," where Elijah holds a one-sided conversation. Zak's comments are clearly set off by quotation marks in the text of the story. The narrator, by contrast, expresses himself in straight narrative. This narrative, although based on hearsay and secondhand information supplied by Zak, is omniscient as well. The narrator speaks from places and knows things that even Zak knows nothing about. As an example I cite Perova's illness:

U Perovoi byl sil'nyi zhar. Doktor, posetivshii ee v etot den' dvazhdy, s nedoumeniem smotrel na rtut', tak vysoko podniavshuiusia po krasnym stupen'kam v goriachem steklian-nom stolbike. (p. 90)

Mme. Perova was worse. The doctor, who had visited her twice that day, had looked with dismay at the mercury that had climbed so high along the red ladder in its glass. (p. 180)

Often, but not always, the narrator masks his omniscience by saying that he imagined or thought such and such must be this way; for instance:

Mne pochemu to kazhetsia, chto kogda ona stala natiagivat' chulki, shelk tseplialsia za nogti ee kholodnykh nog. (p. 90)

I imagine for some reason that when she started pulling on her stockings, the silk kept catching on the toenails of her icy feet. (p. 180)

This confusion of points of view is disorienting and distracting. It weakens Bachmann's story. However, shifting narrative is a technique appropriate to symbolic stories; its distorting quality enhances the central tragic and hysterical mood.

Thus, with the split narrative, the story comes to the reader third-hand. Even though the narrator is the furthest removed character from the action, he is most directly linked to the reader and thus seems more credible. Although he does not know the characters, he is not neutral in his outlook. The narrator sympathizes with Bachmann and Perova, particularly with their human qualities. He sees Bachmann's positive features, and he catches Perova's ready smiles. More curiously, the narrator's subtle comments on the hero and heroine reflect his attitude toward Zak, the other storyteller. He passes no judgment on the manager, but a bitter indictment is implicit. His initial, seemingly objective, description of Zak concludes on a striking note:

Vo vsei ego figure bylo chto-to blagosklonnoe, blistatel'noe i nepriiatnoe. (p. 82)

There was something about his entire figure benevolent, brilliant, and disagreeable. (p. 172)

On the strength of his quasi-omniscience and what he has viewed in the album, the narrator reaches conclusions that immediately contrast with Zak's judgments. There are no editorial comments on

Zak's misjudgments; instead the narrator lets the contrast speak for itself:

"Ne udivliaites'," skazal Zak. "On v bukval'nom smysle neuch: kak pridet v gosti, tak srazu beret chto-nibud' i chitaet."
   Bakhman vdrug pochuvstvoval, chto vse smotriat na nego. On medlenno povernul litso i, podniav rasstrepannye brovi, ulybnulsia chudesnoi, robkoi ulybkoi, ot kotoroi po vsemu litsu razbezhalis' miagkie morshchinki. (pp. 83-84)

"Don't be surprised," said Sack [sic], "he is a barbarian in the literal sense of the word—as soon as he arrives at a party he immediately picks up something and starts reading."
   Bachmann suddenly sensed that everybody was looking at him. He slowly turned his face and, raising his bushy eyebrows, smiled a wonderful, timid smile that made his entire face break out in soft little wrinkles. (p. 173)

Zak's final reflection upon the affair is that Bachmann did not love Perova—in the face of the agonizing love story that he has just related. Further, his preoccupation with false propriety at Perova's death, seen in his anxiety lest her husband find her with Bachmann, reflects his insensitive nature even more. The abrupt conclusion with Zak's coldhearted snub at the railroad station is the narrator's bitter comment on the calculating impresario. The narrator does not temper the ending with a comment. This ostensible denial of the demented Bachmann because of the presence of Zak's companion recalls Nora Shock's blatant rejection of the dead Dobson.
   Zak's distorted viewpoint also recalls the inner narrator Maria in Leskov's "The Night Owls." As in that short story, here, too, the internal, biased storyteller acts in the drama. True to the Leskovian *skaz* technique,[2] Zak's disagreeable personality is distinctively revealed by his speech. He swears and makes off-color puns when relating Bachmann's crazed gestures to his audience:

Ia stolknulsia s nim, kogda posle figi—figi vmesto fugi—on
udalialsia so stseny. (p. 89)

I bumped into him when, after the fig—instead of the fugue—
he was leaving the stage. (p. 179)

Gallicisms, a sign here of affected sophistication, color Zak's
Russian speech as well: *maestro, impresario, madam, sub"ekt, tempera-
mentnaia, angazhement.* This falsity complements his authoritative
and bombastic manner. Throughout the story he rolls his eyes,
flamboyantly plays the part of the impresario, and embodies
everything that the word "entrepreneur" implies. He has only one
purpose: to get Bachmann to play well. He is only interested in
Bachmann the musician.[3] He not only ignores Bachmann the man,
but he also has the greatest contempt for him and likens this
sensitive artist to a rag and a thing (*veshch'*). Perova serves only one
purpose for Zak also. She gets Bachmann to play as never before
and to compose masterpieces:

> No igral on v te dni genial'no. K tomu vremeni otnositsia ego
> simfoniia D-Moll' i neskol'ko slozhnykh fug. (pp. 87-88)

> But in those days there was a genius in his playing. To that
> period belongs his *Symphony in D Minor* and several complex
> fugues. (p. 177)

Zak rightly concludes that Perova's death ruined Bachmann: "Kak
ni kak, ona pogubila ego" (p. 93) ("In any case, she was his
undoing" [p. 183]). Ironically, this obnoxious figure is the most
fully described of all the characters. When first introduced he
seems wholesome and appears to be everything that Bachmann
should be—so much so that he is mistaken for the maestro.

By contrast few details of the lovers' physical appearance are
given. Instead, certain of their manners and habits are described,
and then these distinctive facets of their personality are reiterated
to form impressionistic recurrent images. Perova and Bachmann
are from the start presented in action: limping, reading newspapers, smiling.

Beginning with the first paragraph of the story, Perova shares the spotlight with Bachmann, for in learning of his death the narrator remembers the story of the woman who loved him. Perova's introduction to Bachmann is unexpected. She receives a short note from an acquaintance inviting her to meet Bachmann at her soirée. Here the narrator imagines how she readies herself in an open-necked black dress, with her fan and her omnipresent knobbed walking stick. In characteristic Nabokovian fashion, she even casts "a parting glance at herself in the trifold mirror." However, the reader is given no precise details. He sees only an older woman with a pale, sickly complexion. This feature subtly prepares for her fatal illness. Her limp, her fragile appearance, and her severely pulled back hair liken her to a failed madonna. This image is contracted: she is known to all as the lame madonna (*khromaia Madonna*). Her love for Bachmann is never expressed in words; rather it is shown in the happy motion of her black, glistening fan; in the fluttering of her light temple locks; and most of all by her smile. Nabokov here used gestures and actions rather than features to delineate one of his early heroines. Her love for Bachmann is demonstrated by her constant presence at his concerts and by the fact that she takes no end of punishment from him. She endures him snapping his teeth at her when she helps him with his tie. She tolerates all of his other childish caprices when she admonishes him for his drinking. With Zak, she searches for Bachmann even at the risk of her own life. Her final feverish search through the dank pubs where music explodes—in contrast to the concert hall where music is harmonious—is expanded in the story. Her walk in the blinding rain culminates in her speechless discovery of Bachmann in her room; and her final night of love with him is, as the sympathetic narrator understands it, the most ecstatic moment in their entire affair. This experience leaves a look of happiness on Perova's dead face.[4]

Bachmann is introduced into the story when he is presented to Perova. She, like the reader, has no idea what he looks like. When she arrives at the soirée, Perova first approaches the man in the evening clothes who is loudly denouncing the acoustics of the hall. But it is Zak, a false alarm (*lozhnyi put'*). This structural device heightens the anticipation of what the famous artist looks like.

Bachmann is the reverse of the expected image. He is portrayed as being singularly strange, disheveled, and dirty. However, his flashing, timid smile radiates a warmth and humanity that contradict Zak's appraisal of him. His eccentricity is accentuated by his moving lips and murmurings. His fingers are in perpetual drumming motion throughout the story; and his hands, like Shock's, are almost unreal. These selective details contradict the mastery and perfection that this man can demonstrate at the piano. His odd preparations for his concert performance point to the artist's imbalance. He comes on stage as if released from some evil hands—Zak's, perhaps. His elaborate, detailed, and agonizing adjustment of the piano stool is painfully described. But once at the keyboard, he produces exquisite flights of sound. He knows that Perova is in the front row; indeed, he cannot play without her, such is her effect on him.

For all his artistic maturity, Bachmann is childlike. He is cruel and nasty. He withdraws under blankets for security. His harsh attitude toward Perova points to his latent madness, which is not compensated for by a show of affection or love for Perova. This affair is completely hidden and can only be inferred from Perova's loyalty and happiness and from Bachmann's madness following her death. Bachmann's other passion, his weakness for alcohol, is offset by his innate hospitality toward his fellow drinkers in the bars. Ultimately this carousing, which continues for days at a time, brings the death of his loved one, of his art, and finally of himself. Perova's absence from the theater on the fateful night and her ensuing death break him. He can no longer tolerate music; he mutters: "Stop those sounds! Enough, enough music!" He stops up his ears. Six years later he is found crying before a music box. Now Bachmann's, not Perova's, attire is black, as he mourns her death. His final end in an asylum is as brutal and ignominious a conclusion to his life as is the hero's suicide through the bathroom window in *Zashchita Luzhina*. Both maestros are driven by their art to lunacy.

As one of Nabokov's artist-heroes, even Bachmann's name reflects his musicality. His story is expressed in the symbolic and unusual metaphoric aspects of this piece as well. Symbolically, Perova through her selfless love, support, and indulgence is

Bachmann's muse. Even Zak with all of his materialism concedes that Perova is his inspiration:

On uveriaet, chto eshche nikogda Bakhman tak khorosho, tak bezumno ne igral, i chto potom, s kazhdym razom, on igral vse luchshe i vse bezumnee. (p. 86)

He insists that never before had Bachmann played with such beauty, such frenzy, and that subsequently, with every performance, his playing became still more beautiful, still more frenzied. (p. 175)

In this instance the narrator agrees with Zak.

On a simpler metaphoric level, Bachmann's fugue playing is likened to a cat-and-mouse game:

S nesravnennym iskusstvom Bakhman sklikal i razreshal golosa kontrapunkta, vyzyval dissoniruiushchimi akkordami vpechatlenie divnykh garmonii i—v troinoi fuge—presledoval temu, iziashchno i strastno s neiu igraia, kak kot s mysh'iu,— pritvorialsia, chto vypustil ee, i vdrug s khitroi ulybkoi nagnuvshis' nad klavyshami, nastigal ee likuiushchim udarom ruk. (p. 86)

With incomparable artistry, Bachmann would summon and resolve the voices of counterpoint, cause dissonant chords to evoke an impression of marvelous harmonies and, in his Triple Fugue, pursue the theme, gracefully, passionately toying with it, as a cat with a mouse: he would pretend he had let it escape, then, suddenly, in a flash of sly glee, bending over the keys, he would overtake it with a triumphant swoop. (pp. 175-76)

This image complements a fine metaphoric passage describing the concert hall:

Svetlaia belaia estrada, s lepnymi ukrasheniiami po bokam v vide organnykh trub, i blestiashchii chernyi roial', podniavshii

krylo, i skromnyi grib stula ozhidali v torzhestvennoi
prazdnosti cheloveka s mokrymi miagkimi rukami, kotoryi
seichas napolnit uraganom zvukov i roial', i estradu, i
ogromnyi zal, gde, kak blednye chervi, dvigalis', losnilis'
zhenskie plechi i muzhskie lysiny. (pp. 88-89)

The white, brightly lit stage, adorned by sculptured organ
pipes on either side, the gleaming black piano, with upraised
wing, and the humble mushroom of its stool—all awaited in
solemn idleness a man with moist, soft hands who would soon
fill with a hurricane of sound the piano, the stage, and the
enormous hall, where, like pale worms, women's shoulders and
men's bald pates moved and glistened. (p. 178)

This musical metaphor is repeated in a slightly different
configuration in *Zashchita Luzhina* when Luzhin's chess game is
compared to violin playing (p. 137).[5] These musical images are
particularly striking in view of Nabokov's confession: "Music, I
regret to say, affects me merely as an arbitrary succession of more
or less irritating sounds. Under certain emotional circumstances I
can stand the spasms of a rich violin, but the concert piano and all
wind instruments bore me in small doses and flay me in larger
ones." [6]

Unusual similes generally refer to some quality of Bachmann's:
sea urchin, cat and mouse, boils, monkey, pale worms, cone,
ballerina, little rag. They form a peculiar and rather grotesque
series of images, and this story is unique precisely because of them.
The album of Zak's clippings of Bachmann is compared to a coffin.

Alliterations enhance already "made-strange" images. The initial image of Bachmann's artistry is introduced with repeating *z*
sounds thus:

... zolotoi, glubokii, sumasshedshii trepet ego igry za pe chat
levalsia uzhe na voske, a zazhivo zvuchal v znameniteishikh
kontsertnykh zalakh. (p. 81)

... the golden throb of the deep and demented music he
played was already being preserved on wax, as well as being
heard live in the world's most famous concert halls. (p. 171)

As the ill Perova searches for Bachmann, Nabokov's familiar street sounds are given with the alliterative hushings *sh* and *zh.* The noise of the car thus readily combines with the feverish noise in Perova's temples:

—i shum motora i shipenie shin slivalis' s zharkim zhuzh-zhaniem v viskakh. (p. 90)

. . . and the sound of the motor and the hiss of the tires blended with the hot humming in her temples. (p. 180)

The short story "Bakhman," like the other early symbolic stories, possesses a dimension beyond its literal meaning. Realistic details are not used extensively. They are selective; for instance, only Perova's peculiar sickliness is underscored. It is her limp and turquoise-knobbed walking stick that move through this story, not Perova herself. Bachmann's tale exemplifies Nabokov's absorbed interest in the artist-hero, which Khodasevich had remarked in his article. However, Bachmann is unlike the artists of the realistic stories who achieve tranquillity in searching for the trifles of their daily lives. This hero is not merely a grotesque like Dobson; he is genuinely mad. His life is one of extremes as he rises from artistic eccentricity to the heights of musical perfection, only to tumble finally into total lunacy. In this symbolic story Nabokov's artist-hero is clearly placed in a truly disintegrating world of music, love, and death.

2. "Draka"

In Nabokov's symbolic stories the love theme is present, but generally as an unobtrusive motif. The exception is "Bakhman," where the love affair is prominent only because of the excessive reactions it fosters in the hero and heroine. A love story is the background theme of another early symbolic tale, "Draka" ("The Fight"), which deals with a young Russian writer, reminiscent of the heroes of the realistic stories. The setting is Germany. At first reading, this story strongly recalls "Port." The same émigré sits in a tavern and watches a young woman help her father, a restaurateur. She, like Lialia, has an admirer or fiancé. Nonetheless, she attracts the émigré hero, who falls to musing. In "Port" the nature of this contemplation is clear. In "Draka" the hero's reflections waver between reality and fantasy; and it remains totally unclear if the love story, such as it is, is anything more than a figment of the hero's imagination. This indistinct approach recalls "Groza." This element of fantasy is reinforced by other, more obvious, symbolic techniques, primarily Nabokov's expanded personification of the sun, which underlies the entire piece.

Structurally Nabokov divided "Draka" into two nearly equal sections. Part I acts as an enlarged frame. It describes the narrator's observations and mood and indicates his general sensitivity. The plot in Part I is therefore static and the tone contemplative. On sunny days, the narrator goes to sun and swim at a lake just outside the city. This is doubtless a spot similar to the Berlin forest-lake area described in "Podlets" and later in *Kamera obskura*. There the narrator contentedly observes life around him: nature and people. Particularly he notes an older German who daily suns himself nearby. The narrator's curiosity to know who this man is and what his profession may be raises queries and introduces an element of mystery.

Part II opens with the answers:

Mne professiia ego otkrylas' sovsem sluchaino. (p. 12)

His profession was revealed to me quite by chance.

This signals the exposition, which reveals the names of the characters and sets the scene for the titular fight. Quite by chance the narrator walks into a tavern on a sultry evening to buy a refreshing drink. The tavern-keeper Krause is none other than the narrator's sunbathing partner. He is assisted by his dishwashing daughter Emma. The narrator is as content in the tavern as he is by the lake, and he begins to frequent it. He loves to watch Emma as she gently glances at her rough-looking lover at the bar. Thus all four central characters are presented in the barroom scene: the narrator, Krause, Emma, her suitor.

The rising action of the story begins with the key words, "the last time" *(poslednii raz)*. It immediately raises the question: Why the last time? The hero's subsequent recollection of the painting hanging on the tavern wall depicting the last days of Pompeii with her fleeing denizens figuratively changes the story's key and accelerates the tempo of the action. This is then complemented by a description of an actual oncoming storm outside the tavern. People rush for cover in the subway station as wind and rain lash against the tavern window, recalling the rainstorm in "Blagost'." The darkened and hurried atmosphere contrasts sharply with the sunlit, refreshing peace of the frame and exposition. The narrator senses something unusual as he sits in the tavern. The sullen lover enters and asks for Emma, who has not been seen. Here the restaurant scene from "Port" becomes distorted. The father does not respond. The soaked and chilled lover helps himself to cognac and prepares to leave without paying the twenty pfennigs which Krause then demands. The lover retorts: "I feel I am at home here." Krause follows him out and a street fight ensues between the two.

As the title indicates, this fight is the central event of "Draka." This is one of Nabokov's first uses of this literary theme.[7] It is developed in "Sogliadatai" in the fight between the hero and Kashmarin (pp. 23-26). Boxing is depicted in *Podvig* (pp. 122-25). In *Lolita* Humbert and Quilty fight (pp. 295-307); and there is a tussle between Van and Percy in *Ada* (p. 275). However, in "Draka," despite its central role, the fight does not have the complexity of the later pugilistic scenes, nor is the hero fighting his alter ego or a psychological antagonist. In "Draka" the hero-narrator is merely an observer. His reactions as he watches the confrontation are what are important in "Draka," not the fight itself. In fact, there is little description of the actual fight. The two men scream and shout. Emma runs out with despairing cries, and at the climax Krause knocks down her lover. A crowd surrounds the downed man.

The falling action is a few sentences long. The narrator goes into the tavern to retrieve his forgotten cap. He finds Emma crying at the table. He pats her head, and as he departs he notices that Krause is explaining what has happened to the police. There is no strict conclusion to the event. The narrator has left the scene. The final paragraph of "Draka" is the frame. It does not resolve the action. Instead it offers some possibilities for the ending. The narrator openly admits that he does not know, nor does he care to know, what exactly has transpired. He muses that perhaps this short incident could be twisted completely differently, recalling the options offered for the ending of "Passazhir." For instance, one could sympathetically relate that Emma cried all night and dreamt that her brutal father had mangled her lover. One could say that Emma's happiness had been insulted for the sake of a copper coin. This coin, which clanged when the narrator paid for his first beer, becomes a minor symbol of pride when the lover refuses to pay it and as a result it becomes a cause célèbre for Krause, who fights for it. Figuratively it could represent Emma. The narrator then offers a possibility that reverses the entire meaning of the story. He suggests that perhaps the essence of "Draka" is not just a matter of human suffering and happiness. The narrator wonders if the true essence lies in the play of the shadows on the live bodies and in the harmony of all the gathered minutiae of the hero and now perceived in a single unrepeatable way. This final observation opens up the possibility of a reversal in the plot. Structurally, the central incident—the fight—becomes a story or a daydream within the story. Nabokov's characteristic wavering between reality and fantasy thus emerges: Were the fight and Emma figments of the narrator's imagination? If so, at what point does the story slip from reality to fantasy? In this final frame the plot of "Draka" is therefore further weakened, but the tonal effect is strengthened.

"Draka" acquires the dynamics necessary for the short-story genre, not only through the brief, heated fight, but through Nabokov's skillful use of the temporal element. Time in "Draka" is pinpointed by either day or hour by the use of adverbs, adjectives, and time expressions. There is even an old-fashioned cuckoo clock which at first is described as leisurely striking the dry fractions of time. When Emma suddenly comes through the door under this clock and later is stunned by the fight, the cuckoo pops out with a peep. Thus the clock signals the beginning of the fight, and the two dynamic elements coalesce.

The dominant, contented tone of "Draka" is set by the narrator, an anonymous character. "Draka" is his story and is seen from his viewpoint. Part I is told in the first person. In Part II, when the narrator befriends Krause, the latter engages in a brief one-sided dialogue—a logical device because Nabokov noted that the narrator knows very little German. As in "Britva," the narrator is frustrated by his inability to speak German. (It is implied that he is Russian.) He cannot readily share, much less communicate, his joy over the sunlit surroundings with his beach neighbor in the exposition. Dialogue colors the climax when Krause and the lover argue. Then generalized shouting and pandemonium break out. The heated dialogue serves, like time, to push the story to its emotional peak. Krause repeatedly shouts "Twenty!" The crowd yells and Emma cries: "Otto! . . . Otets! . . . Otto! . . . Otets! . . . " ("Otto! . . . Father! . . ."). Here, of course, Nabokov played with the euphonic *ot* combination, because technically Emma would be shouting, *Vater!* Nabokov's favorite palindrome occurs with this late revelation that Emma's lover is named Otto. Imaginative use of the word "otto" is also found in "Putevoditel' po Berlinu" and in "Skazka." Curiously, this mirror word recurs much later when Humbert Humbert considers using Otto Otto as a pseudonym in *Lolita* (p. 310). Palindromes and acronyms characterize much of Nabokov's fiction. For example, Ada is, like Otto, a perfect mirror *word, particularly in Cyrillic:* A∆A. In "Poseshchenie muzeia" [8] and "The Vane Sisters" [9] Nabokov's wordplay actually holds the key to the stories' meaning.

Throughout "Draka," unobtrusive details point to the hero's typical Nabokovian profession—writing. The narrator's vocation is implied in his comment that the happiness that he felt was as good as if God gave him immortality or a genius praised his book. His contented observations and his stress on the importance of harmonious minutiae are characteristic of all of Nabokov's heroes. In this story the visual observations are, of course, more acute on account of the often-mentioned language barrier of the narrator.

The satisfaction that the narrator feels on the beach he senses in Krause's tavern also. There the narrator, like others of Nabokov's drinking heroes, enjoys his darkened surroundings. It gives him, like Nikitin in "Port," quiet refuge from the sultry world outside. The jolly owner, his daughter, and their customers; the cuckoo clock, the stove, the dirty beer coasters, and the pennants; and Nabokov's Flaubertian posters and advertisements all recall

Nabokov's other bars. The shiny bottles on the shelf behind this
bar are found not only in other taverns but in the barbershop in
"Britva" and on the female acrobats Zita and Arabella's circus
dressing table in "Kartofel'nyi El'f."

On his final tavern visit, the narrator's mood changes. The wind
and rain outside are reflected in the moods of all of the characters
within. He feels that something unusual will soon occur:

Ia mnogo vypil, i dusha moia, zhadnoe, glazastoe moe nutro
trebovalo zrelishch. (p. 3)

I had drunk a lot, and my soul, my entire greedy, big-eyed
guts demanded spectacles.

This attitude conforms in part to a writer's natural desire to
witness or experience something. As the narrator runs outside to
watch the ensuing fight, it is significant that the once ominous
storm now exhilarates him as a gust of the burly wind pleasantly
strikes his face. He marvels at the distorted faces of the men as they
fight. The lamplight reflects the scene on the black, rain-drenched
pavement. He recalls how once in a port dive, he had had a
wonderful fierce fight with an Italian who was as black as a bug.
This "made-strange" simile recalls the Negro whom Nikitin
encounters, also in a port, whose face resembles a wet galosh. The
narrator's caress and final kiss on Emma's hair preludes his
concluding introspection. This brings the story back to its peaceful
sunlit atmosphere.

The tavern keeper Krause is a sympathetically drawn personality. Like the narrator, he worships the sun. Whereas the
narrator is never described and comes to swim with a newspaper
stuffed under his arm, Krause is fully shown as he arrives
punctually at nine. He carefully carries a black umbrella and a
pointedly well folded package. Methodically he undoes it: newspapers, blanket, bath towel. He is lame and is dressed in trousers
and an army-type shirt. Meticulously he strips down to his bathing
trunks and arranges his blanket and umbrella so that he can lie
down to read. He then lies supine on the ground next to the
narrator, who observes him. Krause is equally exact when he

prepares to swim. He douses himself carefully with water, in obvious contrast to the narrator, who dives headlong into the lake. Krause's smiles on the beach and grins in the tavern speak for his basically friendly nature. This kindliness is manifest in his warning about the dogcatcher to those lying on the beach. On the fateful evening Krause, like the others, is hot. He displays a different side of his temperament. His collar is open, and he eats gloomily and fails to respond to the lover's question. Understandably, he is offended by the young man's brashness. However, the fight reveals that Krause, despite his lame leg and his age, is surprisingly agile and strong.

Emma is only sketchily presented. She has a small birdlike face and gentle empty eyes. She wears a plaid dress. She trusts and fondly glances at her lover. She is portrayed in the manner of Nabokov's typical tertiary characters.

Her lover is derogatorily drawn. He is everything that Krause is not, so a conflict between the two is implied. He is a coarse character who, the narrator surmises, must be either a typesetter or a fitter. In true Nabokovian perspective, Emma sees his sharp profile reflected in a mirror. This mirror is bisected by the gold type of Nabokov's ubiquitous advertisement, and his interest in letter shapes manifests itself here. The narrator observes Otto, a sullen chap with white teeth, as he sits throwing dice. On another occasion Otto lazily leans on the counter. As Emma speaks to him, the narrator sees the fitter in profile for himself. The portrait is unattractive: a mournful, evil grimace; wolfish eyes; blue bristle in the hollow of his long, unshaven cheek. His fingernails are described in a typical Nabokov image:

Ia zapomnil takzhe mokruiu ot pivnoi peny ruku montera, bol'shoi palets etoi ruki, szhavshei kruzhku,—gromadnyi chernyi nogot' s treshchinoi poseredke. (p. 3)

In my memory I also retained the fitter's hand which was wet from the beer foam, this hand's thumb, gripping the mug—an enormous black fingernail with a crack down the middle.

This negative physical impression is confirmed by his subsequent insolence. Krause is thus justified in chasing after Otto: this fellow is clearly not worthy of his daughter's affections.

The minor characters are equally colorful. The narrator sees them in clusters, not as individuals. First he notes the familiar tram conductors who are resting and smoking on a green bench. He focuses on their heavy hands, which are described as permeated with metal *(propakhnuvshie metallom ruki)*. Nabokov repeats this metal image when describing the beer: ". . . belogrivoe pivo, chut' otdavavshee metallom" (p. 2) (". . . the white-maned beer, very slightly tasting of metal"). These images in a sense complement the description of Otto's possible profession as a fitter, a man who works with metal. The trammen in their turn are watching a man in a wet apron watering an eglantine flowering along the tracks. By the lake at the edge of the forest, the narrator observes Krause and other passersby; a vendor selling sourballs; two others selling pickles; some rude, but splendidly put-together lads who parrot the vendor's calls; a naked little toddler with wet sand stuck to him; his mother nearby, combing her long, dark hair; athletes playing ball. All personify contentment in microcosm. Besides the four central characters, the figures in the tavern are basically limited to Otto's dice-playing partner, to a sleepy man with appetizing folds of fat on the nape of his neck, and to a coachman with a gray mustache. These last three add color to the dark and greasy tavern scene. In "Podlets" the flower vendor, the paperboy, and the shoeshine man serve the same purpose by quickly conveying a sense of the live city locale.

In "Draka," where atmosphere and the narrator's subjectivity predominate, the sun is a character. Unlike the hot sun in "Port," the sun in "Draka" has a positive effect on the hero, as is indicated by the first and last sentences:

Po utram, esli solntse priglashalo menia, ia ezdil za-gorod kupat'sia. (p. 2)

In the morning, if the sun invited me, I would go out of town to swim.

A mozhet byt' delo vovse ne v stradan'iakh i radostiakh chelovecheskikh, a v igre tenei i sveta na zhivom tele. (p. 2)

Perhaps it isn't a matter of human sufferings and joys after all, but of the play of shadows and light on a live body.

Significantly, the fight does not take place in the daylight but in the shadows of the glistening nocturnal street.

The language of "Draka" is poetic, and the central image of the sun is expressed primarily in tropes. Personification predominates. In Part I the sun, its light and shadows, its heat and sultriness, participate in the action. The sun plays first in the water of the hose, which flies upward like a silver fan and only then falls to the shivering bushes. The sky moves the fir trunks:

Chastye i tonkie stvoly sosen, sherokhovato-burnye [sic] [10] vnizu, telesnogo tsveta povyshe, byli ispeshchreny melkimi teniami, i na chakhloi trave pod nimi valialis', kak by dopolniaia drug druga, loskutki solntsa i loskutki gazct. Vnezapno nebo veselo razdvigalo stvoly. (p. 2)

The close, thin trunks of the firs, somewhat ruggedly brown below, flesh-colored a bit higher, were dappled with minute shadows, and on the stunted grass beneath them, bits of the sun and bits of newspaper lay scattered, as if complementing one another. Suddenly the sky would cheerfully move the trunks aside.

The narrator and Krause watch as the sun plays with the clouds, which are likened to caravans and camels. The dogcatcher's truck passes through sunspots on the beach road. With blind tenderness the sun tumbles on the narrator when he frees himself from his shirt and it dries him after his swim:

. . . solntse vkradchivymi ustami zhadno p'et prokhladnyi biser, ostavshiisia na tele. (p. 2)

... the sun greedily drinks the cool beads remaining on my
body with stealthy lips.

The sun's direct effect is seen on the prostrate bodies that lie on
the gently sloping hill. They show all the shades of the sun's effect.
Some are white with pink spots on the shoulder blades. Others are
hot as honey or the color of strong coffee with cream. Krause's
large bald spot is smoothed by the sun to a red sheen, and the
athletes are black-bodied. The narrator and Krause are brought
together initially by their love for the sun. The athletes throwing
their ball recall the discus throwers in Attica, and the airplane
ascending the sunlit sky is compared to Daedalus.

The sun motif is further enhanced by the figurative contrast of
dry and wet. This is seen in the interaction of the dry sun and the
water of the hose. The swimmers and the sun also interact in an
unusual inverted image of waves of sand and the light smoothness
of the water. In Part II the narrator's initial tavern visit is
occasioned by his need for refreshment from the heat. This thirst is
alleviated by the beer, which acts like water out of a hose and offers
refreshment similar to that of the lake. This cooling beer is
described in a set of poetic images. I cite one alliterative example:

Moi veselyi nemets . . . puskal iz krana tolstuiu zheltuiu struiu,
doshchechkoi srezal penu, pyshno perelivavshuiusia cherez
krai. (p. 2)

My jolly German . . . was letting a thick, yellow stream out of
the faucet, with a little board he skimmed the foam which was
overflowing the brim.

Clearly, "Draka" has some of the placid tone and interest in
minutiae that are characteristic of the realistic stories. However,
the growing enmity between the father and the suitor that is
symbolically suggested by the gathering rainstorm brings the mood
of the story to a violent and brutal climax. This disruption of the
quietude lends the story a distorted dimension. The symbolic view
is complemented by the clear personification of the sun and the
hero's indistinct wavering between waking and dreaming.

3. "Uzhas"

The ambivalence of the hero of "Uzhas" ("Terror") points to a serious emotional problem. The hero no longer daydreams. Instead he fights a losing battle against madness. His growing insanity is exacerbated by a love affair and has no exit. His tragedy is more immediate than Bachmann's because the story entirely concerns him. He is unnamed and is identified as a sensitive writer. Thus the subjective and evocative quality of the story is intense. The first-person narrative approach further amplifies the introspective tone of "Uzhas."

The weak *fabula* of "Uzhas" is at one with the narrative structure. A lengthy exposition sets the scene. This expanded beginning establishes the story's predominating mood, which is indicated by the title "Uzhas." Like Nabokov's other early mood story, "Blagost'," it opens with the artist-narrator arising and facing life around him. In "Blagost'" the narrator feels content-ment. In "Uzhas" he feels the opposite emotion—terror. He recalls that once or twice after long periods of work at night he had looked into the Nabokovian mirror. His reflection struck him as strange and frightening. When told of this reaction, his friends had warned him that it might lead to insanity. The immediacy of this terror is sustained by the narrator's recollection of other frightening experiences, extending as far back as his childhood. (See Chapter III, Note 14.) Once while lying supine in the dark he was overcome by fear. He experienced a panic foretaste of death and realized that he was mortal. Even the woman whom he loved deeply had once evoked fear and terror in him. As he gazed at her, she appeared completely strange to him until she lifted her head. Her smile immediately dispelled his alienation. Nabokov made his particular experience immediate by relating it in the historical present tense. The narrator observes, however, that these three terrifying moments were merely a part of a higher terror that he was to experience later.

The narrator's incipient madness has been revealed in these moments of horror and in the prediction of still another to come. This forms the exposition. The narrator's overwhelming love for his mistress is also described and emphasized by the remark that during their three-year affair he had left her only once and that the emotional strain of that separation was exhausting to him.

The rising action of the narrator's story begins when, at the end of these three years, he is forced to leave again for a fairly extended period. During this separation he endures his greatest terror—the central event of the story. The lovers' last night together is foreboding. They attend the opera, where the lights go out unexpectedly and panic seizes the audience. His beloved becomes so frightened that he takes her home. She rationalizes that it would not have been good to spend their last night together in public at the opera.

The passage of time decelerates as the narrator notes that twenty-four hours later he is in a non-Russian city. Passing time in solitude and without his beloved in unfamiliar surroundings debilitates his already weakened nerves. During the first night he is at least able to dream happily of her, but when reminded of his dream in the light of day, it only horrifies him. The second and third nights are sleepless. The narrator becomes exhausted, more childish and nervous. He tries to calm himself by smoking and working harder, but to no avail. Here the tempo of the story slackens as the narrator's nervousness accelerates. It peaks on the frightening fifth day when the narrator emerges onto the street. Now the city is not just non-Russian; it is strange. His exhaustion is such that his head and legs feel as though they are made of glass. He is torn from the world. His soul no longer accepts houses, trees, and people as familiar. Sitting on a park bench, he becomes totally horrified and fights madness.

The narrator's inability to relate to his immediate surroundings is handled particularly effectively in this story. Nabokov's own ability to view physical objects in an unusual and refreshing manner is a hallmark of his art. The narrator-writer's inability to communicate with these very objects is, in the context of Nabokov's own aesthetic values, comparable to stripping the writer of all his vision. The narrator's nerves are so strained that even Nabokov's faithful dog, who approaches the narrator so trustfully, cannot help. He too is rejected. It will be remembered that in "Port" the dog is a friend whose companionship is accepted.

The rising action of this story nears its climax when the narrator gives up the fight against madness:

Ia uzhe byl ne chelovek, a goloe zrenie, bestsel'nyi vzgliad, dvizhushchiisia v bessmyslennom mire. Vid chelovecheskogo litsa vozbuzhdal vo mne zhelanie krichat'. (p. 203)

I was no longer a man, but a naked eye, an aimless glance moving in an absurd world. The very sight of a human face made me want to scream. (p. 120)

In a stupor he manages to reach the ubiquitous Nabokov hotel. His blindness and passivity are reflected grammatically. He is acted upon: a note is thrust into his hand, a fellow guest bumps into him, the revolving doors take him in. The climax is the remark: "I srazu ves' moi uzhas proshel" (p. 203) ("... and at once my terror vanished" [p. 120]). Technically, this point is masterfully expanded by the use of suspense and surprise: What is written in the note? At the end of a long paragraph it is revealed that the note informs the hero that his loved one is dying. This news has been obliquely anticipated by the statement that the loved one did not fear death and that the couple never spoke of the subject. The minor key sounded by the episode at the opera and the beloved's comment that it was their last night together serves as a preparation for this surprise.

Fright in a darkened theater is used twice in "Uzhas"—first figuratively, when the narrator likens his fear of death to the sudden darkening of a theater, and then as an actual incident. By its association with the figurative image, it acquires an overtone of death. The beloved one dies like Perova in "Bakhman" with the lover at her bedside helplessly watching. Because of the completeness with which the narrator realizes his grief, all of his other emotions are surmounted. Ironically, his loved one's death saves the narrator from insanity, and he knows this. The falling action of this story is brief. It relates that in his beloved's death, half of the narrator dies as well. The half that the narrator cannot see dies with her and the half that she did not know remains. This conclusion contains an implied reversal that points pessimistically to the future. Although he has been rescued from madness, the narrator fully realizes that there will be other moments when neither his beloved nor his fading memories will save him. Thus the threat of hopeless insanity is the crux of the story's conclusion, reversing the entire plot line.

The story's theme of madness and horror is emphasized not only by its title but by Nabokov's depiction of the hero. Like others of his early heroes, this one is an artist, who is, by nature, impressionable. He does not have the equilibrium of the hero of the realistic story "Blagost'." His hypersensitive mind and artistic fervor have detached him from reality. His total and solitary immersion in his writing produces and aggravates recurrent fears and accelerating terror. To reinforce this psychological image, Nabokov used a mirror to draw a physical portrait of the hero—a technique, as I have already noted, employed in other of his early stories. In the realistic story "Port" Nikitin sees himself as a healthy man being shaven in the barbershop mirror. There the image, as in "Sogliadatai" (p. 27) and *Podvig* (p. 201), is merely a "made-strange" device to depict photographically the main character of the story. In "Podlets" the realistic-symbolic mirror reflects Anton Petrovich's physical and psychological deterioration: as Anton Petrovich turns to talk to it, the eyes of the image well up with tears. In "Uzhas" Nabokov made the mirror device still more complex. It does not merely supply an introductory external portrait of the hero and how he sees himself:

> . . . chuzhie, nemigaiushchie glaza, blesk voloskov na skule, ten' vdol' nosa. (p. 96)

> . . . those unblinking alien eyes, that sheen of tiny hairs along the jaw, that shade along the nose. (p. 113)

It also confirms a still deeper mental state in the hero by prompting a distorted reaction from him that borders on madness. These three examples from Nabokov's early stories show his wide-ranging implementation of one and the same device. In "Uzhas" it reaches its most symbolic dimension. Here Nabokov was indebted to Dostoevsky, who used a mirror image in this manner in *The Double,* a work that Nabokov was known to value.[11] In *The Double,* as in "Uzhas," the mirror reflection occurs in the first paragraph and forecasts the hero's divided personality. Nabokov denied that his characters are split, asserting: "There are no 'real' doubles in my novels."[12] However, in "Uzhas," which is not a novel, the hero speaks directly of his *dvoinik.* Thus in this short story, as in *The Double,* the mirror image anticipates and even symbolizes the hero's bifurcated personality. The double hero, with or without the mirror, becomes a basic feature of most of Nabokov's later work, and much has been written on Nabokov's doubles, his own comment notwithstanding. The split hero is developed in "Sogliadatai." In *Otchaianie* and *Lolita,* to name but two novels, the hero is so divided that his alter ego is another actual, named, personality, whether real or imagined.

The woman whom the hero of "Uzhas" loves is, like him, anonymous. The narrator remarks that no one could understand what he found in her. She is uncomplicated, sees the world for what it is, and unquestioningly understands it. Above all, she is mortal and perhaps foresees her death in the opera episode. She is the narrator's blithe spirit in the same way that Chorb's wife is his. The narrator admits:

Bozhe moi, kak ia liubil ee neprimetnuiu milovidnost', veselost', laskovost', ptich'e trepykhanie ee dushi. . . . Ved' delo v tom, chto kak raz ee tikhaia prostota menia okhraniala. (p. 199)

God! how I loved her unassuming prettiness, gaiety, friendliness, the birdlike flutterings of her soul. It was exactly that gentle simplicity of hers that protected me. (p. 116)

Her quiet smiles, laughs, and tears stand in marked contrast to the cataclysmic sense of horror in this story. Her quietude and normalcy provide a structural measure of the narrator's madness. He dreams of her dressed in lace, laughing, but can recall the dream later only with terror. He remembers her mending her silk stockings and recalls her silken legs being pulled out of a heavy boot. These legs are likened to a butterfly emerging from a large cocoon. White lace, silk stockings, images of birds and butterflies connote a grace and fragility that are accentuated by the motifs of gems and color surrounding her: the pearls around her neck; the mother-of-pearl opera glasses; the gold, raspberry, and rose of the opera house. Even in her fright, her eyes sparkle with tears and her mannerisms speak for her. She mangles his cuff, grits her teeth, and rolls up her handkerchief into a ball. Like Chorb's wife she is almost childlike. Andreev wrote that "Sirin's world is full of color, breath, and fragrance, which all come through these pages in spite of the dull sadness inherent in dark human acts" (IV). In this story the beloved one embodies this color, breath, and fragrance. When she lies dying, she is small and delicate against the gigantic pillows. For once she is seen full face. Her hair is pushed aside and shows a distinguishing scar on her temple.

The similarity between the narrator's mistress and Chorb's wife is not the only one in these two stories. The narrator's agony in many ways echoes Chorb's. His separation from his beloved makes the solitary nights insufferable. Compare Chorb's suffering with the narrator's:

Vot tol'ko nochi byli nevynosimy. ("Vozvrashchenie Chorba," p. 8)

Nighttime, though, was unendurable. (pp. 61-62)

. . . eti odinokie nochi byli dlia menia ostrym, bezvykhodnym stradaniem. ("Uzhas," p. 200)

. . . those solitary nights caused me acute unrelieved anguish. (p. 117)

The sounds in the narrator's hotel room—of the falling jacket, for instance—make him jump in much the same way that Chorb is unnerved by the mouse rattling in the wallpaper. In the end the narrator's horror is so great that he completely loses touch with the world around him like Chorb:

Moia sviaz' s mirom porvalas', ia byl sam po sebe i mir byl
sam po sebe,—i v etom mire smysla ne bylo. (p. 202)

My line of communication with the world snapped, I was on
my own and the world was on *its* own, and *that* world was
devoid of sense. (pp. 18-19)

However, unlike Chorb, the narrator is saved by his beloved's
death. In this story the plot moves beyond the gathering together
of meaningful trivia of the loved one's life and the resurrection of
her image. Realistically the narrator notes:

No vremia idet, ee obraz stanovitsia v moei dushe vse
sovershennee i vse bezzhiznennee,—i melochi proshlogo,
zhivye, malen'kie vospominaniia nezametno dlia menia potu-
khaiut. (pp. 204-5)

But time flows, and her image within me becomes ever more
perfect, ever more lifeless. The details of the past, the live
memories, fade imperceptibly. (p. 121)

This story not only moves into the future but moves on a
symbolic plane. The hero is abnormal. The story is full of fear,
horror, screams, nightmares, on the one hand, and fragility
delicacy, and beauty, on the other hand. It deals not with just the
realistic aspects of life, but considers life after death. The problem
of the double and the mirror image recurs here, as we have seen.
Despite its subjectivity, this story is filled with Nabokov's familiar
but ever refreshing motifs. Such trivia as the train platform, the
shaft of light, the butterfly, the trusting dog, the opera, and the
shape of letters punctuate the story. Their concreteness anchors
this symbolic piece.
    The narrator concedes that, even though he is a writer—an artist
of the "word"—he cannot always readily express his intangible
experiences. Three times the "word" escapes him. This almost
becomes a theme in the story. The narrator reflects on cursive
handwriting and wishes that he had some new hitherto unseen

script in which to express himself. Here Nabokov's interest in letter shapes appears.

Despite the narrator's difficulty with words, he expresses himself chiefly in similes. Many of the "made-strange" images take that form. For instance, similes are used in the interlocking technique of which I spoke above. Objects of comparison in one context appear in reality in others, lending an echoing cohesiveness to this story. I pointed out that the image of fear in the opera is used subsequently as an actual experience. Similarly, the image of lying on one's back is used first as an actual experience and then as a simile. The narrator's second moment of horror occurs while he is lying thus. Later he likens a feeling of horror to a frightening memory of his mother leaning over him as he lay flat on his bed. In Nabokov's stories being supine is usually associated with contemplation and even hallucination. In "Passazhir" the narrator eavesdrops on his back. In "Draka" the hero is supine on the beach watching Krause. In *Dar* and *Otchaianie* the central figures are often depicted lying either on their beds or in a wood or park. The narrators of both "Passazhir" and "Uzhas" are released from pondering when they roll over onto their sides. These sketches of supine, pensive heroes are a variation of the double theme. Metaphors are used sparingly because of the already hyperbolic dimension of the subject matter.

Repetition is employed throughout the story, particularly when the narrator experiences his greatest horrors; for instance: "Vysshii uzhas . . . osobennyi uzhas . . ." (p. 198) ("Supreme terror, special terror" [p. 115]), clearly conveying the narrator's nervousness and pointing to his duality. When his loved one's death releases him from this division, he expresses himself directly, without repetition. The language as a whole tends to the "high style." Numerous words are used that, although now completely absorbed into everyday Russian, are derived from Slavonic and lend a lofty air to this story, which grapples with the problems of life and death, sanity and madness, God and devils.

The use of fear vocabulary in connection with the characterization of the hero has already been noted. He cannot escape seeing grotesque visions even in his recollections of his beloved. His image of her is significant, not only because of its distortion, but because it is a fine example of Nabokov's coalescing image. The italics are mine.

V pervuiu noch' ia videl ee vo sne: bylo mnogo solntsa, i ona sidela na posteli v odnoi kruzhevnoi sorochke i do upadu khokhotala, ne mogla ostanovit'sia. I vspomnil ia etot son sovsem sluchaino, prokhodia mimo bel'evogo magazina,—i kogda vspomnil, to pochuvstvoval, kak vse to, chto bylo vo sne veselo,—*ee kruzheva, zakinutoe litso, smekh,*—teper', na iavu, strashno,— i nikak ne mog sebe ob"iasnit', pochemu mne tak nepriiaten, tak otvratitelen etot *kruzhevnoi, khokhochushchii son.* (p. 201)

The first night I saw my girl in dream: sunlight flooded her room, and she sat on the bed wearing only a lacy nightgown, and laughed, and laughed, could not stop laughing. I recalled my dream quite by accident, a couple of hours later, as I was passing a lingerie store, and upon remembering it realized that all that had been so gay in my *dream—her lace, her thrown-back head, her laughter—* was now, in my waking state, frightening. Yet, I could not explain to myself why that *lacy laughing dream* was now so unpleasant, so hideous. (pp. 117-18)

In conclusion, "Uzhas" is a variation of the theme struck in "Bakhman"—an artist's love for a woman. Bachmann goes mad upon the death of Perova, but in "Uzhas" the loved one's death saves the hero from madness, temporarily at least. In "Bakhman" the *siuzhet* is paramount and more realistic. In "Uzhas," as in "Draka," the mood predominates. It is negative and is accentuated by the title and by the unresolved conclusion. The hero will waver between sanity and insanity, finally succumbing to the latter. His grim realization of his fate and that his loved one will not be there to rescue him is the greatest horror of this story and lies beyond its pages. This expressive merging of the themes of beauty and fright and of life and death was immediately recognized by Nabokov's first critics, who singled out "Uzhas" for special reviews.[13]

4. "Katastrofa"

The fatality threatening the young hero of "Uzhas" is actualized in "Katastrofa" ("A Catastrophe," recently retitled "Details of a Sunset").[14] The tram accident mentioned by Frau Ott in "Skazka" provides the central event in this fine early story. The young German hero is hit by a streetcar, wavers between life and death, and finally passes away. Again Nabokov's story has an underlying love theme. Mark Standfuss's joyful love for his fiancée, Klara Heise, completely absorbs and motivates him.

"Katastrofa" is masterfully structured and artistically integrated. It is embellished with elements of suspense and surprise. Typical Nabokovian images and artistic devices are woven through the fabric of the story. The exposition moves directly into the action. The absence of a formal or even lucid presentation of the situation points to the disjointed, symbolic nature of "Katastrofa." Its hero, Mark, is pictured as inebriated, returning home after a bachelor party. His head spins from too much beer and too many happy thoughts of Klara. This introductory, aimless action culminates in Mark's drunken clambering upstairs to his mother. It has a zigzag, almost hesitating rhythm. Mark makes his way up, only to lose hold of his thin walking stick, which then tumbles down the stairs. He falls back to retrieve it, and then gropes his way up once again.

This image of the walking stick *(trost')* is repeated widely in Nabokov's fiction. Like the mirror image, the walking-stick image demonstrates Nabokov's broad artistic use of the motifs peculiar to him. Symbolic aspects of the stick, which are not germane here, have been considered by Rowe.[15] In "Kartofel'nyi El'f," "Bakhman," and even "Sogliadatai" (pp. 15-22), it serves as a realistic detail with no secondary connotation. In *Otchaianie* the walking stick is the clue to the mystery plot. This motif eventually reappears as a cane in Nabokov's realistic novel *Pnin* (pp.164-65). Although Pnin's cane is mentioned parenthetically, the paragraph-long description of it is excessive, and the cane itself is overdecorated. It serves as a superlative example of Nabokov's use of Flaubertian realism. In "Katastrofa" the walking stick has a secondary role. It underlines Mark's intoxicated movements.

Having picked up his stick, Mark finally reaches his mother at the apartment door. This scene echoes the one in "Zvonok" when Galatov appears at his mother's flat, but here it is a physical high point that reflects an emotional joy. Mark's mother's warm but firm parental reception does not dispel his happiness, as does that of Frau Nellis for Galatov. Mark's mother douses his dizzy head, and he falls asleep.

Again a Nabokovian dream provides a structural transition. Nikitin's dream in "Port" has no secondary meaning; it is merely a structural switch. In "Groza" the dream has a symbolic dimension, as it is unclear if the hero ever awakens and if his episode with Elijah is a dream or reality. Here, significantly, Mark's dream is a nightmare of his deceased father beckoning him. This is not only a technical device, bridging the introduction and the rising action, but also stylistically foreshadows Mark's approaching catastrophe, which will also be portrayed as a dream. This latter approach has been used in "Uzhas." In "Katastrofa" the nightmare accentuates the sense of doom that was inconspicuously forecast in the introduction by two seemingly insignificant details: the opening image of the speeding tram, and Mark's almost Gothic view of the coffinlike moving van that he noted on his way.

The rising action begins with a new day, when Mark at work recalls his dream with a shudder and a shake. As in "Uzhas," so here a dream causes a delayed reaction, confirming that the hero has consciously registered his frightening subconscious experience. An internal experience is thus externalized. Mark then falls to musing about his future life with Klara, and more immediately about their evening date. Another typical Nabokovian scene occurs here: Mark sells ties, as Franz does in Dreyer's emporium in *Korol' dama valet.* In "Katastrofa" everything mirrors Mark's joy; even the ties reflect his happiness:

I galstuki, kotorye on predlagal, iarko ulybalis', sochuvstvovali ego schast'iu. (p. 150)

And the neckties he offered his customers smiled brightly, in sympathy with his happiness. (p. 20)

A two-paragraph interruption reveals that while Mark is at work, his mother is visited by Klara's distraught mother. She emotionally relates that Klara has lost her head and has jilted Mark. With this aside, the rising action of "Katastrofa" acquires an element of complex suspense. The reader, but not Mark, knows the catastrophic news that his mother has for him. The action accelerates as Mark heads home once again and reaches the door, pushing it into cold emptiness. Just as he is about to step in, Adolf, his companion, pulls him away for a drink at a bar. The news thus is withheld from him. After the drink, Mark decides to head straight for Klara's. Again the news is withheld; Mark will now learn of Klara's change of heart, not from his sympathetic mother, but from Klara herself. This suspense is compounded by Mark's blindly loving thoughts of his fiancée, which are now out of keeping with reality. Ironically, he feels happiest as the tram speeds him to what will be an emotional catastrophe. He is so absorbed with thoughts of Klara that he misses his tram stop. Rather than waiting patiently for the next stop, Mark jumps off in eager anticipation. Nabokov repeats the image in *Dar* (p. 196). Fedor misses his stop and jumps off of the moving tram, unharmed. In "Katastrofa" Mark is hit.[16]

This climax is enigmatically described: "Odnovremenno pro-izoshlo neskol'ko strannykh veshchei . . ." (p. 153) ("Several odd things occurred simultaneously" [p. 23]). But what precisely happens remains unclear, and the situation is unraveled only obliquely in the falling action. As in "Kartofel'nyi El'f," the climax is clarified only in the conclusion. As a result, another aspect of suspense is introduced. The hero and the reader together are confused as to what has occurred.

The falling action is the strongest part of "Katastrofa." In this section it is slowly revealed that an oncoming vehicle has hit Mark. In his delirium he inverts reality: "Tozhe . . . chut' ne popal pod omnibus . . ." (p. 153) ("That was stupid. Almost got run over by a bus . . ." [p. 23]). Thus the final catastrophe has not been emotional but physical. In a semiconscious state, Mark retraces his steps and rethinks his hopes and dreams. This section thereby parallels the rising action. All that Mark viewed realistically or objectively in that section is viewed fantastically and subjectively in the falling action: Klara's image, the city buildings, streets, the moving van. Consider the contrasting images of the van. First there is a direct view of the van:

. . . tam, chto gromadnye groba, stoiali mebel'nye furgony. Ikh razdulo ot gruza. Bog vest', chto bylo navaleno v nikh. Dubovye bauly, verno, da liustry, kak zheleznye pauki, da tiazhkie kostiaki dvukhspal'noi krovati. Luna obduvala ikh krepkim bleskom. (p. 148)

Several moving vans stood there like enormous coffins. They were bloated from their loads. Heaven knows what was piled inside them. Oakwood trunks, probably, and chandeliers like iron spiders, and the heavy skeleton of a double bed. The moon cast a hard glare on the vans. (p. 18)

The matching grotesque image is punctuated by question marks and suspension points:

Chernyi znakomyi zabor. Rassmeialsia: akh, konechno—furgony . . . Stoiali oni, kak gromadnye groba. Chto zhe skryto v nikh? Sokrovishcha, kostiaki velikanov? Pyl'nye grudy pyshnoi mebeli? (p. 154)

That black fence again. He could not help laughing as he recognized the vans beyond. There they stood, like gigantic coffins. Whatever might they conceal within? Treasures? The skeletons of giants? Or dusty mountains of sumptuous furniture? (pp. 23-24) [17]

These subjective views of the falling action imply that all is not well with the hero. Further, his joyful and distorted dreams of Klara give way to sensations of physical pain that become more frequent as the action falls.

The conclusion is strong. It not only resolves the story by describing the hero's death, but verifies what has occurred in the climax. The irony of the conclusion is that the expected romantic catastrophe that had been strongly intimated in the rising action never comes to pass. Instead, the street catastrophe and death save Mark from heartbreak. The expected confrontation between Mark and Klara, like that of Mashen'ka and Ganin, never happens. This is accented by Mark's final delirious question at the hospital: "Why isn't Klara here . . ." The absence of the question mark is significant; at this point Mark dies.

The entire intense story is tightly held together not only by unity of place, a German city, and of time, twenty-four hours, and the small number of characters, but also by the stylistic interlocking of details. On the first page, two elements of eventual conflict are immediately presented. The significant tram is shown as it moves into the haze of the city. Then Mark appears, moving through this haze. His wisp of hair *(khvostik)* is noted, followed by the statement that Klara loved him for this wisp. Their forthcoming wedding is then mentioned. The *siuzhet* unravels like a moving chain, in a pattern similar to AB BC CD.

The story is related entirely from Mark's viewpoint, but with shifting tenses and varying narrative methods: dreams, nightmares, reveries, subconscious thoughts. This shifting narrative, so integral a part of the symbolic approach, anticipates the more enigmatic narrative shifts in "Sogliadatai." The first page is almost an interior monologue, with Mark drunkenly thinking to himself:

Chto-zh, popletemsia peshkom, khotia ty ochen' p'ian, Mark, ochen' p'ian . . . (p. 147)

Well, might as well just plod along, even though you are pretty drunk, Mark, pretty drunk. . . . (p. 17)

Here the narrator is not designated, and this device of mentally speaking to one's self as if to another person, structurally forecasts a duality in Mark's characterization that is accentuated in the falling action. Mark is also described by an omniscient observer as he wends his way home. The narrative then shifts to the dialogue between Mark and his mother, and that is followed by the prophetic dream. As noted above, Nabokov called attention to this dream by having Mark recall it only the next day, when Adolf's senseless teasing at the store brings it to mind. Mark's dialogue with Adolf gives way to an omniscient description of Mark's thoughts, which in this instance are set off by quotation marks and the speaker is identified:

"O, kak ia schastliv," dumal Mark, "kak vse chestvuet moe schast'e." (p. 152)

"Oh, how happy I am," Mark kept musing, "how everything around celebrates my happiness." (p. 22)

These varied views of Mark in the rising action, although disorienting, prepare for the masterful falling action, where all is described from Mark's semiconscious viewpoint, which realistically wavers between consciousness and unconsciousness. The distortion of the introductory scenes in the falling action further confirms the hero's mental condition. For example, his dazed state on the street is first denoted by his observation of the building rooftops, implying his position:

Tam, v vyshine, Mark razlichal skvoznye portiki, frizy i freski, shpalery oranzhevykh roz, krylatye statui, podnimaiushchie k nebu zolotye, nesterpimo goriashchie liry. Volnuias' i blistaia, prazdnichno i vozdushno ukhodila v nebesnuiu dal' vsia eta zodcheskaia prelest', i Mark ne mog poniat', kak ran'she ne zamechal on etikh gallerei, etikh khramov, povisshikh v vyshine. (p. 154)

Up there, Mark could discern translucent porticoes, friezes and frescoes, trellises covered with orange roses, winged statues that lifted skyward golden, unbearably blazing lyres. In bright undulations, ethereally, festively, these architectonic enchantments were receding into the heavenly distance, and Mark could not understand how he had never noticed before those galleries, those temples suspended on high. (p. 23)

Earlier, the narrator had pointedly observed that the rooftops were rarely noted by passersby. Another such image distortion is that of the swinging lamp, which fluctuates between being Klara's green dress, and a green lamp, which in turn could be a lamp in the street or in the operating room. This lamp recalls one hanging on a similar cord in Chorb's hotel room. The ambiguity of this lamp acts as a transitional image between the street scene and the hospital where Mark dies. Mark's distorted view of his surroundings is supplemented by the thoughts and dreams of Klara. In his delirium, he continues from where he left off at the moment of his accident. He sees the window pane of her room bisected by a green branch. This detail of a bisected rectangle recurs in several of Nabokov's subsequent early works.[18]

In Mark's dream Klara meets him at Nabokov's typical wrought-iron gate. His vision of Klara's party brings to mind the one in Tat'iana's dream of Eugene Onegin. The doctor and Adolf, both of whom Mark has just seen, are the only familiar faces at the snow-white table. By this depiction of Mark's unconscious musings, the double theme hinted at in "Podlets" and later in "Uzhas" enters this story. Nabokov's use of this theme, which is intimated in the rising action when Mark talks to himself, is the most essential feature of the falling action. The split in Mark signals the accident:

Uvidel poodal' svoiu zhe figuru, khuduiu spinu Marka Shtandfussa, kotoryi, kak ni v chem ne byvalo shel naiskos' cherez ulitsu. (p. 153)

He saw, at a distance, his own figure, the slender back of Mark Standfuss, who was walking diagonally across the street as if nothing had happened. (p. 23)

This duality is later reiterated:

. . . Mark uvidel sebia samogo, poodal', sidiashchego riadom s Klaroi—i ne uspel uvidet', kak uzhe sam kasalsia kolenom ee teploi shelkovoi iubki. (p. 155)

. . . Mark saw himself sitting a little way off, beside Klara, and no sooner had he seen it than he found himself brushing his knee against her warm silk skirt. (p. 25)

There is no direct reference to the double per se and no mirroring of Mark's image as in "Uzhas." The doubling device is employed more subtly, forecasting the sophisticated version in "Sogliadatai." In *Dar* the indistinction between the hero's realistic and dreaming actions is comparable to that in "Katastrofa."

The falling action is mental rather than physical, and it nears its nadir when Mark subsides into delirium:

Inostranets na reke sovershaet vysheukazannye molitvy. . . . (p. 156)

The foreigner is offering the aforementioned prayers on the river. . . . (p. 25)

Structurally, this implies his death and restates the alternative that awaited him had he lived—rivalry with the foreign roomer for Klara's love. The action slows and the narrator observes that Mark was tired and wanted to sleep.

The conclusion verifies objectively what has already been suggested:

Mark lezhal zabintovannyi, iskoverkannyi, lampa ne kachalas' bol'she. (p. 156)

Mark was lying supine, mutilated and bandaged, and the lamp was not swinging any longer. (p. 25)

The doctor is there, clicking his tongue like the dentist in "Zvonok." Mark's death is poetically depicted:

A Mark uzhe ne dyshal, Mark ushel,—v kakie sny—neizvestno. (p. 156)

Mark no longer breathed, Mark had departed—whither, into what other dreams, none can tell. (p. 26)

The manner of his death had been metaphorically suggested in the opening sentence of the story by the spark that ran headlong along the tram line and was then extinguished.

Mark is physically portrayed only twice in the story, with very meager details: he is blond, with light eyes, and pink pimples on his chin. Klara is the embodiment of his happiness and indirectly

brings him to his death. As with Mashen'ka and the heroines of
"Blagost'" and "Vozvrashchenie Chorba," she never appears
directly: her effect on others is what is shown. For Mark she is red
hair, a green silk dress, bare arms, and quiet laughter. This sensual
combination recurs in various configurations, culminating in the
likening of her skirt to a green sail and her bright hair to apricot
jam. In the end the green billowing dress becomes the green lamp
looming over Mark. There is no dimension to her personality
except that her affection for Mark in no way matches his for her.
The threat of her former love—the foreign roomer who had left her
home without paying all of his rent—recurs throughout the story.
In the exposition, Mark reassures himself that he has no riv•l in
this man, recalling that Klara swore she had forgotten her former
love. His own mother's admonition is soon followed by the
revelation by Klara's mother that the roomer has returned and
charmed Klara. Mark's concluding incoherent remark about the
foreigner not only ties the story together but reveals that sub-
consciously Mark had felt threatened by this rival. Klara's
inconstancy is negatively judged by the image of her mother's
disapproving face. On the other hand, Klara's tears, which Mark
in his blind love had understood as an expression of affection, now
in retrospect take on hypocritical, even negative connotations.
Mark's blindness to her doubts makes his approaching confrontation with her all the more painful and increases the story's
mounting tension.

The two mothers sitting in the immaculate German kitchen,
crewcut Adolf, and the funny man reading the medical journal on
the tram are the only other significant figures in this story. The
latter two recur in Mark's dream, taking on grotesque proportions:

Sredi nikh byl Adol'f, smuglyi, s kvadratnoi golovoi; byl i tot,
korotkonogii, puzatyi, vse eshche urchashchii chelovek,
chitavshii meditsinskii zhurnal v tramvae. (p. 155)

Among them was Adolf, swarthy, with his square-shaped
head; there was also that short-legged, big-bellied old man
who had been reading a medical journal in the tram and was
still grumbling. (p. 24)

The German city background is obliquely indicated by the names of the central characters. In Cyrillic orthography, Mark Standfuss and Klara Heise look particularly amusing. The vendor who gently and sadly in birdlike fashion whistles "viurstkhen" (*Würstchen*) confirms the locale. A moving van and trams, all urban vehicles, pass through this story as well. As we have noted, in Nabokov's stories the streets are often being worked on. Here the rails are being repaired, as indicated by a black wigwam and red warning lights. The asphalt streets shimmer and shine through the city haze. At times these streets move in Nabokovian fashion.

As in many of the early stories, the city is described particularly effectively at sunset or at night. These Gogolian lyrical asides—for example, concerning the building facades—are both objective (p. 152) and subjective (pp. 153-54). These particular lengthy passages are fine instances of Nabokov's poetic prose, which is rich in this story. All the traditional tropes are implemented. Klara's image is a shorter poetic fragment:

. . . potom zakruzhilas' po komnate,—iubka—zelenyi parus,—i bystro-bystro stala priglazhivat' pered zerkalom iarkie volosy svoi, tsveta abrikosovogo varen'ia. (p. 150)

. . . she began whirling about the room, her skirt like a green sail, and then she started rapidly smoothing her glossy hair, the color of apricot jam, in front of the mirror. (p. 20)

I have already shown that when Mark is injured, the images shift from the normal to the grotesque. There is a parallel linguistic change. For example, when Mark becomes semiconscious, poetic images acquire another dimension. His reveries in delirium are metaphorically described, but this poetry is not an aesthetic expression alone; the metaphor actually reveals the distortions of Mark's mind. The following passage literally describes Mark's warped sense of reality:

Rvanulsia on,—i zelenoe plat'e Klary poplylo, umen'shilos', prevratilos' v zelenyi stekliannyi kolpak lampy. (p. 155)

He writhed, and Klara's green dress floated away, diminished, and turned into the green shade of a lamp. (p. 25)

The city scene is filled with sparkling, glare, and glistening. All colors abound, save blue. Shadows and silhouettes also figure in the descriptions. These chiaroscuro effects are not as numerous as in "Vozvrashchenie Chorba," but the tree casting its shadow is found in both stories, as is the river image. Compare them:

V etom spokoinom germanskom gorode, gde vozdukh byl chut' matovyi, i na reke vot uzhe vos'moi vek poperechnaia zyb' slegka tushevala otrazhennyi sobor. ("Vozvrashchenie Chorba," p. 5)

In that pacific German city, where the very air seemed a little lusterless and where a transverse row of ripples had kept shading gently the reflected cathedral for well over seven centuries. (p. 59)

. . . ognennyi zakat mlel v prolete kanala, i vlazhnyi most vdali byl okaimlen tonkoi zolotoiu chertoi, po kotoroi pro-khodili chernye figury. ("Katastrofa," p. 152)

. . . the flush of a fiery sunset filled the vista of the canal, and a rain-streaked bridge in the distance was margined by a narrow rim of gold along which passed tiny black figures. (p. 21)

In "Port" and "Britva" characters move and their shadows also move and bend, usually along nearby walls or streets. In "Katastrofa" this play of light and shadow is more sophisticated. The light-and-shadow image of Mark climbing up the stairs is succinct and prepares the reader for the hero's fatal division:

Zheltyi klin sveta zakhvatil perila, stupeni, trost',—i Mark, tiazhelo i radostno dysha, podnialsia na ploshchadku, a po stene podnialas' za nim ego chernaia, gorbataia ten'. (p. 149)

A yellow wedge of light encompassed the banisters, the stairs, and his cane, and Mark, panting and pleased, climbed up again to the landing, and his black, hunchbacked shadow followed him up along the wall. (p. 19) [19]

Although "Katastrofa" is set in Nabokov's favored German locale, realistic details of the backdrop do not intrude into Mark's story. He, like other heroes, wavers between reality and unreality. Here, however, this does not point to emotional instability, but to his physical state. In "Katastrofa" Nabokov uses the theme of reality-unreality to indicate a normal reaction to a desperately serious accident. The hero's vacillation is resolved, not by recovery, but by death.

5. "Rozhdestvo"

In "Rozhdestvo" ("Christmas") Nabokov inverted the basic plot line of "Katastrofa." This early symbolic story opens with a death and concludes with a birth. As in "Vozvrashchenie Chorba," "Port," and "Zvonok," the plot centers around man's confrontation with his memories. Specifically, Nabokov varied the pattern of "Zvonok," where a son searches for a parent. In "Rozhdestvo" the parent searches for his son. A lone, grieving father comes face to face with happy memories of his dead son and as a result is spiritually awakened and saved from suicide.

The plot is clearly delineated. Nabokov divided this nine-page story into four sections. In Part I, in the evening, Sleptsov, blind with grief, looks at the funeral wax on his fingers. In Part II, the following morning, he goes outside and recalls his child, whom he has just buried. In Part III, he visits his child's grave, only to be further saddened. In the evening he goes to the child's room and breaks down in tears. He gathers a few of the boy's belongings into a drawer. In the final section, the father brings these treasures into the heated wing of the house and examines them. The poignancy of these momentoes causes him to reject life altogether. At that instant, something snaps and the father opens his eyes. In the warmth of the room, a beautiful butterfly has broken out of his son's treasured cocoon.

This story of the grieving father recalls Chekhov's story "Despair," in which Iona Potapov seeks release from his paternal grief by sharing it with someone. Like "Despair," this story belongs structurally to the twentieth-century short-story form. The tradi-tional rising action—the moment at which the hero loses his freedom of action—occurs before the beginning of the story when Sleptsov's son dies and is buried. The entire story is the intensifica-tion of his grief until the ultimate climax, when the butterfly is released from the cocoon, forcing Sleptsov to open his eyes and to turn from thoughts of suicide. This is not completely unexpected. The father's memories of his child are consistently related to the butterfly. The traditional ending is absent, but a reversal in Sleptsov's mood is implied. The title—"Rozhdestvo"—intensifies this positive tone; it means nativity.

As the mood of "Rozhdestvo" provides the drama, there is little conflict. Instead, the reader is presented with a compressed situation. The location is restricted to Sleptsov's summer home, which until this point has provided only happy memories. Time becomes telescoped to a critical twenty-four-hour period, reflecting Nabokov's more intense and modernistic approach. This temporal element is precisely indicated as the story progresses. It is both explicitly stated and indirectly reflected in the story's setting.

Even though the title connotes joy, a minor note is struck in the opening sentence:

Vernuvshis' po vechereiushchim snegam iz sela v svoiu myzu, Sleptsov sel v ugol, na nizkii pliushevyi stul, na kotorom on ne sizhival nikogda. Tak byvaet posle bol'shikh neschastii. (p. 67)

After walking back from the village to his manor across the dimming snows, Sleptsov sat down in a corner, on a plush-covered chair which he never remembered using before. It was the kind of thing that happens after some great calamity. (p. 153)

Here the central and essentially the only character in the story is introduced. He is solitary and grief-stricken. Nabokov makes Sleptsov's experience immediate by using the second person pronoun and the present tense, thereby involving the reader in the drama:

—kogda vse koncheno, i ty, poshatyvaias', stuchish' zubami,
nichego ne vidish' ot slez. (p. 67)

. . . and you are reeling from grief, your teeth chattering, your
eyes blinded by tears. (p. 153)

Even his name, Sleptsov, phonically suggests that he is blinded:
slepoi meaning "the blind one." In these introductory sentences,
questions are implied: What was this terrible misfortune? Who was
it that died? "Rozhdestvo" has the answer to these questions. It
shows Sleptsov's agony over his son's death.

Sleptsov's mental processes, not his physical motion, give this
story its momentum. This is accomplished by the stream-of-
experience narrative method. The circumscribed setting of this
story further accentuates Sleptsov's mood and thoughts.

Sleptsov has come from St. Petersburg for a few days to his
country estate.[20] This pre-Revolutionary Russian background is
unusual for Nabokov. The entire experience is implicitly unusual
for Sleptsov, as well. He is in his summer home in midwinter. He is
in the wing, not the main part of the house, sitting in an unfamiliar
corner in an unfamiliar chair. He feels strange. The room swims
before his eyes, and he feels as though he were in a doctor's waiting
room. He does not notice his servant Ivan, who brings him light.
All he sees is Ivan's reflected ear and gray cropped hair in the
propped-up mirror. Again the mirror is used in a magnificent
"made-strange" technique. The furniture also plays its appointed
Nabokovian role. The corner and the plush chair are likened to
distant acquaintances of Sleptsov. Nabokov further notes that after
the worst misfortunes, one is most comforted by the unfamiliar.
Even the door of this wing squeaks gently shut when Ivan departs.
Sleptsov, in his turn, prefers not to awaken the familiar part of the
house, perhaps because he does not want to arouse the memories
hidden there.

Nabokov's artistic camera moves in such a way that the reader
essentially sees what Sleptsov sees. This type of highly selective
description characterizes Nabokov's symbolic direction. Shifting
from the chair in the corner to Sleptsov directly, the reader, like
the hero, sees only Sleptsov's hands. Hands are an expressive
feature of any personality and Sleptsov's wax-covered fingers

reveal his immediate tragedy: he has taken part in a funeral. As he distends his fingers, the wax cracks. Like Chorb, Sleptsov stretches his fingers at a critical moment. He breaks his last tangible link with his son.

The following morning, Sleptsov moves from the confines of the house into the quiet sunshine outside. The setting is sympathetic. The floorboards refract the morning sun with agility. The white bench reflects the many-colored window panes:

> ... na beluiu lavku legli raiskimi rombami otrazheniia tsvetnykh stekol. (p. 68)

> ... the reflections of the many-colored panes formed paradisal lozenges on the white-washed cushionless window seats. (p. 154)

This "made-strange" image occurs here in an oblique and nascent form. It contrasts with a similar but more straightforward passage about a pavilion window appearing in *Mashen'ka:*

> In its small diamond-shaped window frames were panes of different-colored glass: if, say, you looked through a blue one the world seemed frozen in a lunar trance; through a yellow one, everything appeared extraordinarily gay; through a red one, the sky looked pink and the foliage as dark as burgundy. Some of the panes were broken, their jagged edges joined up by a spider's web. (pp. 86-87)

Later, in his autobiography, Nabokov was to recall a comparable scene from his childhood: "On the white window ledges, on the long window seats covered with faded calico, the·sun breaks into geometrical gems after passing through rhomboids and squares of stained glass" (p. 105). Likewise, in *Pnin,* Nabokov observed that crystal candlestick reflections "reminded my sentimental friend of the stained glass casements that colored the sunlight orange and green and violet on the verandas of Russian country houses" (p. 146). This realistic image reappears with a symbolic slant in *Lolita:*

One of the latticed squares in a small cobwebby casement window at the turn of the staircase was glazed with ruby, and that raw wound among the unstained rectangles and its asymmetrical position—a knight's move from the top—always disturbed me. (p. 194)

This last example is an elaborate variation of the window-pane image. The reflections are combined here with Nabokov's image of bisected rectangles, chinks of light, and chess moves.

In "Rozhdestvo" this casement window image is followed by another colorful reflecting detail. As Sleptsov moves onward, the icicle hanging from the door reflects a blue-green color. The door, although it does not give way easily to Sleptsov, sweetly cracks open. The reader sees only colorless, salient bits of Sleptsov's clothing: his caracul jacket, his hat, his high boots. The beauty of nature surprises Sleptsov. His teeth no longer chatter from grief, but instead they feel the cold. Like his home, the landscape becomes animate. The snowbanks hug the house, and the fir trees lift their paws out from under the weight of the snow. Like Sleptsov, they are all oppressed with burdens, but they glisten and sparkle nonetheless. Similarly, Sleptsov, although grieving, can still see beauty as he looks at the fountainlike frozen bush. This quiet magnificence comforts him until he spots the snow-covered bridge post. It jars his memory. He angrily reacts and shoves the snow off of the rail and recoils into his grief. Here the stream-of-experience narrative makes his memory highly vivid: it was summer and his son was looking at him. Now the child is dead, and only the memory of laughter under a straw hat, with strong legs in wet sandals, remains for Sleptsov. This vision is the personification of boyish joy and happiness. This phantom child, like Chorb's bride, is lively as he catches his butterflies, and he will be remembered for his fast-moving sandals just as Chorb's wife is recalled by her dancing slippers. Sleptsov drifts into the recent past, remembering the boy's delirium, his queries about a butterfly cocoon, and then his death. Sleptsov's agony wells up as he tries to move away from the vivid tragedy.

Sleptsov cuts a new path into the blinding snow and leans against a solitary tree, looking into the distance where the woods are cut through. As he looks toward the ice-cracked river, he focuses on the blinding, shining church cross. This passage recalls a comparable scene in "Port" when, alone and lost, Nikitin looks at the blinding sunlit sea.

In the afternoon Sleptsov rides to this beckoning church. As at the bridge railing, so here the rail of his son's grave evokes a tormenting response. For Sleptsov, as for Chorb, the rail is painful: it burns through his woolen glove. The memories of his child are less alive under the snow here at the grave than on the snow-covered bridge. The bridge has preserved under its snow countless traces of the fast-moving sandals. This image of tracks and traces recurs in "Rozhdestvo." The trace of wax on Sleptsov's finger, the yellow spot left by the dog in the snow, and Sleptsov's own blue foot tracks indicate Nabokov's absorbing interest in impressions. This artistic observation takes on significance in *Podvig* (p. 205) and *Dar* (p. 97), to name but a few of the later works. These images are all magnifications of the red granular image already discussed. (See above, p. 42.)

Sleptsov returns home disappointed. He has been painfully confronted with memories of his son and is unavoidably drawn to the child's room. In the evening he takes up the lamp himself; neither Ivan nor nature lights his way now. The house reflects his paternal agony. The gallery does not smell of winter. As he enters, the door opens with a heavy wail and the parquet floor cracks agitatedly. The covered furniture seems shrouded. Sleptsov himself is out of proportion and unrecognizable as his shadow and reflection move grotesquely along the walls and windows in Nabokovian fashion.

But a happy past has been retained in his son's room. Now Sleptsov smells, as well as sees, his son's presence. The ripped butterfly net smells of summer in the same way that Chorb's wife's clothes were fragrant with her fine perfume. The clutter of meaningless objects, however, compels the father into heartrending sobs as he drops his head on the child's desk top. This desk and the chest of drawers full of his butterfly collection evoke vivid memories of his son enjoying lepidoptery. Now the butterflies, like the boy, are dead. The father gathers up a few belongings: a blue school notebook-diary, a collapsible butterfly net, tacks, and a little

English biscuit box [21] containing a three-ruble cocoon. Sleptsov puts these souvenirs into a drawer and brings them into the warm wing of the house. Like Chorb, he has a treasure chest of memories.

In the last scene of "Rozhdestvo," Sleptsov is completely out of tune with his surroundings. His face is now visible and is scarred with grief:

Sleptsov, oziabshii, zaplakannyi, s piatnami temnoi pyli, pristavshei k shcheke. (p. 72)

Sleptsov . . . chilled, red-eyed, with gray dust smears on his cheek. (p. 158)

The brilliance of the moonlight does not attract him. Ivan, who had earlier given Sleptsov light, now has brought him a Christmas tree. On its cross-shaped peak he ties a candle. However, Sleptsov rejects Ivan's reminder that it is Christmas Eve in six terse words and distractedly thinks of his tragedy. He delves into the treasures. As he reads his child's notebook, he focuses on the boy's handwriting, a repeated Nabokovian motif:

. . . detskii pocherk podnimaiushchiisia, zavorachivaiushchii na poliakh. (p. 73)

. . . the childish handwriting that slanted up then curved down in the margin. (p. 159)

Sleptsov feels that he is learning the child's secrets, but that not all is revealed. In trying to find his son, Sleptsov has learned much about the child's past and he has also learned that much will remain unknown or unexplained. He becomes inconsolable. His tears are now dry, and he is totally blind to the world around him. To him life is barren and void of miracles. At the moment when he can think of no release from sorrow other than death, Sleptsov hears a snap—a noise that has been metaphorically forecast by the cracking of the wax on his fingers, the creaking doors, the squeaking floors, the echoing woodchops, and the ticking clock. At the sound Sleptsov opens his eyes and sees a glorious butterfly that has broken the cocoon and is gaining its strength. His son's treasure has yielded a new, exquisite life. In burying his own treasure box, his son's casket, Sleptsov has uncovered his son's cache. Birth such as this is beautiful and, above all, miraculous, especially at Christmas. It has opened the eyes of the dying.

This butterfly is the metaphorical transfiguration of Sleptsov's memories of his lost son. In many ways this new life projects his spirit. Its near-human qualities link it to the boy, as seen in the following descriptions; first, of the boy, and then, of the nocturnal lepidoptera. The italics are mine.

(1) Po slizkim doskam, useiannym serezhkami, prokhodil ego syn, lovkim vzmakhom sachka sryval babochku, sevshuiu na perila. Vot on uvidel ottsa. Nepovtorimym smekhom igraet litso pod *zagnutym kraem* potemnevshei ot solntsa solomennoi *shliapy*, ruka terebit tsepochku i kozhanyi koshelek na shirokom poiase, veselo rasstavleny milye, gladkie, korichnevye nogi v korotkikh sarzhevykh shtanakh, v promokshikh sandal'iakh. (p. 69)

There was his son walking along the slippery planks, flecked with aments, and deftly plucking off with his net a butterfly that had settled on the railing. Now the boy sees his father. Forever lost laughter plays on his face, under the turned-down brim of a straw hat burned dark by the sun; his hand toys with the chainlet of the leather purse attached to his belt, his dear, smooth, suntanned legs in their serge shorts and soaked sandals assume their usual cheerful wide-spread stance. (p. 155)

(2) Ono stalo krylatym nezametno, *kak nezametno stanovitsia prekrasnym muzhaiushchee litso.* I kryl'ia—eshche slabye, eshche vlazhnye—vse prodolzhali rasti, raspravliat'sia, vot razvernulis' do predela, polozhennogo im Bogom,—i na stene uzhe byla—vmesto komochka, vmesto chernoi myshi,—gromadnaia nochnaia babochka, indiiskii shelkopriad, chto letaet, kak ptitsa, v sumrake, vokrug fonarei Bombeia.

I togda prostertye *kryl'ia zagnutye, na kontsakh* temnobarkhat-
nye, s chetyr'mia sliudianymi okontsami, vzdokhnuli v poryve
nezhnogo, voskhititel'nogo, pochti chelovecheskogo schast'ia. (p. 75)

It became a winged thing imperceptibly, as a maturing face
imperceptibly becomes beautiful. And its wings—still feeble,
still moist—kept growing and unfolding, and now they were
developed to the limit set for them by God, and there, on the
wall, instead of a little lump of life, instead of a dark mouse,
was a great *Attacus* moth like those that fly, birdlike, around
lamps in the Indian dusk.

And then those thick black wings, with a glazy eyespot on
each and a purplish bloom dusting their hooked foretips, took
a full breath under the impulse of tender, ravishing, almost
human happiness. (p. 161) [22]

The symbolism of the butterfly that culminates in this final
passage is matched by other rich poetic images in "Rozhdestvo."
The story is replete with "made-strange" tropes in the Nabokovian
adjective-noun and noun-verb configurations. I have commented
already upon the personification of the house and its furniture as
devices to reflect Sleptsov's deepening grief. Light, both natural
and artificial, infuses "Rozhdestvo," poetically accentuating the
natural beauty that Sleptsov momentarily rejects. This illumination does not spotlight individual moments, but rather serves as a
brilliant contrasting background to Sleptsov's mental blindness.
Earthly designs are multishaped, rainbow-hued, and glisten and
sparkle. Attributes of color, glass, metal, mineral, and texture recur
in tropes. Nearly all of the colors of the spectrum are indicated.
Metals and minerals are numerous—silvery, metallic, tin, mica.
The related iridescent image of mother-of-pearl is also employed.
This image is comparable to Nabokov's multicolored refractions of
window panes and glass crystals. These early polychromatic
touches are in their turn similar to the peacock or pavonine motifs
that describe iridescence in "Sogliadatai" (p. 84), *Lolita* (p. 165),
and *Transparent Things* (p. 27), for example. These various devices
all convey the impression of many colors at once. Images of
feathers, velvet, and silk reflect Nabokov's fascination with texture.

The following excerpt is a fine example of the poetically integrated style of "Rozhdestvo":

Noch' byla sizaia, lunnaia; tonkie tuchi, kak sovinye per'ia, rassypalis' po nebu, no ne kasalis' legkoi ledianoi luny. Derev'ia—grudy serogo ineia—otbrasyvali chernuiu ten' na sugroby, zagoravshiesia tam i siam metallicheskoi iskroi. (p. 72)

The night was smoke-blue and moonlit; thin clouds were scattered about the sky but did not touch the delicate, icy moon. The trees, masses of gray frost, cast dark shadows on the drifts, which scintillated here and there with metallic sparks. (p. 158)

The child's butterfly collection is this natural beauty in microcosm. It is polychromatic, exquisitely designed, jeweled, and it glitters in the light under the glass lids of the case. Like the snow-covered porch steps that appear to be sprinkled with cinnamon, or the bridge planks scattered with catkin in the summertime, so the mother-of-pearl background of the reddish butterfly's wings is sprinkled with black in Nabokov's granular patterning. The total effect of this wealth of images is climaxed in this final graceful butterfly. Appropriately, this Bombay silk weaver is the most beautiful and probably the first of the Nabokovian lepidopteral images. Soon afterward the butterfly appeared in "Pil'gram," and it has been a hallmark of every significant Nabokov creation since—as a fleeting image at least. Most recently it has recurred in Ada's childhood passion for butterflies. This trait reflects Nabokov's own personal and highly professional love for butterflies.[23] In Chapter 6 of *Speak, Memory*, he explained that this love was first "felt in connection with a rectangle of framed sunlight" (p. 119). Thus Nabokov's fictional butterflies and chinks of light were originally joined in his own early life experience.

"Rozhdestvo" was originally published in the Russian Christmas (Julian calendar) issues of *Rul'* on 6 and 8 January 1925. It stands apart from the other two Christmas stories: the realistic "Putevoditel' po Berlinu" and the realistic-symbolic

"Rozhdestvenskii rasskaz." In fact, "Rozhdestvo" is unique among all of Nabokov's early work. It has definite religious overtones. The sacred details of the blinding church cross, the cross-shaped fir treetop, the wax from the funeral taper, and the Christmas tree candle, all converge in the finale of "Rozhdestvo." The joy and happiness of the newborn, exquisite Bombay butterfly save a desperate man on Christmas Eve. This delicate creature has opened Sleptsov's eyes to God's earthly miracles. "Rozhdestvo" thus stands well apart from Nabokov's other symbolic stories. Fear, grotesques, and madness do not predominate here. On the contrary, in "Rozhdestvo" the despondency, tears, and agony of paternal grief are transformed into beauty, joy, and tender happiness, with exultant revelation implicit in Nabokov's final words.

V

In Conclusion: Some Transparent Things

Nabokov's earliest stories are the product of a unique period in the author's career. They represent the exercises of a youthful writer developing his creative tools. In these pieces we find the young Nabokov's inherent talents most clearly exhibited. As a result, the full scope of the literary range potentially available to the older Nabokov is made manifest. Moreover, these stories were written when Nabokov's emotional dependence on and his literary tie with his Russian mother tongue were most intense. Consequently, in them he achieved a stylistic continuity and refreshing simplicity not recaptured in his later, more prolix English variants of these stories.

The author himself characterized this evolutionary stage: "My passion for good writing put me in close contact with various Russian authors abroad. I was young in those days and much more keenly interested in literature than I am now. Current prose and poetry, brilliant planets and pale galaxies, flowed by the casement of my garret night after night."[1] This period was marked by Nabokov's artistic explorations; by a deliberate literary apprenticeship; and, most importantly, by an impassioned approach to literature. An awareness of these three basic elements is fundamental to the appreciation of Nabokov's earliest stories, which display both realistic and symbolic modi operandi. *style*

To recapitulate: in certain of these stories Nabokov employed a realistic method that borders on naturalism. His device of compiling and enjoying details for details' sake was the legacy of Balzac, Flaubert, and de Maupassant; from the Russian tradition he inherited Gogol's, Turgenev's, Tolstoy's, Chekhov's, and Bunin's direct view of life, with its abundance of minutiae. At the same time the symbolic approach is also very much a part of Nabokov's artistry. This again was a legacy of Gogol as well as of Dostoevsky and Belyi. In a good half of these early stories, Nabokov's technique involves the use of symbols, allegory, parody, and satire. This approach not only entails obliquity and the adumbration of something beyond the printed word but admits artifice, beauty, grandeur, laughter, fear, and the grotesque. Finally, in eight of the early pieces, the realistic and symbolic views are successfully merged. Nabokov's use of this broad-angled technique, as I have noted, was short-lived: in 1930 he turned decisively to the purely symbolic approach.

The themes of the stories of the 1920s, on the other hand, are limited. They often deal with the artist, who in some instances suffers from madness; with confrontations of memories, past moments, and minutiae; and with love affairs. The love theme is explored both in a direct man-to-woman relationship and in Nabokov's more familiar love triangle—as, for example, in "Kartofel'nyi El'f" and "Podlets." The hero of these early stories is nearly always a young man who may waver between reality and fantasy. Although the themes and point of view are as yet undeveloped and narrow, the story structure is varied. The classical divisions of exposition, rising action, climax, falling action, and conclusion are handled traditionally in some of the stories. In others they are inverted and at times unbalanced. A tight plot is paramount in a number of pieces: "Vozvrashchenie Chorba," "Passazhir," "Britva," "Skazka," "Podlets." In others stories, a subjective view predominates: "Blagost'," "Port," "Pis'mo v Rossiiu," "Draka," "Putevoditel' po Berlinu." In nearly all of these stories, the language is innovative and strikingly poetic; it under-lines Nabokov's use of *l'art pour l'art*. "Made-strange" adjectival and verbal phrases are complemented by polychromatism and many figures of speech, particularly similes, metaphors, and diverse personifications—verbal, adverbial, adjectival. This poetic fabric is not as tightly woven as it was to be several decades later; for example, in *Transparent Things*. Nonetheless, a richness of texture is already patent in these earliest works.

The material for Nabokov's craft is "common in experience and uncommon in writing." [2] He chose familiar aspects of life and molded them into unexpected images that recur throughout the early stories and interlock these separate pieces. Ordinary, urban views are presented, usually through windows, and often of Berlin. As the critic Andreev noted, this was a curious attempt of an author to describe alien life from within.[3] Trams, buses, trains; asphalt and often wet, glistening streets under repair; courtyards, shabby hotels, bars, barbershops; city signs; expatriates, young girls, and prostitutes all have a role in Nabokov's stories of the 1920s. The more evocative motifs are nocturnal and daylight shadows, trees and their fluttering leaves, chess, mirrors, doubles, treasure boxes, butterflies, and classical allusions—Orpheus, Zeus, Daedalus, Pompeii.

To Nabokov scholars, the sheer number and variety of these refreshing and youthful pieces give evidence of Nabokov's early promise and developing talent. They reveal the breadth of his techniques far better than any single novel. Some inconsistencies in their quality exist, but these are not exclusively attributable to the author's youth. The financial pressures under which both the young and the established Russian émigré writers were required to write in those days were considerable: their meager income was never sufficient "to keep body and pen together." [4] Doubtless, like his confreres, Nabokov was affected by this unfortunate creative re-straint.

The value of Nabokov's first stories was immediately recognized in Russian émigré literary circles. Most journals and newspapers carried thoughtful critiques of his work. In looking back, Nabokov wrote: "But the author who interested me most was naturally Sirin. He belonged to my generation. Among the young writers produced in exile he was the loneliest and most arrogant one. Beginning with the appearance of his first novel in 1925 and throughout the next fifteen years, until he vanished as strangely as he had come, his work kept provoking an acute and rather morbid interest on the part of the critics." [5]

Never again were Nabokov's Russian works, even his superior later novels, to attract as much considered attention. This was due in part to the subsequent dispersal of the Russian literary groups, and also to the startling novelty of the youthful author's creations. The reactions were mixed.[6] As many as five critics specifically reviewed the volume *Vozvrashchenie Chorba*. (Stories of the 1920s, not appearing in this collection, were not reviewed until the present study.) A. Savel'ev [7] and P. Pil'skii were very laudatory in their appraisal of Nabokov's short stories. G. D. Khokhlov, in reviewing *Vozvrashchenie Chorba*, saw Nabokov's work as a departure from Russian literary tradition.[8] Specifically he felt that Nabokov did not write "as in reality" and that the author's personality and artistic devices were obtrusive. In the earlier review of *Korol' dama valet*, Tsetlin had considered the problems of young émigré writers. He observed that true talent finds ways to adjust to new circumstances and that Nabokov was just such a talent. In his sympathetic review of *Vozvrashchenie Chorba*, Tsetlin noted that, though not all of the stories were equally valuable, they were on the whole masterfully written. He correctly concluded that Nabokov's true talent was still in its period of growth. The fifth review, by S. Nal'ianch in a Warsaw newspaper, has unfortunately not come to hand.[9]

Even in the 1920s and the very early 1930s, Nabokov's work provoked heated debates in the spirit of his controversy with the late Edmund Wilson. Georgii Ivanov, in his review, appearing in the inaugural issue of *Chisla*, termed the stories in *Vozvrashchenie Chorba* "vulgarity without virtuosity." [10] This view was in part based on personal antipathy, and Nabokov seems to have been unperturbed. Later he spoke of the incident as "the amusing case of Georgiy Ivanov, a good poet but a scurrilous critic." [11]

Struve and Andreev, both of whom held Nabokov in high regard, came to his defense.[12] Struve in his article "Tvorchestvo Sirina" surveyed Nabokov's work, including *Vozvrashchenie Chorba*.

In this article Struve contended that Nabokov was the emigration's greatest gift to Russian literature. He saw Nabokov depicting reality in a completely new manner: behind the familiar, he portrayed an illusory, one-dimensional world, and in this type of description imitated neither Russian nor foreign writers, as many had contended.

Andreev's lengthy and penetrating article, "Sirin," considered all of the major works of the 1920s, with a special section on the *Vozvrashchenie Chorba* stories. Andreev found these stories valuable because they brought the reader closer to Nabokov the writer. They enabled the reader to perceive his sense of human sympathy, which was hidden in the novels because their artistic brilliance was too blinding. Andreev noted that there were unsuccessful stories, but recalled Chekhov's observation that bad is the belletrist who writes well from the start; he added that the very instability of the form of certain of Nabokov's creations was consoling and promising. The thesis of Andreev's article was sound: "Sirin is an émigré. . . . From a formal viewpoint Sirin represents a combination of Russian moods and West European forms. Sirin, more clearly and successfully than any other Russian writers, has fulfilled the well-known call of Maiakovskii's companion, the late Lev Lunts—'To the West!' And this has been done while perpetuating the principal direction of Russian literature" (VI).

These criticisms all raised valid points. The question of whether Nabokov's characters were real or cardboard and to what extent his art was artificial clearly occupied his readers. The fundamental question raised by Nabokov's reviewers was whether or not he was a writer in the Russian tradition. I have indicated that I feel he was, but each critic had his own answer. They all agreed that Nabokov's creations were novel, and although recognizing his immaturity, many forecast a brilliant future for him.

Unfortunately, Nabokov's reputation as a Russian writer has never again been so fully appreciated. Today few recall that he had a multilingual literary career. As Berberova has pointed out, Nabokov began writing in Russian, for a time wrote in French, and by pure accident began writing in English.[13] Nabokov achieved little recognition as a writer from the English-reading public until the publication of *Lolita*. Only at that time did his readers turn back to his earlier works, but rarely to the Russian originals. Most of Nabokov's major Russian creations have now been translated into English, making his first career thus better known.

In recent years Nabokov started to publish some English versions of his earliest Russian stories. I have noted in my introductory chapter the recent collections, *A Russian Beauty and Other Stories* (1973), *Tyrants Destroyed and Other Stories* (1975), and *Details of a Sunset and Other Stories* (1976). If Nabokov was not the actual translator, he was the stern supervisor of the work of his son Dmitri. It is an unusual, if not a unique, privilege to have the author direct his own translations.[14]

The reasons behind Nabokov's choice of stories for translation have not always been clear. I have already noted that in the 1930s Struve made the authorized translations of the early stories, "Vozvrashchenie Chorba" and "Passazhir." The selection of "Vozvrashchenie Chorba" was obviously based on its excellence. The brevity of "Passazhir" was a consideration after excellence for its translation, as Nabokov would have preferred a translation of the longer "Zvonok" at that time. However, for some reason these three stories are among the last to be included in recent hardback editions, where they appear as translated by the Nabokovs. Although Nabokov liked Struve's translations of "Vozvrashchenie Chorba" and "Passazhir," he chose to retranslate them, explaining in *Details of a Sunset* that the forty-year-old versions done by Struve were "too tame in style and too inaccurate in sense for [his] present purpose" (p. 58; see also p. 72).

In the late 1940s Struve and his wife translated "Skazka." Although Nabokov also liked that translation, he did not wish to see it printed then because he confessed that he did not like the story at all. The inclusion of "Skazka" in his own English translation in the recent collection *A Russian Beauty* was therefore not prompted by its excellence. Nor was Nabokov's choice of "Kartofel'nyi El'f" for translation predicated on quality. In his introductory remarks to "The Potato Elf," Nabokov explained that this was not his favorite piece but that the earlier unauthorized 1939 version [15] was "full of mistakes and omissions," and he wished to provide a faithful translation of this story. He added: ". . . if I include it in this collection it is only because the act of retranslating it properly is a precious personal victory that seldom falls to a betrayed author's lot." [16]

In the forewords to many of his English versions of his early Russian novels, Nabokov explained his approach to the English translator. His foreword to *King, Queen, Knave* best sheds light on this process:

> By the end of 1966, my son had prepared a literal translation of the book in English, and this I placed on my lectern beside a copy of the Russian edition. I foresaw having to make a number of revisions affecting the actual text of a forty-year-old novel which I had not reread ever since its proofs had been corrected by an author twice younger than the reviser. Very soon I asserted that the original sagged considerably more than I had expected. I do not wish to spoil the pleasure of future collators by discussing the little changes I made. Let me only remark that my main purpose in making them was not to beautify a corpse but rather to permit a still breathing body to enjoy certain innate capacities which inexperience and eagerness, the haste of thought and the sloth of word had denied it formerly. (pp. vii-viii)

A comparison of Nabokov's Russian and English short-story texts is a study in itself. I have already cited some variations, and the bilingual reader has surely spotted the other changes evinced by my parallel quotations of Nabokov's own Russian and English texts. I wish, however, to point to a few of the "little changes," even if I trespass on the province of "future collators" whom Nabokov anticipated in the foreword to *King, Queen, Knave.*

In general the English renderings appear surprisingly faithful to the original. Only on closer scrutiny does one find variations. The most obvious is that proper nouns are often changed: Frau Ott becomes Frau Monde; Frau Nellis becomes Frau Kind, born Countess Karski; and in "A Matter of Chance" the old lady, Mar'ia Pavlovna Ukhtomskaia, is elevated to the rank of a princess. In that same story Max the waiter is given a last name,

Fuchs, and Luzhin's crystalline powder bears a new brand name, as Merk becomes Kramm. The nomenclature of the butterflies and moths in "Rozhdestvo" also changes in translation.

Other revisions are made to some allusions in the original texts which would be familiar only to the Russian reader. Thus in "Rozhdestvo" the citation "Frigate Pallas" is now identified as Goncharov's "Frigate." The allusion to Mayne Reid in "Zvonok" is updated to Jack London in "The Doorbell." The Berlin newspaper in "Sluchainost' " becomes *Rul'* in "A Matter of Chance." In that same story "the revolution in Berlin" becomes "a Communist revolution in Berlin," consequently, "they aren't doing so well" become "the sovetchiks aren't doing so well." Dates in these stories, which originally were given relative to Nabokov's time of writing, now are given as calendar dates; for example, "five years before" is specified as 1919.

Some poetic images are rephrased. In "Sluchainost' " Luzhin calculates the details of his death "as if he were *solving* a chess problem." In the 1974 version this image is changed to "*composing* a chess problem." This is more in keeping with his future namesake in *Zashchita Luzhina* and with Nabokov himself. Another colorful simile, "from underneath the large flat slice of bread, a piece of ham stuck out like a pink tongue," is not found in the English "A Missed Chance," nor is the interesting inverting mustache/eyebrow image, which is, however, retained in the English version of "Uzhas." In this last "eyes" become "octopus eyes."

There is a critical addition in the opening paragraph of "Christmas," where the action takes place after "the funeral service is over." In "Rozhdestvo" the reader only knows that "it's all over," thus raising questions which are only answered some paragraphs later. I feel that Nabokov, by being explicit in the English version, destroyed much of this story's original effect. On the other hand, plot clues in "Sluchainost' " and "Skazka" are so obscured in the English renderings as to be lost. As I have already observed, in "Sluchainost' " the critical date 1 August 1915 in the wedding ring is masked as 1-VIII-1915; and in "Skazka" Frau Ott's play on the number thirteen has a double entendre in Russian which is not offered clearly in English.

Finally, in Nabokov's updated English stories he sometimes left

Russian-language phrases intact. These, I imagine, were retained so as not to destroy the original Russian flavor of these stories. Because of the miscellaneous and picayune nature of Nabokov's revampings, I hesitate to draw any conclusions, particularly as this analysis is not intended to be exhaustive. Generally, any substantive changes were for elucidation, and on the whole, Nabokov's "rewriting" was remarkably faithful to his original work.

Nabokov's recent interest in his earliest prose [17] is seen not only in the translation and republication of the stories but in certain cases in their "reincarnation" in somewhat different form. Elements of Nabokov's earliest stories are thus found in his recent novel, *Transparent Things.* Andreev's remarks about Nabokov's early repeating images being preparatory études for his later work have proved singularly apt. Conscious recurrent elements and, more significantly, unconscious authorial reminiscences [18] link Nabokov's immature Russian stories with his mature English work. Aspects of the artistic approach, the plot line, the characterizations, the symbols, and the images that occur in his earliest rich and diverse pieces are found in *Transparent Things.* This bond is evident despite the language difference and the three- to four-decade gap in time of composition. Nabokov's own views on the timeless and placeless character of an author's craft are relevant here: "I have always maintained, even as a schoolboy in Russia, that the nationality of a worthwhile writer is of secondary importance. ... The writer's art is his real passport. His identity should be immediately recognized by a special pattern or unique coloration. His habitat may confirm the correctness of the determination but should not lead to it. Locality labels are known to have been faked by unscrupulous insect dealers." [19]

In Nabokov's view, the distinctive features of the writer's art, not his habitat or nationality, are the key to his identity. Moreover, he justified any repetition of these distinctive features by saying: "Derivative writers seem versatile because they imitate many others, past and present. Artistic originality has only its own self to copy." [20] As a result, in Nabokov's strong opinion, it is natural for his works to be similar and even iterative, despite linguistic and temporal gaps. However, what is most remarkable about the link between these two sets of work is that none of the many intervening creations have been so similar in pattern and coloration.

Of foremost importance is that Nabokov's early realistic-symbolic method, basic to his first stories, is also fundamental to *Transparent Things*. The symbolic approach is manifest particularly in the bifurcation of the hero's personality and in his concern with time: past, present, and future. Nabokov has placed these two literary themes within a wider symbolic frame: the relationship of life to death. Death is something of a cliché in Nabokov's first stories. In *Transparent Things*, on the other hand, it becomes a major theme and the genuine concern of an older author. The hero both consciously and unconsciously tries to understand the intangibles of life and death by seeking tangibles in the realia of life. Hugh Person searches for the very same minutiae of the real world that Nabokov's earliest heroes had sought. Likewise "the special pattern or unique coloration" of Nabokov's artistic devices and linguistic effects join his first and latest works.

Nabokov labeled *Transparent Things* a novel. However, it is only one hundred pages long and could be considered an expanded short story. It deals with only one major figure, Hugh Person. The central and essentially the single event of the work is the hero's return to the source of his memories, in order to recapture the image of his dead wife. This *recherche du temps perdu* follows to a striking degree the plot of "Vozvrashchenie Chorba." [21] Like Chorb, Person is a man in search:

What had you expected of your pilgrimage, Person? A mere mirror rerun of hoary torments? Sympathy from an old stone? Enforced re-creation of irrecoverable trivia? A search for lost time in an utterly distinct sense from Good-grief's dreadful *"Je me souviens, je me souviens de la maison où je suis né"* or, indeed, Proust's quest? . . . Practically all the dreams in which she had appeared to him after her death had been staged not in the settings of an American winter but in those of Swiss mountains and Italian lakes. He had not even found the spot in the woods where a gay band of little hikers had interrupted an unforgettable kiss. The desideratum was a moment of contact with her essential image in exactly remembered surroundings. (pp. 94-95)

Person, too, seeks a hotel room that he had once shared with his wife—a twist of a theme in the earlier story, in which Chorb is given his old room by coincidence. Both heroes plan to spend the critical night of the story with a young woman. This fairly simple plot is complicated artistically by the inversion of time. Distorted time, basic to the structure of "Vozvrashchenie Chorba," is fully developed in Nabokov's later novel. The plot of *Transparent Things* begins at the end of Person's life. At the conclusion of the novel the beginning and the end coalesce in time. The hero's four visits to Switzerland are stages in his life and are fully inverted. As past, present, and future fall into place, the plot sequence does as well; the story loses its enigmatic quality and becomes more "transparent." This use of time as a structural device is strengthened by Nabokov's employment of time as a poetic image in the novel. To note just one example, the three young women in Witt are symbolically named by Person his Past, Present, and Future Tenses.

As with many of Nabokov's early stories, shifting time sequences complement the hero's vacillation between reality and fantasy, waking and dreaming, fact and fiction, consciousness and subconsciousness. Person wavers between sanity and madness. Like Bachmann, he has moments of complete unreason—but they result not from a loss of love or an aberration of artistic genius. They derive from a weakness in his own personality, foreshadowed by his somnambulism and acrophobia. This basic instability recalls another early hero in "Uzhas" who moves in a world of unreason.

Person, like Chorb and the narrators of "Putevoditel' po Berlinu," "Draka," and "Groza," is concerned with literature. He is an editor, working on the manuscripts of Mrs. Flankard and Mr. R. Like the early heroes, he is an alien—an American in Switzerland. As in the early stories, his love affair is the major theme. Person is in love with the spirited Armande. She runs effortlessly up mountainsides and as briskly skis down them, with Person barely but faithfully in pursuit, recalling Chorb's trailing of his bride. In Person's case, however, his devotion is unjustified. His Armande is a vixen and recalls the ladyloves in "Blagost'," "Kartofel'nyi El'f," and "Katastrofa" who are insincere in their affection toward the Nabokovian heroes. Her only resemblance to Chorb's bride is that she, too, is half Russian through her mother.

Basically her mother, Madame Chamar, is everything that her nubile, graceful daughter is not: "Her unwieldy corpulence could be moved only by means of one precise little wiggle; in order to make it [out of the chair] she had to concentrate upon the idea of trying to fool gravity until something clicked inwardly and the right jerk happened like the miracle of a sneeze" (p. 39). Later she wearily descends the stairway with "the jelly of a bare forearm wobbling"—thus recalling Chorb's mother-in-law, Frau Keller, who "having plunked out a plump leg, in her turn crawled out of the car." Frau Keller's hair is dyed red, and Madame Chamar in similar fashion retains her "youth" with "the purple arches of her pastel eyebrows." Like Frau Keller, she wears an elaborate dress with flounces, recalling Nabokov's description of other matrons in the opening chapters of *Transparent Things:* "Each old woman in turn spread the same flower-patterned dress against her bosom" (p. 12). Like the Kellers, Madame Chamar does not approve of her daughter's admirer, but nevertheless she gives Armande's childhood albums to Person. Structurally, these volumes tell Person the heroine's past visually, not aurally, in much the same way that Zak's albums tell the story of Perova's affair to the narrator of "Bakhman."

Images of Nabokov's earliest stories recur in *Transparent Things;* for example, the cheap and dreary hotels that form the background of many of the early stories.[22] The action of *Transparent Things* begins when Person "extricate[s] his angular bulk from the taxi," much as Frau Keller did in "Vozvrashchenie Chorba," and notes the Ascot Hotel, "a dreadful building of gray stone and brown wood" (p. 3). Street scenes with glistening asphalt are very much a part of the world of *Transparent Things.* As in most of the early stories,[23] the hero's urban microcosm is pointedly under repair: "A lot of construction work was going on around Witt, scarring and muddying the entire hillside" (p. 37).

Nabokov's early Belyi-like fascination with numerals, letters, and their configurations is a motif threaded through the late novel. There is Nabokov's ubiquitous city sign: "An electric sign, DOPPLER, shifted to violet through the half-drawn curtains and illumined the deadly white papers he had left on the table" (p. 77). The figures on the photograph booth and on Madame Chamar's front door, which has "Villa Nastia" signed "in French cursive," are characteristic examples. Person recalls the critical hotel room precisely because of its number: "He saw a very black 313 on a very white door and recalled instantly how he had told Armande . . . : 'Mnemonically it should be imagined as three little figures in profile, a prisoner passing by with one guard in front of him and another behind'" (p. 95). These last key numbers and the significance of their design reflect Nabokov's interest in palindromes such as "otto," which we noticed as far back as "Putevoditel' po Berlinu" and "Draka." As in the first stories, so in *Transparent Things* these letters and numbers not only attract the hero but decorate the urban backdrops on billboards, marquees, shop windows, and street signs.

In the early stories[24] a friendly dog is the only animal that Nabokov noted, save one or two horses. Frequently this dog nuzzles into the lap of the hero. Significantly he reappears in *Transparent Things,* and now with something of a function. He signals that Person has recaptured a memory. Initially, the typically overaffectionate dog chases Person when he makes his first visit to Armande. On his pilgrimage, the dog reemerges:

> . . . a large, white, shivering dog crawled from behind a crate and with a shock of futile recognition Hugh remembered that eight years ago he had stopped right here and had noticed that dog, which was pretty old even then and had now braved fabulous age only to serve his blind memory. (p. 87)

Later Person hears a dog yapping within hotel room No. 313 and notes it as a mark of the room's occupancy. Thus, he ". . . carried away a feeling of satisfaction, the sense of having recovered an important morsel of that particular past" (p. 95).

Nails, legs, and feet and the impressions they leave are curious, yet constant Nabokovian images.[25] The "made-strange" nail image recurs in various sizes, shapes, and hues in the early stories. In *Transparent Things* this motif occurs at a critical juncture in the novel: "Trying for the best hold, he had clutched her around the neck from behind, his square-nailed thumbs digging into her violet-lit nape" (p. 81). Having killed Armande, Person then perceives his fingernails as "bashful claws."

Mention of legs and feet recurs in *Transparent Things.* Person's first recollection of Armande is almost metonymic: "Spoke to a girl on the train. Adorable brown naked legs and golden sandals" (p. 27). Footprints themselves, as in "Rozhdestvo" (pp. 69-70) and "Pis'mo v Rossiiu" (p. 47), are a memory image for the hero in *Transparent Things:* "It was not worthwhile continuing that lone climb. Had she passed here, had her soles once imprinted their elaborate pattern in that clay?" (p. 90). This passage clearly recalls Chorb's similar pilgrimage through the rocks and his memories of his lively bride. A clear instance of Nabokovian authorial reminiscence is found in a twist of the aforementioned nail-and-foot image. In *Transparent Things* Person hates the sight of his feet: "What a jaggy chill he experienced at the mere thought of catching a toenail in the silk of a sock (silk socks were out, too)!" (p. 85). This directly evokes the passage in "Bakhman" where the narrator imagines Perova pulling on her stockings and catching the silk on "the toenails of her icy feet."

Nabokov's most familiar motifs, chessmen and butterflies, are secondary images in both the first and the late prose pieces. The chess image is as fleeting in *Transparent Things* as it is in "Rozhdestvo" and "Podlets." Person is released from prison early because he has taught his fellow inmates how to play chess. The butterfly found in "Rozhdestvo" as a central image, and in "Uzhas," as a minor metaphor appears in *Transparent Things* several times. When Person peruses the albums of Armande, the second volume "burst[s] into color to celebrate the vivid vestiture of her adolescent molts" (p. 41). This metaphor is made concrete on the same page when Person notes a Denton mount of a birdwing butterfly on the Chamar mantelpiece. Later Person's long-remembered kiss for Armande is metaphorized as the pebble-butterfly kiss.

The lepidopteral image is more highly developed in the description of Person's pilgrimage:

He noticed a large white butterfly drop outspread on a stone. Its papery wings, blotched with black and maculated with faded crimson, had transparent margins of an unpleasant crimped texture, which shivered slightly in the cheerless wind. Hugh disliked insects; this one looked particularly gross. Nevertheless, a mood of unusual kindliness made him surmount the impulse to crush it under a blind boot. With the vague idea that it must be tired and hungry and would appreciate being transferred to a nearby pincushion of little pink flowers, he stooped over the creature but with a great shuffle and rustle it evaded his handkerchief, sloppily flapped to overcome gravity, and vigorously sailed away. (p. 90)

Person's reaction to butterflies is an unusual one for the author, himself a passionate lepidoperist, to ascribe to his hero. Perhaps Nabokov is signaling a peculiarity in Person's character. Even in this instance, the butterfly finally evokes gentleness in Person. Nabokov's distinctive "made-strange" themes seem to stress the abnormality of Person's personality. As the butterfly image underlines an idiosyncrasy, so do the images of mirrors, moving furniture, dripping water, and open windows accentuate Person's derangement.

Contrary to what might be expected, the mirrors in *Transparent Things* are not used to stress Person's madness; instead, they describe him quickly and unobtrusively. Very early in the novel, Person sees himself in a mirror:

. . . the no less rapt mirror in the lift reflected, for a few lucid instants, the gentleman from Massachusetts, who had a long, lean, doleful face with a slightly undershot jaw and a pair of symmetrical folds framing his mouth in what would have been a rugged, horsey, mountain-climbing arrangement had not his melancholy stoop belied every inch of his fantastic majesty. (p. 4)

Person has his "last interview" with the mirror when he plucks a black hair out of a red nostril.

Moving furniture is another thread in Nabokov's special pattern that links his first work with the later. In *Transparent Things* the lively furniture is evidence of Person's instability: ". . . Hugh, in his sleep, had imagined that his bedside table, a little three-legged affair, . . . was executing a ferocious war dance all by itself" (p. 21). This dancing table foreshadows the night table that actually collapses when Person kills Armande.

Water, which trickles and flows in "Pis'mo v Rossiiu" (p. 44) and "Podlets" (p. 106), attracts Person's attention in *Transparent Things:* "The tap expostulated, letting forth a strong squirt of rusty water before settling down to produce the meek normal stuff" (p. 5). Again: "He heard a toilet flush upstairs and with a guilty wince slapped the thick book shut" (p. 41). Just before Person murders Armande, he again hears dripping water: "He lay open-eyed for a while listening to another tenacious small sound, the pinking of waterdrops on the linoleum under a defective radiator" (p. 78).

Many of Nabokov's early heroes look out on an alien world through a frame, usually that of a window.[26] Similarly, in *Transparent Things* open windows and their vistas—often into courtyards or city streets—are a dominant image. When Person's father looks out of his hotel window to examine the weather, he glimpses the wet, shiny pavement before the venetian blind tumbles down. Later through a window Person notices "a tremendous crater full of excavating machines" (pp. 4-5). Nabokov established Person's acrophobia with this window motif:

> He opened wide both casements; they gave on a parking place four floors below; the thin meniscus overhead was too wan to illumine the roofs of the houses descending toward the invisible lake; the light of a garage picked out the steps of desolate stairs leading into a chaos of shadows; it was all very dismal and very distant, and our acrophobic Person felt the pull of gravity inviting him to join the night and his father. (p. 19)

Person closes the window and, like the heroes of "Blagost' " and "Podlets," he spends the remainder of the night in an armchair.

Person's forays with Armande out of hotel windows echo his childhood somnambulism. The two elements, acrophobia and somnambulism, combine in Person's climactic dream:

> Giulia, or Julie, wore a Doppler shift over her luminous body and prostrated herself on the sill, with outspread arms still touching the wings of the window. He glanced down across her, and there, far below, in the chasm of the yard or garden, the selfsame flames moved. (p. 80)

At Person's own death, exit through the window frame is barred: "The window banged with such force that its panes broke into a torrent of rubies, and he realized before choking to death that a storm outside was aiding the inside fire" (p. 103). This death of the hero at the window echoes the final scene in *Zashchita Luzhina*.

Nabokov's window views out of rooms are complemented by the rays of light that fall into them. The light beams that pour into Nabokov's early stories continue in *Transparent Things:* "Actually all that impinged on the darkness was an angled beam from the living room, the door of which he had left ajar" (p. 78); ". . . she would never see, the little rug doing its duty to receive the first square of sun and the first touch of Hugh's sticking-plastered toes" (p. 101).

Transparent Things is as polychromatic as the early stories. Although mournful and transparent blacks and browns pervade the first pages of the novel, colors, particularly the favorite purple shade, predominate. As always, this last color recurs in variations: dingy lilac, plumbeous plumb, mauve, purple, violet. Person's nightmare after a dinner of melted cheese, young potatoes, and a bottle of green wine later inverts into a recollection of a colorful childhood dream. A boy is encircled by the vegetables of his first picture book. Slowly in the dream these colored vegetables spin and form a transparent ring of banded colors. At Person's death all of these colors blur again, this time in iridescent dizziness. Finally, at the window, ". . . a long lavender-tipped flame dance[s] up to stop him with a graceful gesture of its gloved hand" (p. 104).

Tropes, particularly metaphors, personifications, and similes occur in abundance in *Transparent Things*. As in the early stories, Nabokov's sharp observation of commonplace elements is matched by the precise word. For instance, in the natural world he perceives "the sullen overcast sky," "scarred melancholy mountains," "tossing, demonstrative trees," and "round-browed gray rocks." The aforementioned lengthier passages are all fine examples of Nabokov's extended use of tropes.

Inevitably, differences exist between the earliest work and *Transparent Things*. Clearly this late work is mature and more involuted. The most obvious difference between Nabokov's work of the 1920s and the 1970s is the language. The early stories were originally written in Russian, of course, and *Transparent Things,* in

English; but Nabokov commented: "I think of myself as an American writer who was once a Russian one." [27] Here he implied that his American work bears the mark of his earliest pieces. The language in *Transparent Things*, although English, literally reflects Nabokov's native Russian tongue. Not only do Person's fiancée and her mother speak Russian, but, as Karlinsky has established, there are many allusions to the Russian language and literature in the novel.[28]

To those who fully appreciate both Nabokov's Russian and English works, the similarity of means of expression, differences in language notwithstanding, is remarkable. The "special pattern or unique coloration" is particularly exciting when it is encountered in both of his tongues. In this regard I again quote Nabokov's wistful remark: "None of my American friends have read my Russian books and thus every appraisal on the strength of my English ones is bound to be out of focus." [29] Except for Karlinsky and Slonim, [30] most critics of *Transparent Things* missed the rich heritage of this novel. The earliest stories hold critical literary clues to *Transparent Things,* and Nabokov, by translating his earliest stories into English, helped bring all of his work into focus.

The authorial translation of these earliest stories and their reprise in *Transparent Things* is critical in still another respect. It underlines my contention that Nabokov's artistically broad-ranging early stories are more than youthful probings. These stories clearly bear the promise of Nabokov's eventual versatility and talent, which has been fulfilled in his last prose. And Nabokov, in rescuing these first stories from their disintegrating Russian versions, lent new value to his earliest creations and substantiated their instrinsic worth.

Appendix

The short stories are listed below in chronological order with place and date of their original publication. The asterisk indicates that the story subsequently appeared in *Vozvrashchenie Chorba: Rasskazy i stikhi.*

"Udar kryla"	*Russkoe Ekho*	Jan. 1924
"Mest' "	*Russkoe Ekho*	20 Apr. 1924
* "Blagost' "	*Rul'*	27 Apr. 1924
* "Port"	*Rul'*	24 May 1924
* "Kartofel'nyi El'f"	*Russkoe Ekho*	8, 15, 22, 29 June 1924
repr.	*Rul'*	15, 17, 18, 19 Dec. 1929
"Sluchainost' "	*Segodnia*	22 June 1924
* "Katastrofa"	*Segodnia*	13 July 1924
* "Bakhman"	*Rul'*	2, 4 Nov. 1924
* "Groza"	*Rul'*	Aug. 1924?
* "Rozhdestvo"	*Rul'*	6, 8 Jan. 1925
* "Pis'mo v Rossiiu"	*Rul'*	29 Jan. 1925
"Draka"	*Rul'*	26 Sept. 1925
* "Vozvrashchenie Chorba"	*Rul'*	12, 13 Nov. 1925
* "Putevoditel' po Berlinu"	*Rul'*	24 Dec. 1925
"Bogi"	*Segodnia*	1926? (It is not in the issues of 1924 or 1925, as previously thought)

223

"Britva"	*Rul'*	19 Feb. 1926
* "Skazka"	*Rul'*	27, 29 June 1926
* "Passazhir"	*Rul'*	6 Mar. 1927
* "Uzhas"	*Sovremennye Zapiski*	30 (1927), 214-20
* "Zvonok"	*Rul'*	22 May 1927
* "Podlets"	*Rul'*	June-Dec. 1927?
"Rozhdestvenskii rasskaz"	*Rul'*	25 Dec. 1928

Notes

Preface

1. *Nabokov: The Man and His Work,* ed. L. S. Dembo (Madison, Wisc.: Univ. of Wisc. Press, 1967), pp. 19-20.

2. V. Nabokov, *The Annotated Lolita,* ed. A. Appel, Jr. (New York: McGraw-Hill Book Co., 1970), pp. 318-19.

3. Nabokov, *A Russian Beauty and Other Stories* (New York: McGraw-Hill Book Co., 1973); *Tyrants Destroyed and Other Stories* (New York: McGraw-Hill Book Co., 1975); *Details of a Sunset and Other Stories* (New York: McGraw-Hill Book Co., 1976). Ardis Publishers is currently reprinting some of Nabokov's early stories in their original Russian versions.

4. March 1975, p. 144.

Chapter I

1. Nabokov, *Speak, Memory: An Autobiography Revisited* (New York: Putnam, 1966), pp. 265-66.

2. A. Field, *Nabokov: His Life in Art* (Boston: Little, Brown & Co., 1967), p. 57; G. Struve, *Russkaia literatura v izgnanii* (New York: Chekhov Publishing House, 1956), pp. 21-22.

3. Nabokov, *Strong Opinions* (New York: McGraw-Hill Book Co., 1973), p. 161.

4. *Speak, Memory,* p. 281.

5. *Mashen'ka* (Berlin: Slovo, 1926). The English edition is *Mary*, tr. M. Glenny with the author (New York: McGraw-Hill Book Co., 1970). Unless otherwise indicated, all page references to this work are to the English edition.

6. *Korol' dama valet* (Berlin: Slovo, 1928). As in the original edition, no commas will be used here in the title. The English edition is *King, Queen, Knave*, tr. D. Nabokov with the author (New York: Capricorn Books, 1970). Unless otherwise indicated, all page references to this work are to the English edition.

7. *Zashchita Luzhina* (Berlin: Slovo, 1930). The English edition is *The Defense*, tr. M. Scammel with the author (New York: Capricorn Books, 1970). Unless otherwise indicated, all page references to this work are to the English edition.

8. See the Appendix for a complete chronological listing of these stories with their original place of publication.

9. *Vozvrashchenie Chorba: Rasskazy i stikhi* (Berlin: Slovo, 1930); reissued (Ann Arbor, Mich.: Ardis Publishers, 1976). Russian quotations of the fifteen stories contained in this collection are taken from this edition. The Appendix gives full references for these stories.

10. "Draka," *Rul'*, 26 Sept. 1925, pp. 2-3; "Britva," *Rul'*, 19 Feb. 1926, pp. 2-3; "Rozhdestvenskii rasskaz," *Rul'*, 25 Dec. 1928, pp. 2-3. Russian quotations are from these newspaper editions and the English translations are mine.

11. Field, *Nabokov: A Bibliography* (New York: McGraw-Hill Book Co., 1973), pp. 104-7.

12. "Sluchainost'," *Segodnia*, 22 June 1924, pp. 7-8. Russian quotations are from this newspaper edition.

13. "A Matter of Chance," *Tyrants Destroyed*, pp. 143-55. English quotations of this story are from this edition.

14. These stories also appeared earlier in English translations in separate issues of various magazines.

15. "The Potato Elf," *A Russian Beauty*, pp. 221-51. English quotations are from this edition.

16. "An Affair of Honor," which previously appeared in *Nabokov's Quartet* (New York: Pyramid Publications, 1968), pp. 11-49, has now been included in *A Russian Beauty*, pp. 83-115. English quotations are from this edition.

17. "Bachmann," *Tyrants Destroyed*, pp. 171-83. English quotations are from this edition.

18. "A Nursery Tale," *Tyrants Destroyed*, pp. 41-58. English quotations are from this edition.

19. "Terror," *Tyrants Destroyed,* pp. 113-21. English quotations are from this edition.

20. "The Return of Chorb," *Details of a Sunset,* pp. 59-70; "The Passenger," *Details of a Sunset,* pp. 73-80. These stories were translated earlier by G. Struve as "The Return of Tchorb," in *This Quarter,* 4 (June 1932), 592-602 and "The Passenger," in *Lovat Dickson's Magazine,* 2 (June 1934), 719-24. My English quotations are from *Details of a Sunset.*

21. "Details of a Sunset" [Katastrofa], pp. 15-26; "A Letter that Never Reached Russia" [Pis'mo v Rossiiu], pp. 83-87; "A Guide to Berlin" [Putevoditel' po Berlinu], pp. 91-98; "The Doorbell" [Zvonok], pp. 101-15; "The Thunderstorm" [Groza], pp. 119-23; "Christmas" [Rozhdestvo], pp. 153-61. English quotations are from this collection. (Some of these translations had first appeared in magazines.)

22. Well after my study was written, Nabokov's *Details of a Sunset* was published with so many of these early stories appearing in their English variants. There will therefore be some understandable inconsistencies between my earlier more literal short translations and the subsequent more poetic renderings of Nabokov which I now give in the longer excerpts. The latter, although not always exact, have been included because they are not only the author's own, but sometimes shed light on the original Russian text. Another reason for supplying English translations is for the benefit of the non-Russian-reading scholar. However, it must be remembered that my analysis is of the *Russian* stories of the 1920s and not of their English renderings in the 1970s, which Nabokov himself carefully dubbed "Englished stories" (Foreword, *A Russian Beauty*). (For my views on these Englished pieces, see Chapter V.) If a given phrase or passage has no page reference, the translation is mine to note a stylistic or linguistic point. All other stories, remaining untranslated by Nabokov, are translated by me and also carry no reference. These translations also seek to capture the literal, rather than the smoother poetic, meaning.

23. *Speak, Memory,* p. 276.

24. Struve, pp. 24-29; N. Berberova, *The Italics Are Mine* (New York: Harcourt, Brace & World, Inc., 1969), pp. 31-35.

25. *Speak, Memory,* pp. 280-88.

26. *Dar* (New York: Chekhov Publishing House, 1952). The English edition is *The Gift,* tr. M. Scammel with the author (New York: Capricorn Books, 1970). My textual references are to the English edition. The foreword is not numbered by page.

27. *Speak, Memory,* p. 283.

28. *Ania v strane chudes* (Berlin: Gamaiun, 1923); reissued (New York: Dover Publications, 1976).

29. Field, p. 58.

30. *King, Queen, Knave*, p. viii.

31. *Ibid.*

32. "Sogliadatai," *Sovremennye Zapiski*, 44 (1930), 91. The English edition is *The Eye*, tr. D. Nabokov with the author (New York: Phaedra, 1965). My textual references are to the English edition.

33. "Ultima Thule," *Novyi Zhurnal*, 1 (1942), 49-77. The English version appeared in *A Russian Beauty*, pp. 149-82.

34. "Solus Rex," *Sovremennye Zapiski*, 70 (1940), 5-36. The English version appeared in *A Russian Beauty*, pp. 185-218.

35. *Pale Fire* (New York: Putnam, 1962).

36. The first edition was published in 1955.

37. *Ada or Ardor: A Family Chronicle* (New York: McGraw-Hill Book Co., 1969).

38. *Podvig* (Berlin: Petropolis, 1932). The English edition is *Glory*, tr. D. Nabokov with the author (New York: McGraw-Hill Book Co., 1971). My textual references are to the English edition.

39. This story was published in Russian in *Russkie Zapiski*, 2 (1937), 33-42. The English version appeared in *Nine Stories* (Norfolk, Conn.: New Directions Books, 1947).

40. In its English translation, this work is labeled a novel.

41. A. Appel, "An Interview with Vladimir Nabokov," *Nabokov: The Man and His Work*, p. 21.

42. *The Works of Edgar Allan Poe* (New York: A.C. Armstrong & Son, 1884), VI, 117.

43. Nabokov noted that as a young boy he "relished especially" the works of Poe and Flaubert. *The Annotated Lolita*, pp. xliii-xliv.

44. *Oeuvres complètes du Gustave Flaubert: Correspondance* (Paris: L'Imprimerie Nationale, 1927), IV, 464. The translation is mine.

45. This has been discussed by Berberova in "Nabokov i ego *Lolita*," *Novyi Zhurnal*, 57 (1959), 96.

46. *The Annotated Lolita*, pp. 313, 316-17.

47. *Strong Opinions*, p. 33.

48. *Saturday Review of the Arts*, Jan. 1973, p. 30.

49. "Vladimir Weidle on Sirin," *The Complection of Russian Literature*, ed. A. Field (New York: Atheneum, 1971), p. 239.

50. V. Khodasevich, "O Sirine," *Vozrozhdenie*, 13? Feb. 1937, reprinted in *Literaturnye stat'i i vospominaniia* (New York: Chekhov Publishing House, 1954), p. 252. A partial English translation by M. H. Walker is found in *Nabokov: Criticism, Reminiscences, Translations and Tributes* (New York: Simon & Schuster, 1970), p. 96.

51. "Sirin," *Nov'*, (Oct. 1930). This journal, which was published for a

brief period in Tallinn, Estonia, is virtually unobtainable. I have a xerographic copy through the kindness of N. Berberova. It is without page numbers, so references in my text are cited by the section numbers given by Andreev. The translation is mine. A partial English translation is found in *The Complection of Russian Literature,* p. 231.

52. I shall give all Russian titles but Nabokov's in English translation. Nabokov's works will be given in their original titles.

53. *Nikolai Gogol* (Norfolk, Conn.: New Directions Books, 1944).

54. L. Foster, "Nabokov in Russian Emigré Criticism," *Russian Literature Triquarterly,* 3 (1972), 330.

55. Struve, "Current Russian Literature: II. Vladimir Sirin," *Slavonic and East European Review,* 12 (1934), 436; "Nabokov as a Russian Writer," *Nabokov: The Man and His Work,* p. 47.

56. "V. Sirin," *Segodnia,* 12 Jan. 1930, p. 5.

57. I am very grateful to N. Berberova for her many kind discussions with me on this point in 1972-73.

58. Andreev noted Nabokov's debt to Gogol: "Sometimes there is an excess of separate detail. In places the author's tone is interrupted by intonations which are not his own. At times we hear Gogol: his running start into lyrical digressions about Berlin at eventide" (II).

59. The following discuss this point: Struve, "Current Russian Literature," pp. 439-40; S. Karlinsky, "Nabokov and Chekhov: The Lesser Russian Tradition," *Nabokov: Criticism . . .,* pp. 7-16.

60. The following discuss this point: M. Tsetlin, rev. of *Korol' dama valet,* by V. Sirin, *Sovremennye Zapiski,* 37 (1928), 536-37; Struve, *Russkaia literatura v izgnanii,* p. 284; Struve, "Current Russian Literature," p. 440.

61. *Speak, Memory,* pp. 285-86.

62. *King, Queen, Knave,* p. x.

63. Struve has noted the influence of Belyi on Nabokov, although from a slightly different viewpoint in "Tvorchestvo Sirina," *Rossiia i Slavianstvo,* 17 May 1930 and in *Russkaia literatura v izgnanii,* p. 284.

64. *Mimesis: The Representation of Reality in Western Literature,* tr. W. Trask (New York: Doubleday & Co., 1953).

65. In the foreword to the English edition of *Korol' dama valet* Nabokov noted: "Speaking of literary air currents, I must admit I was a little surprised to find in my Russian text so many '*monologue intérieur*' passages— no relation to *Ulysses,* which I hardly knew at the time; but of course I had been exposed since tender boyhood to *Anna Karenin,* which contains a whole scene consisting of those intonations, Eden-new a hundred years ago, now well used" *(King, Queen, Knave,* p. x). As I have noted above, Tolstoy's approach, as exemplified by his detailed and often irrelevant

descriptions in *War and Peace* and *Anna Karenina*, for instance, left their mark on Nabokov's realistic manner as well.

66. *Strong Opinions*, p. 3.

67. Appel, "An Interview with Vladimir Nabokov," p. 21.

68. In his article on Nabokov, Khodasevich explained that Nabokov's death theme is an artistic device: "Peculiar to Sirin is the realization, or perhaps only a deeply felt conviction, that the world of literary creativity, the true world of the artist, conjured through the action of images and devices out of apparent simulacra of the real world, consists in fact of a completely different material—so different that the passage from one world into the other, in whichever direction it is accomplished, is akin to death. And it is portrayed by Sirin in the form of death" (pp. 250-51).

69. *Sovremennye Zapiski*, 43 (1930), 191-207. Struve has indicated that this story was composed in 1929, in "Current Russian Literature," p. 440. The English version, "The Aurelian," appearing in *Nabokov's Dozen* ([Garden City, N.Y.: Doubleday, 1958], pp. 76-89), is dated "Berlin, 1931." This is incorrect.

70. "Nabokov i ego *Lolita*," pp. 92 ff.

71. *Kamera obskura* (Paris: Sovremennye Zapiski, 1932). The English edition is *Laughter in the Dark* (New York: Bobbs-Merrill Co., 1938).

72. *Otchaianie* (Berlin: Petropolis, 1936). The English edition is *Despair* (New York: Putnam, 1966).

73. *Priglashenie na kazn'* (Paris: Dom Knigi, 1938). The English edition is *Invitation to a Beheading*, tr. D. Nabokov (New York: Capricorn Books, 1965).

74. Much of Nabokov's parodic element is lost in the English translation in *A Russian Beauty*. The Bunin passage occurs on pages 196-97. Shakespeare is parodied on page 195, Pushkin on page 190, and business style is found in a passage on page 210. I am grateful to N. Berberova for pointing out these examples to me.

75. *The Annotated Lolita*, p. 319.

76. *The Real Life of Sebastian Knight* (Norfolk, Conn.: New Directions Books, 1941).

77. *Bend Sinister* (New York: Henry Holt, 1947).

78. *Conclusive Evidence: A Memoir* (New York: Harper & Bros., 1951), translated into Russian as *Drugie berega* (New York: Chekhov Publishing House, 1954) and revised as *Speak, Memory* (1966).

79. Appel, "The Road to *Lolita*, or the Americanization of an Emigré," delivered at the annual meeting of AATSEEL, 29 Dec. 1973.

80. *Pnin* (New York: Doubleday, 1957).

81. *Transparent Things* (New York: McGraw-Hill Book Co., 1972).

82. *Look at the Harlequins* (New York: McGraw-Hill Book Co., 1974).
83. N. Berberova in conversation; Field, p. 129.
84. *Strong Opinions,* p. 154.
85. This is the subject of Chapter V.

Chapter II

1. Flaubert, VIII, 317. The translation is mine.
2. Struve, "Nabokov as a Russian Writer," p. 47.
3. *Strong Opinions,* pp. 10-11. Another comment on realism can be found on p. 118.
4. Struve, *Russian Literature under Lenin and Stalin, 1917-1953* (Norman, Okla.: Univ. of Okla. Press, 1971), p. 44. Zamiatin has made a similar, less succinct observation in "On Synthetism," *A Soviet Heretic: Essays by Yevgeny Zamyatin,* ed. and tr. M. Ginsburg (Chicago: Univ. of Chicago Press, 1970), pp. 85-86.
5. *Strong Opinions,* p. 7.
6. Karlinsky, "Nabokov and Chekhov: The Lesser Russian Tradition," *Nabokov: Criticism . . .,* p. 16.
7. R. Wellek, *Concepts of Criticism,* ed. S. G. Nichols (New Haven, Conn.: Yale Univ. Press, 1963), p. 253.
8. In these early stories *meloch'* (trivia), *pustiaki* (trifles), and *obyknovennye veshchi* (commonplace things) are reiterated.
9. Appel, "An Interview with Vladimir Nabokov," p. 38.
10. This directly echoes Ganin's attempt to resurrect the image of his loved one in *Mashen'ka:* "He was a god, recreating a world that had perished. Gradually he resurrected that world, to please the girl whom he did not dare to place in it until it was absolutely complete. But her image, her presence, the shadow of her memory demanded that in the end he must resurrect her too—and he intentionally thrust away her image, as he wanted to approach it gradually, step by step, just as he had done nine years before" *(Mary,* p. 56). Although in this work the heroine is alive, she is every bit as elusive as Chorb's dead wife. Thus in many respects *Mashen'ka* foreshadows "Vozvrashchenie Chorba," written two years later.
11. This action may be seen to anticipate an episode in *Lolita* (p. 108) in which the parent and child are inverted. Humbert Humbert withholds the news of Charlotte Haze's death from her daughter Lolita in a similar manner. Humbert telephones Lolita's camp and leaves a message for the girl, saying only that her mother is ill.
12. Russian formalist critics distinguished these structural elements. The *fabula* is the chronological order of the motifs, while the *siuzhet* is their artistically ordered presentation, which often is quite different. B.

Tomashevskii, "Tematika: Prozaicheskoe povestvovanie," *Teoriia litera-tury: Poetika* (Leningrad: Gosizdat., 1928), p. 199.

13. K. P. Kempton, *The Short Story* (Cambridge, Mass.: Harvard Univ. Press, 1947), p. 131.

14. S. O'Faolain, *The Short Story* (London: Collins, 1948), p. 157.

15. *Appleton's Journal* (1869), as quoted in Kempton, p. 154.

16. O'Faolain, p. 155.

17. *Poshlost'* is a Russian noun which unfortunately has no precise English translation. Nabokov discussed this term at length in his Gogol study. He wrote: "English words expressing several, although by no means all aspects of *poshlust* [sic] are for instance: 'cheap, sham, common, smutty, pink-and-blue, high falutin', in bad taste' " (p. 64). To this Nabokov also added "the falsely important, the falsely beautiful, the falsely clever, the falsely attractive" (p. 70). It has been also defined as self-satisfied, bourgeois mediocrity, or vulgarity.

18. Kempton, pp. 103, 180.

19. Field incorrectly has said Italy (p. 146).

20. Field, p. 43.

21. Shklovskii, in his analysis of Tolstoy, noted that "making-strange" is the artist's refusal to view a thing in the conventional light. This is done by removing an object or word from its normal context, calling it by a different name, refusing to recognize it, and rescuing it from being a verbal cliché with no evocative response. In short, it is making a word or object appear strange. V. B. Shklovskii, "Iskusstvo kak priem," *O teorii prozy* (Moskva: Izdat. Federatsiia, 1929), pp. 7-23.

22. Khodasevich, p. 253.

23. In a literary inversion, Nabokov's hero in *Mashen'ka* dreams of a southern French port. In the conclusion he sets off for Provence.

24. This same image repeats in *Mashen'ka* (p. 167).

25. A garnet-red lamp in Europe years ago went with "low haunts," according to Humbert in *Lolita* (p. 291).

26. This expression *v glubine* is repeated in this story (p. 18 twice and p. 24).

27. Nabokov noted that Tamara's twin sister is Mashen'ka in the novel of that name *(Mary,* pp. xi-xii).

28. Tsetlin, rev. of *Vozvrashchenie Chorba,* by V. Sirin, *Sovremennye Zapiski,* 42 (1930), 530-31.

29. Foreword to *The Eye.*

30. Field has translated *truby* as sewer pipes (p. 141). They could also be water pipes or heating pipes. They are utility pipes in Nabokov's recent English version *(Details of a Sunset,* p. 91).

31. Nabokov divided many of his stories into sections. He marked these divisions variously, with Roman and Arabic numerals, dashes, double spaces. My analyses are based on these divisions.

32. In *Dar,* written some ten years later, Nabokov was to view a German conductor and his tram passengers in a more jaundiced light: "The Russian conviction that the German is in small numbers vulgar and in larger numbers—unbearably vulgar was, he knew, a conviction unworthy of an artist; but nonetheless he was seized with a trembling, and only the gloomy conductor with hunted eyes and a plaster on his finger, eternally and painfully seeking equilibrium and room to pass amidst the convulsive jolts of the car and the cattle-like crowding of standing passengers, seemed outwardly, if not a human being, then at least a poor relation to a human being" (p. 93).

33. Nabokov attributed "the first little throb of *Lolita*" to a newspaper story about a caged ape in Paris "who after months of coaxing by scientists produced finally the first drawing ever charcoaled by an animal, and this sketch, reproduced in the paper, showed the bars of the poor creature's cage" *(Strong Opinions,* pp. 15-16).

34. Karlinsky has noted: "It is his [Nabokov's] training in lepidoptery that gives this writer the precision of observation . . ." ("Nabokov and Chekhov: The Lesser Russian Tradition," p. 13). I maintain that Nabokov's lepidoptery is a contributing but not exclusive factor in his precise vision. Struve has suggested this point in his earlier article "Notes on Nabokov as a Russian Writer." He has written: "Suffice it to say that his keenness of vision, and the sharpness and colorfulness of the verbal garb in which that vision is clothed, seem to me to be closely related to his lepidopteric pursuits and habits" (p. 56).

35. In the English variant Nabokov added rather horrifying details to the child's recollection. The italicized words in the following passage indicate the emendations: "He will remember the billiard table and the coatless evening visitor who used to draw back his sharp white elbow and hit the ball with his cue, and the blue-gray cigar smoke, and the din of voices, *and my empty right sleeve and scarred face,* and his father behind the bar, filling a mug *for me* from the tap" (p. 98). In his prefatory note Nabokov wrote: "Despite its simple appearance, this *Guide* is one of my trickiest pieces. Its translation has caused my son and me a tremendous amount of healthy trouble. Two or three scattered phrases have been added for the sake of factual clarity" (p. 90).

36. Struve has noted: "The critic in 'Passazhir'. . . bears a certain resemblance to the well-known Russian impressionist-critic Julius Aikhenvald, who was a friend of Nabokov's." *A Century of Russian Prose and*

Verse: From Pushkin to Nabokov, ed. Struve et al. (New York: Harcourt, Brace & World, Inc., 1967), pp. 164-65. This point was recently confirmed by Nabokov in *Details of a Sunset* (p. 72).

37. The narrator's professed love for sleepers reflects Nabokov's literary fascination for the broader railway theme, best expressed in *Podvig:* "From that year on Martin developed a passion for trains, travels, distant lights, the heartrending wails of locomotives in the dark of night, and the waxworks vividness of local stations flashing by, with people never to be seen again" (p. 24).

Chapter III

1. In Russian these names sound less alike: Il'ia and Elisei.

2. Lilac does not figure solely as a color image in Nabokov's work. It often appears as an actual bush. Like the birch, it seems to have a Russian connotation for him. Nabokov wrote: "Lilacs—those Russian garden graces, to whose springtime splendor, all honey and hum, my poor Pnin greatly looked forward—crowded in sapless ranks along one wall of the house" *(Pnin,* p. 145). A Persian lilac bush appears in "Skazka" (p. 55).

3. Professor Struve has kindly informed me that Grushevskii's association with Cairo enabled knowledgeable Russian readers to link him to the journalist Aleksandr Iablonovskii *(grusha* meaning pear echoes *iabloko* meaning apple), for whom Cairo was a stop in his travels westward from Russia. Nabokov knew him well, as he was a regular contributor to *Rul'.* In the English version Nabokov destroys this association by having Grushevskii meet Nikolai in the Canary Islands.

4. For Nabokov, memory and the sense of smell were intricately joined. Remember that in "Vozvrashchenie Chorba" the perfumed clothes of Chorb's bride elicit a response from the prostitute (p. 14). In *Mashen'ka* Ganin recalls his loved one's perfume, and this is followed by an explanation on the part of the author: "She used a cheap, sweet perfume called 'Tagore.' Ganin now tried to recapture that scent again, mixed with the fresh smells of the autumnal park; but, as we know, memory can restore to life everything except smells, although nothing revives the past so completely as a smell that was once associated with it" (p. 93).

5. A variant is found in the opening scene of *Mashen'ka* when Mashen'ka's childhood sweetheart and husband become acquainted in the dark, stalled elevator of the pension in which they both live. Eventually, the ceiling bulb "blazes forth" to reveal the diverse characters of the "rivals," not to themselves, but to the readers.

6. This detail has an autobiographical source. In *Conclusive Evidence* Nabokov wrote: "My father's mother, born Baroness Korff, was a

descendant of Karl Heinrich Graun (1701-59), one of the most eminent composers of his time. He is portrayed, standing somewhat aloof, with folded arms, in Menzel's popular picture of Frederic the Great playing the flute (reproductions of it kept following me through all the German boarding houses I stayed in during my years of exile)" (p. 31).

7. Professor Struve has pointed this out to me. He has noted that when *Lovat Dickson's Magazine* was considering publishing a Nabokov short story, Nabokov very much wanted Struve to translate "Zvonok" instead of "Passazhir," but the magazine wanted something shorter and "Passazhir" was picked.

8. The surname Luzhin surfaces five years later as the name of the hero of *Zashchita Luzhina.*

9. There is no such break in the English version.

10. She becomes a princess in the English version.

11. In the English version Nabokov identified this newspaper as *Rul'.* Apropos here are Nabokov's less charitable remarks in his introduction to this English version: *"Sluchaynost,* one of my earliest tales, written at the beginning of 1924, in the last afterglow of my bachelor life, was rejected by the Berlin émigré daily *Rul'* ('We don't print anecdotes about cocainists,' said the editor . . .) and sent, with the assistance of a good friend, and a remarkable writer, Ivan Lukash, to the Rigan *Segodnya,* a more eclectic émigré organ" *(Tyrants Destroyed,* p. 142).

12. The English version gives the date more obscurely.

13. The italics are mine.

14. This repeating simile, found on p. 7 of the 1924 Russian text, is absent in the recent English variant. It reappears in a more symbolic form in "Uzhas," written three years after "Sluchainost' ": ". . . v detstve, ia prosnulsia, i prizhav zatylok k nizkoi podushke, podnial glaza, i uvidal sproson'ia, chto nad reshetkoi izgolov'ia nakloniaetsia ko mne neponiatnoe litso, beznosoe, s chernymi, gusarskimi usikami pod samymi glazami, s zubami na lbu,—i vskriknuv, privstal, i mgnovenno chernye usiki okazalis' broviami, a vse litso—litsom moei materi, kotoroe ia sperva uvidal v perevernutom, neprivychnom vide" (p. 202) (". . . in my childhood, on waking up, I raised my still sleepy eyes while pressing the back of my neck to my low pillow and saw, leaning toward me over the bed head, an incomprehensible face, noseless, with a hussar's black mustache just below its octopus eyes, and with teeth set in its forehead. I sat up with a shriek and immediately the mustache became eyebrows and the entire face was transformed into that of my mother which I had glimpsed at first in an unwonted upside-down aspect" [p. 119]).

15. This image is repeated almost word for word in the final sentence of

Mashen'ka: "As his train moved off he fell into a doze, his face buried in the folds of his mackintosh, hanging from a hook above the wooden seat" (p. 169).

16. These two Nabokovian barbershops predate the barbershop scene in *Lolita* where Humbert gets a haircut in Kasbeam (p. 215). In his afterword to *Lolita,* Nabokov noted that this Kasbeam barber "cost [him] a month of work" (p. 318). With two such well developed forerunners, this remark is surprising. Perhaps Nabokov had forgotten his barbershops of thirty years before and the Kasbeam barber was an unconscious recurrent motif. Shaving scenes also figure frequently in Nabokov's fiction.

17. Field has discussed the confrontation theme in his Nabokov analysis, but omits "Britva" as an example (p. 145).

18. Field has incorrectly called him Novogordtsev (pp. 172-73).

19. Field has incorrectly noted that Golyi had written a continuation of Novodvortsev's work (p. 172).

20. *Oeuvres complètes de Gustave Flaubert: Madame Bovary* (Paris: L'Imprimerie Nationale, 1930), pp. 45-46. The translation and italics are mine.

21. Oblomovism is a state of indecision and sluggishness, as typified by the hero of Ivan Goncharov's classic novel *Oblomov.* The Russian suffix *shchina* gives this word a negative connotation, absent in the English *ism.* Novodvortsev is overjoyed that the critic ranks his art with that of the Russian literary master.

22. "Rozhdestvenskii rasskaz" appeared in *Rul'* on 25 Dec. 1928. It was never republished. Nabokov's earlier Christmas story "Rozhdestvo" was published in *Rul'* on 6 and 8 Jan. 1925, which is Christmas according to the Julian calendar used by the Russian Orthodox church. These differing Christmas publication dates indicate that, as time went on, both December 25 and January 7 came to be used as occasions for marking Christmas by newspapers.

23. Curiously, Nabokov used "fairy tale" when describing the nature of Erwin's fantasy in the English version (p. 47).

24. *Entsiklopedicheskii slovar',* ed K. K. Arsen'ev (S. -Peterburg: Brokgauz-Efron, 1900), XXX, 162; A. Kviatkovskii, *Poeticheskii slovar'* (Moskva: Izdat. Sovetskaia Entsiklopediia, 1966), p. 270.

25. Nabokov in his preface to the English version noted that this story "required some revamping here and there" (p. 40). In the Russian original Frau Ott says: "V polnoch' pridete na ulitsu Gofmana—znaete gde eto? Tam otyshchete nomer trinadtsatyi" (p. 59) ("At midnight come to Hoffmannstrasse—know where that is? There you will find number

thirteen"). This is a literary clue that in the end Erwin will find the woman who is Number Thirteen at Hoffmannstrasse. This detail is less obvious in the English version: ". . . at midnight you are to come to Hoffmann Street. Know where that is? Look between Number Twelve and Fourteen" (p. 51). Here Frau Monde (Ott) also avoids, superstitiously, mentioning the number thirteen. Possibly it has the submeaning of a warning to look carefully at girl Number Thirteen. Also the Russian "You will find" has become "Look [for]" in the English variant.

26. In a modern short story, this section is generally abbreviated. I cite here Chekhov's "The Man in a Case" and "The Lady with a Dog."

27. In the English version Gospozha Ott becomes Frau Monde.

28. *Nabokov's Quartet*, p. 7.

29. Karlinsky, "Nabokov and Chekhov," p. 10.

30. Nabokov focused on shoes and socks five times in this story. I have noted his interest in shoes and socks in my analysis of "Port."

31. This image has been discussed by Berberova, "The Mechanics of *Pale Fire,*" *Nabokov: Criticism . . .,* p. 153. It is also analyzed by W. W. Rowe, *Nabokov's Deceptive World* (New York: New York University Press, 1971), p. 125.

32. *Nabokov's Quartet*, p. 7.

33. I have indicated Nabokov's preoccupation with furniture in the analysis of "Pis'mo v Rossiiu." In that story the furniture pointedly does not move, implying the hero's contented state and thus underscoring Nabokov's realistic method. By contrast, in "Podlets" Nabokov has clearly endowed this everyday furniture with a deeper meaning. Its movement both literally and figuratively substantiates the hero's unbalanced state.

34. This onomatopeia echoes the noun *uboi* (p. 125), which means "slaughter."

35. I am grateful to G. Struve for all of this information.

36. Nabokov was always interested in magicians. In 1939 he wrote "Volshebnik," which has never been published. It was essentially a rough draft for *Lolita.* Field, pp. 328-30.

37. *A Russian Beauty,* p. 220.

38. Instead of the Russian transliteration Shok, I use the less contrived anglicization Shock. This criterion explains my use of the germanized Erwin instead of the transliterated Ervin, above; and of Bachmann instead of Bakhman, Standfuss instead of Shtandfus, Heise instead of Gaize, Adolf instead of Adol'f, below, etc. In his translations often Nabokov either simplified the name spelling or adapted it to the given story's milieu.

39. Rowe, p. 77.

40. Nabokov, "Rowe's Symbols," *New York Review of Books,* 7 Oct. 1971, p. 8.

41. Rowe, pp. 77-78.

'42. Nabokov's interest in the cinema and cinematic effects is also reflected in his story "The Assistant Producer" *(Nine Stories,* p. 59), and in his own filmscript for *Lolita (Lolita: A Screenplay,* New York: McGraw-Hill Book Co., 1974). This Nabokovian theme has been well studied, for example, by D. Stuart, *"Laughter in the Dark:* Dimensions of Parody," *Nabokov: Criticism . . .,* p. 72, and by A. Appel, *Nabokov's Dark Cinema* (New York: Oxford Univ. Press, 1974).

Chapter IV

1. Field in his synopsis of this story has many inaccuracies (pp. 178-80).

2. *Skaz* is a Russian noun which, again unfortunately, has no precise English translation. However, the *skaz* technique is familiar in English literature and means "stylistically individualized inner narrative placed in the mouth of a fictional character and designed to produce illusion of oral speech." This excellent definition is by Hugh McLean in "On the Style of the Leskovian Skaz," *Harvard Slavic Studies* (Cambridge, Mass.: Harvard Univ. Press, 1954), II, 299. It is based on B. M. Eikhenbaum, "Illiuziia skaza," *Skvoz' literaturu: Sbornik statei* (Leningrad: Academia, 1924), pp. 152-56.

3. In Nabokov's early work Zak develops into Valentinov, the manager in *Zashchita Luzhina,* who in turn becomes one of a series of antagonists for Nabokov's sympathetic heroes, culminating in the haunting figure of Quilty in *Lolita.*

4. Perova's marriage does not present the traditional late-nineteenth-century and early-twentieth-century conflict portrayed in the dramas of Anna Karenina and the Lady with the Dog. Perova's husband is incidental to the story and is uncaring.

5. In his prefatory remarks to the English version of "Bakhman," Nabokov noted more basic parallels between "Bakhman" and *Zashchita Luzhina:* "I am told that a pianist existed with some of my invented musician's peculiar traits. In certain other respects he is related to Luzhin, the chess player of *The Defense"* (p. 170).

6. *Speak, Memory,* pp. 35-36.

7. The other is in *Mashen'ka* (p. 105), written at the same time.

8. *Sovremennye Zapiski,* 68 (1939), 76-86. The English version appears in *Nabokov's Quartet,* p. 11.

9. *Nabokov's Quartet*, p. 87.

10. This misprint, *burnye* (rough) instead of *burye* (brown) is only one of the many typographical mistakes in the early Russian editions of Nabokov's work. Most of the errors are missing punctuation marks.

11. Appel, "An Interview with Vladimir Nabokov," p. 37.

12. *Ibid.*

13. M. Osorgin, rev. of "Uzhas," by V. Sirin, *Poslednie Novosti,* 27 Jan. 1927; Iu. Aikhenval'd, "Literaturnye zametki," *Rul',* 2 Feb. 1927, pp. 2-3; Diks, rev. of "Uzhas," by V. Sirin, *Zveno,* 13 Feb. 1927.

14. Nabokov explained this title change in his introduction to the English version: "I doubt very much that I was responsible for the odious title *('Katastrofa')* inflicted upon this story . . . I have now given it a new title, one that has the triple advantage of corresponding to the thematic background of the story, of being sure to puzzle such readers as 'skip descriptions,' and of infuriating reviewers" (p. 16).

15. Rowe, pp. 109, 120, 134.

16. Remember that in "Skazka," which is also dated 1927, a man is hit by a tram. (By coincidence Nabokov's friend Aikhenval'd, who figures prominently in "Passazhir," was struck and killed by such a streetcar in Berlin in 1928, after a party at Nabokov's home.)

17. Curiously, this moving van is to reappear in the long opening sentence of *Dar.*

18. In *Zashchita Luzhina* there is the cracked chessboard (p. 23) and the cracked bathroom window (p. 254) through which Luzhin jumps to his death. A "dragon-shaped crack travers[es]" the ceiling in "Solus Rex" *(A Russian Beauty,* p. 188). No doubt this image in some manner reflects the various moves of chessmen.

19. In *Ada* the shadow both ascends and descends: "There he recalled with anguish . . . he with his dancing light behind her hurdies and calves and mobile shoulders and streaming hair, and then shadows in huge surges of black geometry overtaking them, in their winding upward course, along the yellow wall" (p. 209); "With the tartan toga around him, he accompanied his black double down the accessory spiral stairs leading to the library" (p. 115).

20. This home and the surrounding locale very closely resemble Voskresensk in *Mashen'ka.* The latter, according to Nabokov, is a fictional representation of his childhood country house in Rozhdestveno *(Mary,* p. xii).

21. Nabokov recalled his own childhood biscuit box: "There was dim Miss Rachel, whom I remember mainly in terms of Huntley and Palmer

biscuits (the nice almond rocks at the top of the blue-papered tin box, the insipid cracknels at the bottom) which she unlawfully shared with me" *(Speak, Memory,* p. 86).

22. I am grateful to the McGraw-Hill Book Company for permission to quote these long, copyrighted excerpts from Nabokov's story "Christmas," appearing in their collection, *Details of of a Sunset and Other Stories* (1976).

23. Nabokov wrote: "My pleasures are the most intense known to man: writing and butterfly hunting" *(Strong Opinions,* p. 3).

Chapter V

1. *Speak, Memory,* pp. 283-84.

2. G. Munson, *Robert Frost: A Study in Sensibility and Good Sense* (New York: G. H. Doran Co., 1927), p. 87. Frost's literary formula is apt for Nabokov as well.

3. "Sirin," III.

4. *Speak, Memory,* p. 283.

5. *Ibid.,* p. 287.

6. More detailed analyses of Nabokov in émigré criticism may be found in my article "Nabokov as Viewed by Fellow Emigrés," *Russian Language Journal,* 99 (1974), 18-26, and in Foster, pp. 330-33.

7. "Russkie novinki," *Rul',* 31 Dec. 1929, pp. 2-3.

8. *Volia Rossii,* 2 (March 1930), 190-92.

9. *Za Svobodu,* 209 (Aug. 1930?), as cited in *Nabokov: A Bibliography,* p. 186.

10. Field, p. 88. A portion of this review is quoted in Struve, *Russkaia literatura v izgnanii,* p. 281. Nabokov discussed it in *Strong Opinions,* p. 39.

11. *Strong Opinions,* p. 39.

12. K. Zaitsev, in his review of this issue of *Chisla,* published in *Rossiia i Slavianstvo,* 5 April 1930, also spoke for Nabokov and seriously questioned Ivanov's literary ethics.

13. Stated in a lecture at Princeton University.

14. A series of articles on Nabokov's translations is found in *Nabokov: The Man and His Work,* pp. 266-333.

15. "The Potato Elf," tr. S. Bertensson and I. Kosinka, *Esquire,* Dec. 1939, p. 70.

16. *A Russian Beauty,* p. 220.

17. Other stories, dating from the early 1930s, have appeared in English translation as well, in *A Russian Beauty* and *The New Yorker.* They also figure in the recently published collection, *Tyrants Destroyed.*

18. This is Nabokov's term for an artist's unconscious repetition of his artistic devices and is found in his translation of *Eugene Onegin,* Bollingen

Series LXXII (New York: Pantheon Books, 1964), I, x. Berberova has noted this Nabokovian literary trait in her articles "Nabokov i ego *Lolita*," pp. 106-108, and "The Mechanics of *Pale Fire*," *Nabokov: Criticism* . . ., p. 153.

19. Appel, "an Interview with Vladimir Nabokov," pp. 19-20.

20. *Strong Opinions,* p. 95.

21. Variations of this memory theme are central also to "Port," "Rozhdestvo," and "Uzhas." Karlinsky notes the very strong parallels between "Vozvrashchenie Chorba" and *Transparent Things* in his fine article "Russian Transparencies," *Saturday Review of the Arts,* Jan. 1973, p. 44.

22. "Port" (p. 23), "Vozvrashchenie Chorba" (p. 9), "Uzhas" (p. 203), "Zvonok" (p. 29), and "Podlets" (p. 135).

23. "Putevoditel' po Berlinu" (pp. 94-95), "Vozvrashchenie Chorba" (p. 11), "Katastrofa" (p. 148), "Draka" (p. 2).

24. "Port" (p. 19), "Skazka" (p. 55), "Uzhas" (p. 203), "Kartofel'nyi El'f" (p. 168, metaphorically), "Groza" (pp. 79-80).

25. "Draka" (p. 3), "Putevoditel' po Berlinu" (p. 96), "Skazka" (p. 51), "Passazhir" (p. 141).

26. "Blagost' " (p. 158), "Port" (p. 23), "Vozvrashchenie Chorba" (p. 14), "Passazhir" (p. 144), "Rozhdestvenskii rasskaz" (p. 2), "Kartofel'nyi El'f" (p. 172), "Groza" (p. 77), "Podlets" (p. 136).

27. Appel, "An Interview with Vladimir Nabokov," p. 19.

28. "Russian Transparencies," p. 45.

29. *Lolita,* p. 318.

30. M. Slonim, "Posledniaia kniga V. Nabokova," *Russkaia Mysl',* 8 Mar. 1973, p. 8.

Bibliography of Works Cited

Aikhenval'd, Iu. "Literaturnye zametki." *Rul'*, 2 Feb. 1927, pp. 2-3.

Andreev, N. "Sirin." *Nov'*, 3 (Oct. 1930). In English: "Nikolay Andreev on Vladimir Sirin." *The Complection of Russian Literature*. Ed. A. Field. New York: Atheneum, 1971, pp. 231-38.

Appel, A. *Nabokov's Dark Cinema*. New York: Oxford Univ. Press, 1974.

———. "An Interview with Vladimir Nabokov." *Nabokov: The Man and His Work*. Ed. L. S. Dembo. Madison, Wisc.: Univ. of Wisc. Press, 1967, pp. 19-44.

Auerbach, E. *Mimesis: The Representation of Reality in Western Literature*. Trans. W. Trask. New York: Doubleday & Co., 1953.

Berberova, N. *The Italics Are Mine*. New York: Harcourt, Brace & World, Inc., 1969, pp. 316-35.

———. "The Mechanics of *Pale Fire*." *Nabokov: Criticism, Reminiscences, Translations and Tributes*. Ed. A. Appel and C. Newman. New York: Simon & Schuster, 1970, pp. 147-59.

———. "Nabokov i ego *Lolita*." *Novyi Zhurnal*, 57 (1959), 92-115.

Carroll, L. *Alice in Wonderland [Ania v strane chudes]*. Trans. V. Nabokov. Berlin: Gamaiun, 1923; reissued in New York: Dover Publications, 1976.

A Century of Russian Prose and Verse: From Pushkin to Nabokov. Ed. G. Struve et al. New York: Harcourt, Brace & World, Inc., 1967.

Dembo, L. S., ed. *Nabokov: The Man and His Work.* Madison, Wisc.: Univ. of Wisc. Press, 1967.

Diks. Rev. of "Uzhas," by V. Sirin. *Zveno,* 13 Feb. 1927.

Eikhenbaum, B. M. "Illiuziia skaza." *Skvoz' literaturu: Sbornik statei.* Leningrad: Academia, 1924.

Entsiklopedicheskii slovar'. Ed. K. K. Arsen'ev. S.- Peterburg: Brokgauz-Efron, 1900.

Field, A. *Nabokov: A Bibliography.* New York: McGraw-Hill Book Co., 1973.

———. *Nabokov: His Life in Art.* Boston: Little, Brown & Co., 1967.

Flaubert, G. *Oeuvres complètes du Gustave Flaubert: Correspondance.* Paris: L'Imprimerie Nationale, 1927.

———. *Oeuvres complètes de Gustave Flaubert: Madame Bovary.* Paris: L'Imprimerie Nationale, 1930.

Foster, L. "Nabokov in Russian Emigré Criticism." *Russian Literature Triquarterly,* 3 (1972), 330-41.

Karlinsky, S. "Nabokov and Chekhov: The Lesser Russian Tradition." *Nabokov: Criticism, Reminiscences, Translations and Tributes.* Ed. A. Appel and C. Newman. New York: Simon & Schuster, 1970, pp. 7-16.

———. "Russian Transparencies." *Saturday Review of the Arts,* Jan. 1973, pp. 44-45.

Kempton, K. P. *The Short Story.* Cambridge, Mass.: Harvard Univ. Press, 1947.

Khodasevich, V. "O Sirine." *Vozrozhdenie,* 13? Feb. 1937. Also in *Literaturnye stat'i i vospominaniia.* New York: Chekhov Publishing House, 1954, pp. 245-54. In English: Trans. M. H. Walker. *Nabokov: Criticism, Reminiscences, Translations and Tributes.* Ed. A. Appel and C. Newman. New York: Simon & Schuster, 1970, pp. 96-101.

Khokhlov, G. D. Rev. of *Vozvrashchenie Choba,* by V. Sirin. *Volia Rossii,* 2 (March 1930), 190-92.

Kviatkovskii, A. *Poeticheskii slovar',* Moskva: Izdat. Sovetskaia Entsiklopediia, 1966.

McLean, H. "On the Style of the Leskovian Skaz." *Harvard Slavic Studies.* Cambridge, Mass.: Harvard Univ. Press, 1954, II, 299.

Munson, G. *Robert Frost: A Study in Sensibility and Good Sense.* New York: G. H. Doran Co., 1927.

Nabokov, V. *Ada or Ardor: A Family Chronicle.* New York: McGraw-Hill Book Co., 1969.

———. "An Affair of Honor." *Nabokov's Quartet.* New York: Pyramid Publications, 1968, pp. 11-49. Also in: *A Russian Beauty and Other Stories.* New York: McGraw-Hill Book Co., 1973, pp. 83-115.

———. *The Annotated Lolita.* Ed. A. Appel, Jr. New York: McGraw-Hill Book Co., 1970.

———. "The Assistant Producer." *Nine Stories.* Norfolk, Conn.: New Directions Books, 1947.

———. "The Aurelian." *Nabokov's Dozen.* Garden City, N.Y.: Doubleday, 1958, pp. 76-89.

———. "Bachmann." *Tyrants Destroyed and Other Stories.* New York: McGraw-Hill Book Co., 1975, pp. 171-83.

———. *Bend Sinister.* New York: Henry Holt, 1947.

———. "Britva." *Rul',* 19 Feb. 1926, pp. 2-3.

———. "Christmas." *Details of a Sunset and Other Stories.* New York: McGraw-Hill Book Co., 1976, pp. 153-61.

———. "Cloud, Castle, Lake." *Nine Stories.* Norfolk, Conn.: New Directions Books, 1947.

———. *Conclusive Evidence.* New York: Harper & Bros., 1951.

———. *Dar.* New York: Chekhov Publishing House, 1952.

———. *The Defense.* Trans. M. Scammel with the author. New York: Capricorn Books, 1970.

———. *Despair.* New York: Putnam, 1966.

———. *Details of a Sunset and Other Stories.* New York: McGraw-Hill Book Co., 1976.

———. "Details of a Sunset." *Details of a Sunset and Other Stories.* New York: McGraw-Hill Book Co., 1976, pp. 17-26.

———. "The Doorbell." *Details of a Sunset and Other Stories.* New York: McGraw-Hill Book Co., 1976, pp. 101-15.

———. "Draka." *Rul',* 26 Sept. 1925, pp. 2-3.

———. *Drugie berega.* New York: Chekhov Publishing House, 1954.

———. *The Eye.* Trans. D. Nabokov with the author. New York: Phaedra, 1965.

———. *The Gift.* Trans. M. Scammel with the author. New York: Capricorn Books, 1970.

———. *Glory.* Trans D. Nabokov with the author. New York: McGraw-Hill Book Co., 1971.

———. "A Guide to Berlin." *Details of a Sunset and Other Stories.* New York: McGraw-Hill Book Co., 1976, pp. 91-98.

———. "Inspiration." *Saturday Review of the Arts,* Jan. 1973, pp. 30, 32.

———. *Invitation to a Beheading.* Trans. D. Nabokov with the author. New York: Capricorn Books, 1965.

———. *Kamera obskura.* Paris: Sovremennye Zapiski, 1932.

———. *King, Queen, Knave.* Trans. D. Nabokov with the author. New York: Capricorn Books, 1970.

———. *Korol' dama valet.* Berlin: Slovo, 1928.

———. *Laughter in the Dark.* New York: Bobbs-Merrill Co., 1938.

———. "A Letter that Never Reached Russia." *Details of a Sunset and Other Stories.* New York: McGraw-Hill Book Co., 1976, pp. 83-87.

———. *Lolita: A Film Screenplay.* New York: McGraw-Hill Book Co., 1974.

———. *Look at the Harlequins.* New York: McGraw-Hill Book Co., 1974.

———. *Mary.* Trans. M. Glenny with the author. New York: McGraw-Hill Book Co., 1970.

———. *Mashen'ka.* Berlin: Slovo, 1926.

———. "A Matter of Chance." *Tryants Destroyed and Other Stories.* New York: McGraw-Hill Book Co., 1975, pp. 143-55.

———. *Nikolai Gogol.* Norfolk, Conn.: New Directions Books, 1944.

———. "A Nursery Tale." *Tyrants Destroyed and Other Stories.* New York: McGraw-Hill Book Co., 1975, pp. 41-58.

———. "Oblako, ozero, bashnia." *Russkie Zapiski,* 2 (1937), 33-42.

———. *Otchaianie.* Berlin: Petropolis, 1936.

———. *Pale Fire.* New York: Putnam, 1962.

———. "The Passenger." *Details of a Sunset and Other Stories.* New York: McGraw-Hill Book Co., 1976, pp. 73-80. Also: Trans. G. Struve. *Lovat Dickson's Magazine,* 2 (June 1934), 719-24.

———. "Pil'gram." *Sovremennye Zapiski,* 43 (1930), 191-207.

———. *Pnin.* New York: Doubleday, 1957.

———. *Podvig.* Berlin: Petropolis, 1932.

———. "Poseshchenie muzeia." *Sovremennye Zapiski,* 68 (1939), 76-86.

———. "The Potato Elf." *A Russian Beauty and Other Stories.* New York: McGraw-Hill Book Co., 1973, pp. 221-51. Also: Trans. S. Bertensson and I. Kosinka. *Esquire,* Dec. 1939, pp. 70-71, 228, 230-35.

———. *Priglashenie na kazn'.* Paris: Dom Knigi, 1938.

———. *The Real Life of Sebastian Knight.* Norfolk, Conn.: New Directions Books, 1941.

———. "The Return of Chorb." *Details of a Sunset and Other Stories.* McGraw-Hill Book Co., 1976, pp. 59-70. Also: "The Return of Tchorb." Trans. G. Struve. *This Quarter,* 4 (June 1932), 592-602.

———. "Rowe's Symbols." *New York Review of Books,* 7 Oct. 1971, p. 8.

———. "Rozhdestvenskii rasskaz." *Rul',* 25 Dec. 1928, pp. 2-3.

———. *A Russian Beauty and Other Stories.* New York: McGraw-Hill Book Co., 1973.

———. "Sluchainost'." *Segodnia,* 22 June 1924, pp. 7-8.

———. "Sogliadatai." *Sovremennye Zapiski,* 44 (1930), 91-152.

———. "Solus Rex." *Sovremennye Zapiski,* 70 (1940), 5-36. In English: *A*

Russian Beauty and Other Stories. New York: McGraw-Hill Book Co., pp. 185-218.

―――. *Speak, Memory: An Autobiography Revisited.* New York: Putnam, 1966.

―――. *Strong Opinions.* New York: McGraw-Hill Book Co., 1973.

―――. "Terror." *Tyrants Destroyed and Other Stories.* New York: McGraw-Hill Book Co., 1975, pp. 113-21.

―――. "The Thunderstorm." *Details of a Sunset and Other Stories.* New York: McGraw-Hill Book Co., 1976, pp. 119-23.

―――. *Transparent Things.* New York: McGraw-Hill Book Co., 1972.

―――. *Tyrants Destroyed and Other Stories.* New York: McGraw-Hill Book Co., 1975.

―――. "Ultima Thule." *Novyi Zhurnal,* 1 (1942), 49-77. In English: *A Russian Beauty and Other Stories.* New York: McGraw-Hill Book Co., 1973, pp. 149-82.

―――. "The Vane Sisters." *Nabokov's Quartet.* New York: Pyramid Publications, 1968, pp. 87-108.

―――. *Vozvrashchenie Chorba: Rasskazy i stikhi.* Berlin: Slovo, 1930; reissued in Ann Arbor, Mich.: Ardis Publishers, 1976. All of Nabokov's Russian stories cited in my book and not individually indicated in this bibliography are contained in this collection. For a more detailed listing, see the Appendix.

―――. *Zashchita Luzhina.* Berlin: Slovo, 1930.

Nal'ianch, S. Rev. of *Vozvrashchenie Chorba,* by V. Sirin. *Za Svobodu,* 209 (Aug. 1930?).

Naumann, M. "Nabokov as Viewed by Fellow Emigrés." *Russian Language Journal,* 99 (1974), 18-26.

O'Faolain, S. *The Short Story.* London: Collins, 1948.

Osorgin, M. Rev. of "Uzhas," by V. Sirin. *Poslednie Novosti,* 27 Jan. 1927.

Pil'skii, P. "V. Sirin." *Segodnia,* 12 Jan. 1930, p. 5.

Poe, E. A. *The Works of Edgar Allan Poe.* New York: A. C. Armstrong & Son, 1884.

Pushkin, A. *Eugene Onegin.* Trans. V. Nabokov. Bollingen Series LXXII. New York: Pantheon Books, 1964.

Rowe, W. W. *Nabokov's Deceptive World.* New York: New York Univ. Press, 1971.

Savel'ev, A. "Russkie novinki." *Rul',* 31 Dec. 1929, pp. 2-3.

Shklovskii, V. B. "Iskusstvo kak priem." *O teorii prozy.* Moskva: Izdat. Federatsiia, 1929.

Slonim, M. "Posledniaia kniga V. Nabokova." *Russkaia Mysl',* 8 Mar. 1973, p. 8.

Struve, G. "Current Russian Literature: II. Vladimir Sirin." *Slavonic and East European Review,* 12 (1934), 436-44.

———. "Nabokov as a Russian Writer." *Nabokov: The Man and His Work.* Ed. L. S. Dembo. Madison, Wisc.: Univ. of Wisc. Press, 1967, pp. 45-56.

———. *Russian Literature under Lenin and Stalin, 1917-1953,* Norman, Okla.: Univ. of Okla. Press, 1971.

———. *Russkaia literatura v izgnanii.* New York: Chekhov Publishing House, 1956, pp. 278-90.

———. "Tvorchestvo Sirina." *Rossiia i Slavianstvo,* 17 May 1930.

Stuart, D. *"Laughter in the Dark:* Dimensions of Parody." *Nabokov: Criticism, Reminiscences, Translations and Tributes.* Ed. A. Appel and C. Newman. New York: Simon & Schuster, 1970, pp. 72-95.

Tomashevskii, B. "Tematika: Prozaicheskoe povestvovanie." *Teoriia literatury: Poetika.* Leningrad, Gosizdat., 1928, p. 199.

Tsetlin, M. Rev. of *Korol' dama valet,* by V. Sirin. *Sovremennye Zapiski,* 37 (1928), 536-38.

———. Rev. of *Vozvrashchenie Chorba,* by V. Sirin. *Sovremennye Zapiski,* 42 (1930), 530-31.

Weeks, Edward. Rev. of *Tyrants Destroyed,* by V. Nabokov. *The Atlantic Monthly,* March 1975, p. 144.

Weidlé, W. "Vladimir Weidle on Sirin." *The Complection of Russian Literature.* Ed. A. Field. New York: Atheneum, 1971, pp. 238-40.

Wellek, R. *Concepts of Criticism.* Ed. S. G. Nichols. New Haven, Conn.: Yale Univ. Press, 1963.

Zaitsev, K. "Chisla." *Rossiia i Slavianstvo,* 5 April 1930.

Zamiatin, E. *A Soviet Heretic: Essays by Yevgeny Zamyatin.* Ed. and trans. M. Ginsburg. Chicago: Univ. of Chicago Press, 1970.

Index

Index